Quod scriptura, non iubet vetat

The Latin translates, "What is not commanded in scripture, is forbidden:'

On the Cover: Baptists rejoice to hold in common with other evangelicals the main principles of the orthodox Christian faith. However, there are points of difference and these differences are significant. In fact, because these differences arise out of God's revealed will, they are of vital importance. Hence, the barriers of separation between Baptists and others can hardly be considered a trifling matter. To suppose that Baptists are kept apart solely by their views on Baptism or the Lord's Supper is a regrettable misunderstanding. Baptists hold views which distinguish them from Catholics, Congregationalists, Episcopalians, Lutherans, Methodists, Pentecostals, and Presbyterians, and the differences are so great as not only to justify, but to demand, the separate denominational existence of Baptists. Some people think Baptists ought not teach and emphasize their differences but as E.J. Forrester stated in 1893, "Any denomination that has views which justify its separate existence, is bound to promulgate those views. If those views are of sufficient importance to justify a separate existence, they are important enough to create a duty for their promulgation ... the very same reasons which justify the separate existence of any denomination make it the duty of that denomination to teach the distinctive doctrines upon which its separate existence rests." If Baptists have a right to a separate denominational life, it is their duty to propagate their distinctive principles, without which their separate life cannot be justified or maintained.

Many among today's professing Baptists have an agenda to revise the Baptist distinctives and redefine what it means to be a Baptist. Others don't understand why it even matters. The books being reproduced in the *Baptist Distinctives Series* are republished in order that Baptists from the past may state, explain and defend the primary Baptist distinctives as they understood them. It is hoped that this Series will provide a more thorough historical perspective on what it means to be distinctively Baptist.

The Lord Jesus Christ asked, *"And why call ye me, Lord, Lord, and do not the things which I say?"* (Luke 6:46). The immediate context surrounding this question explains what it means to be a true disciple of Christ. Addressing the same issue, Christ's question is meant to show that a confession of discipleship to the Lord Jesus Christ is inconsistent and untrue if it is not accompanied with a corresponding submission to His authoritative commands. Christ's question teaches us that a true recognition of His authority as Lord inevitably includes a submission to the authority of His Word. Hence, with this question Christ has made it forever impossible to separate His authority as King from the authority of His Word. These two principles—the authority of Christ as King and the authority of His Word—are the two most fundamental Baptist distinctives. The first gives rise to the second and out of these two all the other Baptist distinctives emanate. As F.M. Iams wrote in 1894, "Loyalty to Christ as King, manifesting itself in a constant and unswerving obedience to His will as revealed in His written Word, is the real source of all the Baptist distinctives:' In the search for the *primary* Baptist distinctive many have settled on the Lordship of Christ as the most basic distinctive. Strangely, in doing this, some have attempted to separate Christ's Lordship from the authority of Scripture, as if you could embrace Christ's authority without submitting to what He commanded. However, while Christ's Lordship and Kingly authority can be isolated and considered essentially for discussion's sake, we see from Christ's own words in Luke 6:46 that His Lordship is really inseparable from His Word and, with regard to real Christian discipleship, there can be no practical submission to the one without a practical submission to the other.

In the symbol above the Kingly Crown and the Open Bible represent the inseparable truths of Christ's Kingly and Biblical authority. The Crown and Bible graphics are supplemented by three Bible verses (Ecclesiastes 8:4, Matthew 28:18-20, and Luke 6:46) that reiterate and reinforce the inextricable connection between the authority of Christ as King and the authority of His Word. The truths symbolized by these components are further emphasized by the Latin quotation - *quod scriptura, non iubet vetat*— *i.e.,* "What is not commanded in scripture, is forbidden:' This Latin quote has been considered historically as a summary statement of the regulative principle of Scripture. Together these various symbolic components converge to exhibit the two most foundational Baptist Distinctives out of which all the other Baptist Distinctives arise. Consequently, we have chosen this composite symbol as a logo to represent the primary truths set forth in the *Baptist Distinctives Series.*

Notes
on the
Principles and Practices
of
Baptist Churches

FRANCIS WAYLAND
1796-1865

NOTES

ON THE

PRINCIPLES AND PRACTICES

OF

BAPTIST CHURCHES.

BY

FRANCIS WAYLAND.

With a Biographical Sketch of the Author by John Franklin Jones

---

NEW YORK:
SHELDON, BLAKEMAN & CO., 115 NASSAU STREET.
BOSTON: GOULD & LINCOLN.
CHICAGO: S. C. GRIGGS & CO.

1857

he Baptist Standard Bearer, Inc.
NUMBER ONE IRON OAKS DRIVE • PARIS, ARKANSAS 72855

Thou hast given a *standard* to them that fear thee;
that it may be displayed because of the truth.
— *Psalm 60:4*

Reprinted 2006

by

THE BAPTIST STANDARD BEARER, INC.
No. 1 Iron Oaks Drive
Paris, Arkansas 72855
(479) 963-3831

THE WALDENSIAN EMBLEM
lux lucet in tenebris
"The Light Shineth in the Darkness"

ISBN# 1579785468

PREFACE.

THE present volume contains the papers which lately have appeared in *The Examiner*, over the signature of "Roger Williams." It was the intention of the author to limit the series to eight or ten numbers; subject after subject was, however, suggested to him for discussion, until it attained its present magnitude. It assumes a more permanent form, in compliance with what is supposed to be the wish of its former readers.

The main object of the author has been to present a popular view of the distinctive belief of the Baptist denomination, and to urge upon his brethren a practice in harmony with their profession. That this humble effort to promote the spirituality and efficiency of a portion of the church of Christ may be accepted by the Master, is the earnest prayer of the author.

PROVIDENCE, October 28, 1856.

CONTENTS.

I.
PAGE

Baptists have no Authoritative Confessions of Faith.—The Absence of such Confession a Cause of Union rather than Division....... 13

II

Baptist Views of the Trinity, the Law, Human Depravity, the Atonement, Particular and General............................... 16

III.

Extent of the Atonement.—Regeneration.—Preaching Christ.—Manner of Preaching, and Reason of it...................... 20

IV.

Baptist Preaching formerly extempore, that is, without written preparation.—Advantages of this mode of preaching for the cultivation of Pulpit Eloquence............................. 23

V.

Objections to unwritten Discourses.—These not peculiar to this mode of Public Address... 27

VI.

Language of our early Preachers universally understood.—Their Discourses abounded in illustrations drawn chiefly from the Scriptures... 30

VII.

Objection answered.—Men of Sense desire Preaching which will move their Consciences.—Error of the older Preachers.—Our Error the Opposite.. 35

VIII.

Ministers decreasing in Number.—Older Preachers urged Men to immediate Repentance.—Their Preaching Experimental........ 39

IX.

Effects of Preaching on Experimental Religion on Saints and Sinners.—Discriminating Preaching necessary to the Success of the Gospel. 43

X.

Baptist Views of Qualifications for the Ministry.—We are bound by the Apostolic Rule.—Our Circumstances not essentially different from those of the early Christians............................ 47

XI.

It is possible to believe our Principles and act at variance with them.—Change in Thirty-five Years.—The Reason of the Saviour's Rule 52

XII.

By carrying out these Views we should have such a Ministry as Christ has appointed, a more numerous Ministry, a Ministry adapted to the various wants of Men.—Consequences of the opposite view... 57

CONTENTS. vii

XIII.

Objections considered.—Frequent Changes of Ministers.—Ministerial Support.—Our condition demands a Ministry that can in part support itself.—Labor with the hands degrades no one.—Dr. Alexander's friend Mr. Shelburne.................................. 62

XIV.

What should be done to improve our Ministry.—Education of our Children.—Ministers' Duty in this Matter.—Higher Education for those designed for it.—Theological Seminaries.—These views eminently favorable to Ministerial Education.................. 72

XV.

Universal Obligation resting on all the Disciples of Christ to labor personally for Him.—Sunday-schools.—Colporteurs.—General Inefficiency of Professors of Religion........................ 79

XVI.

Baptists acknowledge the sole Authority of the New Testament in opposition to Tradition and Decrees of Councils.—Baptism; the Mode of Administering this Ordinance which we consider obligatory.. 85

XVII.

Subjects of Baptism.—Reason why Baptists do not Baptize Infants.—We are not convinced by the views given in favor of Infant Baptism.—Its effect upon the Church 93

XVIII.

Mode of Admission to the Ministry by the Church.—No better Method.—But Churches must do their Duty in this Matter.—Entering the Ministry merely as an agreeable Profession........ 99

CONTENTS.

XIX.

Evidences of a Call to the Ministry our own Consciousness and the Consciousness of our Brethren.—Duty of a Church to a Candidate.—Mistakes in this Matter.. 106

XX.

Ordination.—Its Nature.—Importance of examination of the Candidate.—In no other manner can the Ministry be improved 114

XXI.

The points in which we differ from other Sects important.—The manner in which we have escaped the errors into which others have fallen... 121

XXII.

Hereditary Membership at variance with the idea of the Spirituality of the Church.—Tendency of Infant Baptism to establish Hereditary Membership... 125

XXIII.

Other Truths to which Baptists have borne Testimony.—The Spirituality of the Church of Christ.—The Right of Private Judgment.—The Sufficiency of the New Testament as our Rule of Faith and Practice.—The Separation of the Church from the State.......... 130

XXIV.

Approximation of other Sects to the Principles held by Baptists.—The Spirituality of the Church.—The Sufficiency of the New Testament as our Rule of Faith.—Liberty of Conscience.......... 139

XXV.

Points in which we have erred by imitation of others.—Church Music 147

XXVI.

Change of opinion respecting Church Music.—Church Architecture . 153

XXVII.

Sabbath Services.—Posture in Prayer.—Reading Notices.—Formula in Baptism.—Services at Weddings and Funerals 158

XXVIII.

Relations between the Church and the Congregation.—Gradual change in this respect.—Unfortunate position of a Minister 165

XXIX.

Preaching to build up a Society.—Vestry Services.—Church Discipline.—Amusements.—Honesty in Mercantile Dealing 171

XXX.

Independence of the Churches.—Can a Church properly be represented? 177

XXXI.

Attempts to form a Baptist representation have failed.—Baptist General Convention.—Missionary Union.—No one of all our Benevolent Associations represent the Baptist Denomination.... 183

XXXII.

Love to the Saviour the bond which must unite Baptists to each other.—Errors to be avoided in conducting Benevolent Associations.—The special object of a Church must not be transcended. —Infant Dedication.—Concluding Reflections 190

XXXIII.

Importance of Public Worship.—The Duty of the Disciples of Christ to maintain it.—With us, this Duty requires a universal effort.—Difficulties peculiar to our condition 199

XXXIV.

Facilities in our Condition for Extension.—Our latest Statistics show a great need of Ministers of the Gospel 206

XXXV.

In our present condition what is to be done?—Can Theological Seminaries and Colleges supply our Need?—The answer given by Statistics.—We need a great number of Ministers, and we need that every Minister be made as efficient as possible............ 212

XXXVI.

The Gifts which Christ, on his Ascension, received for his Church.—These Gifts bestowed in Answer to Prayer.—What is Effectual Prayer 219

XXXVII.

Duty of Baptists in new Settlements, where their number is small, to know each other, meet together for Worship, organize Sabbath-schools, and seek out for Gifts for the Ministry among themselves. 226

XXXVIII.

Duty of feeble Churches to rely, under God, on themselves; to cultivate Talent for the Ministry among their own Members.—Always hold Worship on the Sabbath.—Pay a Ministering Brother for his Time and Expenses; be not ashamed of him if he be a Laboring Man 232

XXXIX.

Objection, We are Few and Weak, etc.—Would this justify your Course in Converts from Heathenism, or in the Times of the Apostles?—This excuse savors of Pride, not Humility.—Example of the Church in Hamburg.. 240

CONTENTS.

XL.

Churches in Cities.—Their special Need of Opportunity to labor for Christ.—Its Effect upon Individual Piety 247

XLI.

Means to be used to Improve the whole Ministry.—Theological Seminaries.—Colleges.—Academies............................. 255

XLII.

Our great Reliance for the Improvement of the Ministry is on the Ministry itself.—What a Minister may do in this Work.—The Blessings that will follow such Labor........................ 261

XLIII.

Ministers competent to this Work.—Without them it can not be done.—Suggestions to those that have the Ministry in View..... 269

XLIV.

Object of Education.—Education not confined to the study of books.—Difficulty of acquiring the habit of continuous thought.—Aids in acquiring it... 276

XLV.

Pulpit Assistants.—Different Classes of Sermons.—Doctrinal Sermons.—Practical Sermons................................... 283

XLVI.

Experimental, Expository, and Hortatory Sermons............... 289

XLVII.

Texts.—Why should a Text be taken at all?—How may it be used? 296

XLVIII.

Moral Requisites for Understanding the Scriptures.—Intellectual Preparation.—A Knowledge of the Meaning of the Words, of the Context, and of the Manners and Usages of the Time........... 303

CONTENTS.

XLIX.

Construction of a Sermon.—What is a Sermon?—Acquaintance with the Human Heart, how acquired.—Necessity of unflinching mental effort 309

L.

Importance of Self-reliance.—Saving Fragments of Thought.—Introduction and Close of Sermons.—Style proper for Sermons.—Mistakes on this Subject 316

LI.

Delivery of a Sermon.—The Natural Tones of Emotion.—Length of Sermons.—All the Services of Worship to be in Harmony with the Sermon.—Foppery.—Talking in the Pulpit 323

LII.

Week-day Services.—Lecture or Conference Meetings.—Pastoral Visits.—Conversation on Religion.—Conclusion 330

BAPTIST

PRINCIPLES AND PRACTICES.

I.

BAPTISTS HAVE NO AUTHORITATIVE CONFESSIONS OF FAITH.—THE ABSENCE OF SUCH CONFESSION A CAUSE OF UNION RATHER THAN DIVISION.

The question is frequently asked, What is the creed, and what are the acknowledged standards of the Baptist churches in this country? To this, the general answer has ever been, "Our rule of faith and practice is the New Testament." We have no other authority to which we all profess submission. To this it will be replied by Christians of other denominations, We all make the same profession, but we have also our authorized confessions, creeds, and formularies, to which every one who enters our churches must subscribe; they are framed by our highest ecclesiastical tribunals, and they, to a greater or less extent, govern the profession of all our members. It is in this manner alone that our unity is preserved, and our members protected from the seductions of error.

To this we answer, Whether an established confession of faith is desirable or not, with us it is impossible. We believe, in the fullest sense, in the independence of every individual church of Christ. We hold that each several church is a Christian society, on which is conferred by Christ the entire power of self-government. No church has any power over any other church. No minister has any authority in any church, except that which has called him to be its pastor. Every church, therefore, when it expresses its own belief, expresses the belief of no other than its own members. If several churches understand the Scriptures in the same way, and all unite in the same confession, then this expresses the opinions and belief of those who profess it. It, however, expresses their belief, because all of them, from the study of the Scriptures, understand them in the same manner; and not because any tribunal has imposed such interpretations upon them. We can not acknowledge the authority of any such tribunal. We have no right to delegate such an authority to any man, or to any body of men. It is our essential belief that the Scriptures are a revelation from God, given not to a Pope, or a congregation of Cardinals, or an Archbishop, or a bench of Bishops, or a General Assembly, or a Synod, but to every individual man. They were given to every individual that he might understand them for himself, and the word that is given him will judge him at the great day. It is hence evident that we can have no standards which claim to be of any authority over us. This, however, in no manner prevents those who are agreed from working together, and co-operating in every form of Christian effort, and uniting in every manifestation of brotherly love.

If the question be asked, How are we saved from divisions and heresies? we reply, by asking again, How are other denominations saved from them? Have creeds and confessions any power either to create or to preserve unity? Have they done it in the Papal, the Episcopal, the Lutheran, or the Presbyterian churches? Nay, where a creed is most strictly imposed, and even established by law, *there* is the divergence in sentiment from it the most remarkable. A large proportion, perhaps the majority, of the members of the Lutheran church, believe no more in the doctrines of Luther than in the doctrines of Confucius.

We reply, secondly, that this very absence of any established creed is in itself the cause of our unity. If the Bible be a book designed for every individual man, and intended to be understood by every man, then the greatest amount of unity attainable among men of diversified character, will be produced by allowing every one to look at it and study it for himself. Here is an inspired record allowed to be pure truth. The nearer the opinions of men approach to its teachings, the nearer they approach to each other. Here is a solid and definite basis of unity. It is such a unity as is adapted to the nature of man as an intelligent and accountable being. Other foundation can no man lay than that which is laid. If we stand upon this, we can not be far distant from each other.

And the fact has proved the truth of this remark. I do not believe that any denomination of Christians exists, which, for so long a period as the Baptists, have maintained so invariably the truth of their early confessions. The confessions of the persecuted Baptists in the time of Charles II. are almost identical with those of our churches of the present day in this country, though probably not one in ten thousand of our members ever heard of their existence. The churches which boast of standards of faith and practice, are in this respect certainly much less fortunate than ourselves. Abundant evidence of this remark will be seen in the following numbers.

While there is, however, this general belief, it may be of use to present a brief view of our principles and practice, that we ourselves may have the means of verifying it, and knowing the harmony which exists between us and our brethren. The writer of this paper has, therefore, thought that a few miscellaneous notes on this subject might be acceptable to his brethren. He pretends to no learning in ecclesiastical history. He has no leisure for extensive research, or indeed for any research whatever. He has, however, had some opportunity for knowing the opinions and practices of Baptists in the northern States, and these he proposes to present as he may find now and then a leisure moment. They bind no one, but are the simple record of the observation of an individual.

II.

BAPTIST VIEWS OF THE TRINITY, THE LAW, HUMAN DEPRAVITY, THE ATONEMENT, PARTICULAR AND GENERAL.

THE theological tenets of the Baptists, both in England and America, may be briefly stated as follows: they are emphatically the doctrines of the Reformation, and they have been held with singular unanimity and consistency.

In England and America, Baptists have been always

Trinitarian. They believe, without exception, that there is one only living and true God, and that this God is revealed to us as Father, Son, and Holy Spirit. Among the Baptists in England, and their descendants in America, I have never known or heard of a church that has adopted the Unitarian belief. I do not say that persons professing Unitarian sentiments may not have been convinced of the obligation of the disciples of Christ to be baptized by immersion. The belief in baptism by immersion may be entertained by a man of almost any persuasion, but this alone does not unite him with us. He remains in other respects as he was before. Our churches, with one accord, always and every where have held Unitarianism to be a grave and radical error.

They have also always held that the Law of God, or, as it used to be called, the first covenant, required sinless obedience, and that without sinless obedience we could, on legal ground, make no claim to salvation.

They believe that all men have broken the law; that they are, therefore, under condemnation; that the carnal mind is enmity against God; that it is not subject to the law of God, neither indeed can be, so that they that are in the flesh can not please God; and that by the deeds of the law no flesh can be justified. Such being the case, justification by works is absolutely impossible, and the whole world is guilty before God.

It is, so far as I know, universally believed that this depravity came upon us through the sin of Adam. In regard to the manner of the transmission of depravity, there may have been some differences of opinion. The more common belief among us has been, that a man, in consequence of his connection with Adam, is born with a sinful nature. There may be some who believe that from circumstances in our constitution, created by the fall of our first parents, every man becomes sinful, but the number of these is probably small. As to the fact of man's universal guilt and desert of punishment, there is no difference whatever.

The belief of the Baptists in regard to the Atonement has also been singularly uniform. They have always held, that salvation by works having by sin become utterly impossible, our only hope of eternal life rests upon the obedience and death of the Mediator, Christ Jesus. We are saved, not in virtue of what we have done, or can do, but merely and entirely in virtue of what Christ has done for us, and we become partakers of the salvation which he has wrought out for us, solely by repentance and faith in the Lord Jesus.

The extent of the atonement has been and still is a matter of honest but not unkind difference. Within the last fifty years a change has gradually taken place in the views of a large portion of our brethren. At the commencement of that period Gill's Divinity was a sort of standard, and Baptists imbibing his opinions were what may be called almost hyper-Calvinistic. A change commenced upon the publication of the writings of Andrew Fuller, especially his "Gospel Worthy of all Acceptation," which, in the northern and eastern States, has become almost universal. The old view still prevails, if I mistake not, in our southern and western States. This, however, does not interrupt the harmony which should subsist among brethren. Dr. Baldwin and Dr. Stillman differed in opinion on this subject ;

the former following Fuller, the latter adhering to Gill. No two ministers, however, ever lived in more fraternal intercourse, exchanging with and aiding each other, and rejoicing in each other's prosperity, as it became the servants of one common Lord. I have known men believing the atonement to be limited, preach with great acceptance in New England, where the contrary belief prevails almost universally, and the contrary has been even more frequently the case. Men, in this respect, differ amicably; and it is found that when their hearts are warmed with the love of God and desire for the salvation of souls, they all preach very much alike.

It is difficult at the present day to conceive to what extent the doctrine of the limited atonement, and the views of election which accompanied it, were carried. I once knew a popular minister, who used to quote the passage, "God so loved the world," etc., by inserting the word *elect* before world: "God so loved the *elect* world," etc. I was, in the early part of my ministry, settled in a respectable town in Massachusetts. One of my members, a very worthy man, and the son of a Baptist minister, and reputed to be "very clear in the doctrines"—(this was the term applied to this form of belief)—had an interesting family wholly given up to worldliness. I wished to converse with them on the subject of personal religion, and mentioned to him my desire. He kindly but plainly told me that he did not wish any one to converse with his children on that subject. If they were elected, God would convert them in his own time; but if not, talking would do them no good, it would only make them hypocrites. He was, I believe, the last pillar of Gillism then remaining in the church.

III.

EXTENT OF THE ATONEMENT.—REGENERATION.—PREACHING CHRIST.— MANNER OF PREACHING, AND REASON OF IT.

In my last number I referred to the change which had taken place, in the opinions of Baptists, on the subject of the atonement. The question mainly at issue was the *extent* of the gospel sacrifice; in other respects there has ever been, I believe, an entire harmony. It may be well to state briefly what I suppose to be the prevailing belief, in this doctrine, at present. In the northern and eastern States, it is generally held that the whole race became sinners in consequence of the sin of the first Adam; and that, on the other hand, the way of salvation was opened for the whole race by the obedience and death of the second Adam. Nevertheless, this alone renders the salvation of no one certain, for, so steeped are men in sin, that they all, with one consent, begin to make excuse, and universally refuse the offer of pardon. God, then, in infinite mercy, has elected some to everlasting life, and, by the influence of the Holy Spirit, renders the word effectual to their salvation and sanctification. In his offer of mercy he is perfectly honest and sincere, for the feast has been provided, and it is spread for all. This does not, however, interfere with his gracious purpose to save by his sovereign mercy such as he may choose. There is here sovereignty, but no partiality. There can be no partiality, for none have the semblance of a claim; and, if any one perishes, it is not from the want of a full and free provision, but from his own wilful perverseness. Ye will not come to me, that ye may have life.

As to the doctrine of Regeneration, its nature, being an entire renovation of the moral character in consequence of a change of the affections, there has always been great unanimity among us. So it has been always held that the evidence of this change of the affections is found, not only in the internal character, but in the outward life. In all these respects, the doctrines of the Baptists in the northern and eastern States approach very nearly to those of the first President Edwards, and the writers of that class.

Those who remember the Baptist preachers forty or fifty years since, will, I think, call to mind the fact that Christ Jesus was, in a particular manner, the burden of their discourses. The character of Christ, his wonderful love, his sufferings and death, his character as prophet, priest, and king, his teachings, his example, his infinite excellency, the glory which he was shortly to bestow upon the believer, his nearness to us at all times, specially in the hour of trial and death, were frequently the topics of their discourses. Thus, the late John Williams, the first pastor of Oliver-street church, speaking to a friend on the morning of his sudden death, said, "I love President Edwards, he *always speaks so sweetly of Christ.*"

But, it may be said, there is nothing peculiar in these sentiments; they are held by other denominations of Christians. Did not Congregationalists, Presbyterians, and other Calvinistic preachers, treat on all these subjects? I answer yes, but there was still a difference, very observable, between the Baptist preachers some forty or fifty years since, and their brethren holding the same doctrinal sentiments. Whether I can convey an accurate conception of this difference or not, I am not sure, but I will mention a few of the most obvious particulars.

In the first place, our ministers were commonly, I might almost say universally, men of no classical education. They were men who had left some secular—generally mechanical—employment, for the sake of preaching the gospel, and, in doing this, they had suffered, not prospective, but actual loss. They were impelled to the ministry by the conviction that they could not conscientiously do any thing else.

There was frequently a struggle in their minds in thus giving up all for Christ, not unlike a second conversion. As the result of this, it followed that they threw their whole souls into the work, in the form of a second and unalterable consecration. This, I think, gave an earnestness and persistence to their efforts, and a simplicity of reliance on the power and grace of Christ to aid them, and render their work effectual, which have not been so apparent in later times.

There was at this period, to a very considerable extent, a prejudice against learning. This was by no means unnatural. They saw that education, rather than piety, was in many denominations the test of ministerial qualification; and, instead of assigning to it its proper and subordinate place, they abjured it altogether. This was, doubtless, an error. Are not we now liable to the very error against which they contended? Be this as it may, there was, undoubtedly, in most parts of our country, a prejudice against men who were "college learned." A brother whom I knew, was, for a while, settled in one of the best Baptist churches in any city. He had received a collegiate education. After laboring for a while unsuccessfully, he returned to the eastward. One of the members of the church was asked why they allowed him to leave. His reply was, "He is a good man, a pious man, humble and devout, but he is spoiled by too much learning." The fact was that his delivery was rather tame: he aimed, probably, at correctness rather than power, at propriety rather than impressiveness—by-the-by, a very common error—and they ascribed these imperfections to the fact that he had been through college.

IV.

BAPTIST PREACHING FORMERLY EXTEMPORE, THAT IS, WITHOUT WRITTEN PREPARATION.—ADVANTAGES OF THIS MODE OF PREACHING FOR THE CULTIVATION OF PULPIT ELOQUENCE.

IN my last notes, I mentioned the fact that our ministers of the last generation were not classically educated, and that they were generally men impelled to leave their secular employments by a conviction that they could not otherwise answer a good conscience toward God.

I mention another peculiarity. They almost universally preached without notes. It was not uncommon to distinguish extempore from written discourse by different appellations.

Delivery without notes was alone called *preaching*, but when a manuscript was used, it was called merely *reading*. Baptists generally considered the latter a very different thing from preaching, and they disliked it extremely. They rarely attended the ministry of other denominations, even occasionally, where it was practiced. As ministers from the East, however, came westward with their written discourses, the people gradually became accustomed to them, but it cost a severe struggle before they would tolerate the change. It was no uncommon thing to see several of the oldest and best members of our churches rise and leave the house when a minister opened his book and began to read from his manuscript. If I do not misremember, I have several times seen this myself.

Now the effect of this mode of introduction to the ministry must be manifest. Let us picture to ourselves a young man of limited education and retired pursuits, who would hardly dare to open his lips in mixed society, impressed with the conviction that it is his duty to preach Christ. He must stand up, without any aid from writing, and deliver a discourse to a mixed assembly. The pecuniary sacrifice which he must make is nothing in his eyes—this he has willingly made; but how shall he occupy the attention of an audience? He has no accumulated treasures of reading or study on which he can rely. He has read little except his Bible, but he has been in the habit of studying that carefully and prayerfully. He knows that there will be before him men older, wiser, and better educated than himself. The danger of breaking down, and retiring in utter confusion from the great assembly, the fear of losing his recollection of what he had mentally prepared, the conscientious dread of so stating the truth that souls may be lost through his imperfection, and the fear lest he should offend God by this fear of man that bringeth a snare, all fill him with apprehension. He looks to man for aid, but from this source no help comes. He looks to God, and hears the command repeated, "Son of man, preach the preaching that I bid thee." He turns his thoughts inward, and the voice utters, "Woe is me if I preach not the gospel." In an agony he resorts to prayer. He can find no refuge but in the promises of God. Christ has said, "Go ye into all the world, and preach the gospel to every creature, and lo, I am with you always." He begins to take courage, but his faith is only a bruised reed. He wrestles with God for help from on high. His faith gains strength by the effort. Another promise serves as a cordial to his soul. One after another, every earthly trust is abandoned, and he is at last enabled to cast himself wholly on the promised aid of the Holy Spirit. Trembling, hoping, fearing, he goes forth to meet the people. His knees smite one against another, as he ascends the pulpit stairs. In a voice scarcely audible, he calls upon God for his blessing upon the congregation. He commences his sermon. His own voice seems strange to him. Gradually he forgets himself, and loses his fears. As a prophet from God he delivers his message. The powers of his mind begin to react. He is transported beyond himself. He would that the whole world were present to hear the story of redeeming love. He pours out his soul in earnest entreaty. He warns the ungodly, as though he and they were already in view of the judgment-seat. Words, burning and impressive, come unbidden to his bursting heart. The time will not allow him to say half that fills his soul. He sits down, and thanks God for fulfilling his promise, but fears that it can never be thus with him again. When he attempts to preach again the same conflict is renewed, until, in preaching, this becomes the habit of his soul. This is the school in which our older preachers were nurtured, and it is difficult to imagine a better school for the cultivation of pulpit eloquence.

Take now the other case. A young man, just in opening youth, is converted. He feels a desire to become a minister of the gospel. He is encouraged by his friends to pursue a course of preparatory study. He devotes several years to secular learning. He learns, in college, to write on any subject of science or literature. He pursues the study of theology. He learns to write on a sacred theme. He prepares, thoughtfully, a written discourse. He writes it over and over again, and it receives the last criticism of his instructors. It is in accurate and elegant English, and "fit to preach before any congregation." He has asked for the blessing of God in writing it. He does the same before delivering it. He takes it in his pocket, and reads it before an assembly. He is at first a little fluttered at the novelty of his position, but he has no fear of failure, for he knows the sermon to be perfectly accurate in doctrine and expression. Where is there here the room for burning enthusiasm, for that power which transports men? No one can move others without being deeply moved himself. It is in this earnest and deep-felt trust in God that the power of the old ministers consisted.

V.

OBJECTIONS TO UNWRITTEN DISCOURSES.—THESE NOT PECULIAR TO THIS MODE OF PUBLIC ADDRESS.

In my last number I ventured to offer some remarks on written and unwritten discourses. My readers, if perchance I am so fortunate as to have any, may possibly inquire whether I intend, in this manner, to characterize these two modes of discourse in general? I reply, this is not my object. I only intended to compare them as schools for the cultivation of popular discourse; and for the sake of illustrating the kind of preaching which has, until lately, distinguished the Baptist pulpit.

While on this subject, however, I may perhaps be permitted to add a word or two further.

The former habit of unwritten discourse was, I know, liable to various objections. In the first place, it frequently led to a sing-song delivery, which was peculiarly unpleasant. The speaker generally began in an under-tone, and seemed oppressed with a consciousness of the responsibility which weighed upon him. Gradually he warmed with his subject, and became animated. At the same time he began to fall into a measured cadence, rising and falling at regular intervals, and measuring every sentence by a strict and invariable cantilation. As he became more in earnest, the tone became more distressing, until it was carried to the utmost capacity of the speaker's lungs. This habit was so prevalent, that I have known it to be adopted by men of very good education.

This is a serious drawback to the power of unwritten discourses. I think it arises from bashfulness in a young speaker. It is easier, when we are embarrassed, to sing than to speak in our natural tones. The one requires a degree of self-possession not demanded by the other. Hence, Methodists and Quakers have generally fallen into it. Among the latter it exists in all its former intensity, especially among the female preachers of that sect.

This, however, is not necessarily associated with unwritten discourse. Lawyers always speak without writing, and they never fall into it. In legislative assemblies we never hear it. The English Baptists rarely read their discourses, and yet they have no tone. Robert Hall, the first preacher of his age, spoke from a brief memoranda. Among our preachers in this country, I have not heard a sermon *toned* for many years. The way in which this habit may be prevented is obvious. The young man who wishes to improve his talent for preaching, should commence in the conference-room, or in a small assembly, where he will be able to maintain complete self-command, and cultivate the tones of earnest conversation. These form the true foundation of all good speaking. When he can speak with ease here, let him proceed a step further, and address larger assemblies. In this manner he will carry with him his natural tones of earnest address, and will be saved from a habit which must render his manner unacceptable to a large portion of his audience. Many of the Methodist ministers, by following this mode of preparation, have attained to distinguished excellence as pulpit orators.

But it will be said that this manner of preaching is unfavorable to study and reflection, and that a preacher thus falls into mere common-place exhortation, without order, plan, or object. This may be true, but not by necessity. There would seem to be greater need of a plan in an unwritten than a written discourse, for without some plan an extempore preacher is liable at every moment to break down. But do we escape this difficulty by written discourses? Are not written discourses frequently, in fact, extempore, without either plan or object? Do we not many times hear the complaint concerning them, that the discourse was well written, but that no one could discover what the speaker was aiming at? Are not written discourses frequently occupied in proving what no one ever doubted, or in generalizing some important truth until it has lost all practical application. In this respect, therefore, the difference is not so great as is commonly supposed.

But it is also said that men who preach without writing naturally tend to sameness, that they have but few sermons, and that whatever be the text, these sermons are sure to be repeated, until an audience grows weary of hearing the same ideas in the same words month after month, if not Sabbath after Sabbath. This may be true, and it must be confessed there is danger of it. But is the danger removed by adopting the other method? Are not written sermons preached over and over again, until the manuscript is worn out by use? Is it not the fact, that many ministers have a stock of sermons that will last for a year or two, and that by changing from place to place, these last them during a lifetime?

The fact is, that richness of illustration, appositeness of subject, and variety in treating it, do not depend upon the manner of address. The cause lies deeper. A man who treats the ministry as a profession, and performs its duties perfunctorily, will soon grow tame, and will produce but small moral effect on his audience. He will prepare for the pulpit with difficulty, and hence we will hear from him the constant complaint of the intense labor of preparation. This will be the case whatever be the mode of address which he adopts. But let him put his own soul into the work. Let him make the conversion of souls, not next year, but day by day, the business of his life. Let him follow up his Sabbath labors by visiting from house to house, calling sinners to repentance, and building up saints in their most holy faith. Let him read the Bible until it is as familiar to him as a household word, lifting up his soul for the teachings of the Holy Spirit, and he will have no difficulty in finding subjects for sermons. The gospel will be in him a well of water springing up into eternal life.

VI.

LANGUAGE OF OUR EARLY PREACHERS UNIVERSALLY UNDERSTOOD.—THEIR DISCOURSES ABOUNDED IN ILLUSTRATIONS DRAWN CHIEFLY FROM THE SCRIPTURES.

But I find myself to have wandered as far from the plan of my discourse, as the most extemporaneous of extempore preachers. It is time for me to return, if I can, and pick up my thread where I left it.

I was remarking that there was formerly a difference

between Baptist and other evangelical ministers, although both believed essentially the same doctrines. In attempting to explain this fact, I referred to the education of the larger part of them, and to the mode in which they entered the ministry. This led me to consider some of the aspects of written and unwritten discourse. I might easily pursue this subject further, but I can tarry upon it no longer. I will leave it by recommending to every Baptist minister the reading of the memoir of the late Dr. A. Alexander, by his son, Dr. Alexander, of New York. It is a most interesting biography of one of the best men and most remarkable preachers of our times. So thoroughly had he trained himself to unwritten discourse, that although a voluminous author, he declared that were he on trial for his life, he would rather make his defense without writing or even meditating a plea, but merely by possessing himself thoroughly of the principles of the case, and leaving every thing else to the excitement of the occasion.

The circumstances to which I have referred, will serve to explain the peculiarity and the success of our early ministers.

In the first place, they were taken from the middle walks of life, adding to the scanty education of their youth such acquisitions as they were able under great difficulty to secure. They were in general very desirous of improvement, and availed themselves of every opportunity that presented itself for gaining knowledge. One of them, who settled early in what was then the wilderness of western New York, has told me how he snatched the hours and half hours of morning and evening for mental improvement, while he was laboring to clear up his farm. As the country settled around him he was a constant attendant on the courts of justice, for the purpose of learning how lawyers constructed a plea, and of gaining from their example ease and self-possession in delivery. With this kind of training it is obvious that the language of these preachers was not the English of books, but the English of common conversation, rendered sober and solemn by the thought to which it gave utterance. This is really the language by which the masses of men are to be moved. You may explain a doctrine, or enforce a duty in so refined and eloquent English, that not one in ten of a common audience will ever understand you. Men never enter fully into the conceptions of a speaker, unless there is a common medium of communication between them. The more perfectly this medium is understood by both parties, the more ready and perfect is the transmission of the thought. The *common people* heard *Christ* gladly. The apostles were observed to be *unlearned* and *common* men, while they were filling Jerusalem with their doctrine. Suppose John Bunyan had been senior wrangler at Cambridge, could he ever have written the Pilgrim's Progress? He might then have written a Paradise Lost for scholars, but could he have written a book for all ages, all conditions, and for men of all nations, and tongues, and languages?

It was this plain and honest Anglo-Saxon that our fathers used in preaching. Hence the people flocked to hear them, because they heard in *their own language* the wonderful works of God. They left the pulpits where the truth was adorned with every grace of classic eloquence, which they could neither understand nor feel, and came to attend upon ministrations which uttered what seemed to them new truth, while it was really the very truth which they had heard oftentimes before. The difference was, it was in the one case clothed in the English of books, in the other in the English of conversation.

Again, it is obvious that men accustomed for years to the ordinary avocations of life, lose the capacity for following a closely connected series of reasoning. The mind grows weary, some link in the chain is lost, then follows indistinctness of connection, so that the end is irrevocably severed from the beginning. I remember once to have heard a very able man deliver a discourse admirable throughout, perfectly conclusive, and elegantly written, to an audience of common and plain people, with here and there an educated man. He saw by their countenances that he had utterly failed to fix the attention of the mass, and was mortified. "I might," said he, "just as well have delivered a lecture on noses." And he was right. The discourse gratified highly a very small portion of his audience, while to the remainder it was almost unintelligible. Had he delivered the same ideas in the language of simple, earnest conversation, breaking up the continuity here and there by illustrations which reflected light on its more abstract principles, he would have carried with him his whole audience. The ten or fifteen who admired the style as it was delivered, might have expressed less admiration, but the truth would have been as strongly fixed in their minds, and the eight or nine hundred would have been deeply interested. Which of these is the best method of preaching the gospel? Which of them would St. Paul have chosen?

This was the advantage of the early Baptist preachers. They delivered their message in such a manner that every body understood them. But besides this, they were not often enticed into the fields of literature or science. They occupied themselves mainly in the study of the Scriptures. From the Bible they drew all their illustrations. From the Bible they proved all their doctrines. Their language in prayer was almost wholly the language of the Scriptures. This gave great point to all their sayings, and it placed them in a region of thought with which all their audience was familiar. They rarely quoted from learned authorities, for the simple reason that they did not know of their existence. They never attempted to prove a doctrine of revelation by an appeal to natural religion, or to the necessary relations of things. They had not read John Foster's Essay, and therefore had no fear of creating an "aversion in men of taste to evangelical religion." They believed the Bible to be the word of God, and they felt themselves called upon to preach it, and to quote it as ultimate truth, though it seemed to the Jews a stumbling-block, and to the Greeks foolishness. They did not gain the mighty and the noble, but they roused the masses. They were reviled by the tens, but the hundreds and the thousands were converted unto God.

VII.

OBJECTION ANSWERED.—MEN OF SENSE DESIRE PREACHING WHICH WILL MOVE THEIR CONSCIENCES.—ERROR OF THE OLDER PREACHERS.—OUR ERROR THE OPPOSITE.

It will be said, in answer to my remarks in the last number, that men so illiterate would not be tolerated in any pulpit at the present day. The mass of the people are well taught in our common schools, and they would be repelled from such uncouth ministrations. There is undoubted force in this objection, until we consider all the facts in the case. There would be no men so illiterate in the pulpit now, were the principles to which I have referred, adhered to. The preachers, it may well be supposed, would not, by any possibility, be excluded from the increased advantages of their contemporaries. They would have as good opportunities for education as their hearers. There were no common schools, or high schools, or academies open to all, when the old ministers entered upon their work. Those who came after them would, with the men of their own age, receive the benefit of increased advantages for the acquisition of knowledge.

Suffer me to illustrate my meaning by relating an anecdote. I happened to be present at a great meeting a short time since, assembled to deliberate on the subject of ministerial education. Among the speakers was a learned brother, who urged the absolute necessity of the most advanced education for every candidate for the ministry, and, as it seemed to some, spoke rather sneeringly of those who entered upon the work of a clergyman without the most extended acquisitions. He enforced his argument by mentioning the fact, that he had lately overheard some boatmen, on a canal-boat, discussing some of the latest theories in geology, and using them as arguments against the authenticity of revelation. He found himself in want of the knowledge which these common men possessed, and felt obliged to burnish up, and enlarge his knowledge of physical science. The argument seemed conclusive, until a plain brother rising, asked the question, "Where did these boatmen gain this knowledge?" Here was a learned man, deep in Latin, Greek, German, and metaphysics, ignorant of what was known by common boatmen. The fact is, that many of our academies, at the present day, furnish a better education than most of our colleges did thirty or forty years since. And another fact, equally evident, is, that it would be far better if our ministers were more familiar with the knowledge of the common people, even if it were acquired at the loss of much which is included in what is called a thorough training for the ministry.

And once more, we deceive ourselves in our estimate of what thoughtful and intellectual men want. I have known a few eminent men in the several professions. They have told me that they do not want this sort of aliment. They have enough of the intellectual in their daily work. They want discourses directed to the conscience, that shall make them feel their moral obligations, and render the Sabbath something very different from all the other days of the week. Our intellectual discourses, in general, have about as much of religion as would be suitable for a sober lecture before an

Athenæum, or an article in a respectable Review. I have frequently listened to discourses from the pulpit, which I certainly would not have read on the Sabbath, for the simple reason that I should have considered them too secular for the holy day.

But here—for I wish to tell the whole truth—the preaching of the older ministers was liable to many objections. Men were apt to use too great freedom in the pulpit. They told many anecdotes, and these were sometimes strongly tinctured with the ludicrous. There was occasionally a want of sobriety in address, and the preacher manifestly aimed too low; instead of trying to please the judicious, he was satisfied if he split the ears of the groundlings. The peculiar humor of the speaker was, at times, too apparent; and, if a man of lively imagination, he would court a smile when he should win a tear. Such was the case with the late John Leland, and men of his class. He was a man of rare endowments, clear-headed, and gifted with great power of moving men. His audiences were frequently bathed in tears, and, it is said, were as frequently excited to laughter. This is bad, and should be always reprehended. And yet few men now living have been as successful in the conversion of sinners as this very John Leland. The men of whom I write aimed at one portion of an audience. We aim at the opposite portion. In both cases there is an error. The souls of learned and unlearned, of wise and unwise, are all of equal value in the sight of God. We should study such a mode of address as will be acceptable and useful to all. The common people heard Christ gladly, and yet the Scribes and Pharisees—the aristocracy in rank and intellect in Jerusalem—asked, Whence hath this man this *wisdom?* for he taught as one having authority, and not as the Scribes. It is wrong to exclude from the benefit of the proclamation of the gospel any portion of our hearers. To close the ears of one out of ten to our preaching is a sin. But is it not equally a sin to close the ears of nine out of ten; while the tenth is the very man who is least likely of them all to derive any benefit from our teachings?

This, however, is a single instance of a wide-spreading and most lamentable error. We select our music and hire our performers for the sake of pleasing those who spend their evenings at the opera, while the taste of a man whose soul is melted by Mear and Old Hundred, is sneered at. We write our sermons for judges, barristers, doctors of the law, learned authors, and professors of science, just as if we had them for our audience. We build churches for the accommodation of men and women who come to them in splendid equipages, or in the hope that we shall, by these means, attract them to come, while the lowly wayfaring man can not afford to attend upon our ministrations. Some denominations have for centuries done thus, and they may do it, if their gospel is supported by the power of the state. But when Baptists do it, whose whole power is in the people, and whose only friends from the beginning have been the people, it indicates that we know not what manner of spirit we are of.

VIII.

MINISTERS DECREASING IN NUMBER.—OLDER PREACHERS URGED MEN TO IMMEDIATE REPENTANCE.—THEIR PREACHING EXPERIMENTAL.

It may be objected to what I have written that all this is very well, but that it would be impossible ever to induce men to enter the ministry if we subjected them to so severe a trial. This deserves a moment's consideration. In the first place, I would ask, What is the way of supplying the church with ministers, which the Lord has appointed? It is probable that He knew the necessities of his church as well as we, and was able to foresee what would be the best manner of supplying them. Do we find in the New Testament any of those requisites enumerated which many persons now deem indispensable? By what right do we establish rules which Christ has not established?

But turn to the facts. For about thirty or forty years we have changed our views on this subject. Has the supply of ministers increased? Has it not sensibly diminished? Nay, has it not so diminished as to cause the gravest apprehensions for the safety of the denomination? Formerly we were obliged to repress the earnestness with which men were pressing into the ministry. Now we are unable, with every inducement that can be presented, to urge men into it. The number is diminishing, and men frequently ask, Is the quality improving? It is said that this deficiency in ministers is owing to the fact that we have but few revivals now in comparison with former years. But why have we so few revivals? We are under a system which was intended to increase the *efficiency* of the ministry. It would seem, then, that while we have been laboring to improve the ministry, we have decreased its number, and diminished its power. We are obliged to call in the aid of colporteurs to do its work, and these are increasing in all denominations.

This leads me to refer to a peculiarity which has until lately distinguished our preachers. They aimed at the immediate conversion of men. The Baptists of the time of Charles II. were so peculiar in this respect, that they considered their practice of sufficient importance for insertion in their Confession of Faith. Thus the London Confession, Article 25, asserts: "The preaching of the gospel to the conversion of sinners is absolutely free, no way requiring as absolutely necessary, any qualifications, preparations, or terrors of the law, but only and alone the naked soul, a sinner and ungodly, to receive Christ crucified, dead and buried and risen again, who is made a Prince and a Saviour for such sinners as through the gospel shall be brought to believe on him."—*Hansard Knollys Society's* Publications, page 37, of Baptist Confessions.

From the manner in which our ministers entered upon their work, it is evident that it must have been the prominent object of their lives to *convert* men to God. They did not enter the ministry as a learned and respectable profession, as a place of literary leisure, as an introduction to a professorship, or presidency of a College, or to a secretaryship or agency of a Society, but because they believed that they were called to the work of turning men to God. Nothing but just such a conviction would have drawn them aside from their previous pursuits. Hence they labored directly for this object. The great doctrines which they preached were the depravity and moral helplessness of man, his just condemnation under the holy law of God, the way of salvation by repentance and faith on the Lamb of God who taketh away the sins of the world ; and these were always followed by earnest entreaties to their hearers to flee from the wrath to come. They preached with the hope that at every sermon some one would submit himself to Christ ; and unless this result followed their labors, they felt that they had labored in vain. They had little to do with the " public mind," " the benefits which Christianity confers on our civil institutions," or with any of the common means so frequently resorted to to render the gospel of Christ respectable. There were perishing sinners before them. They held in their hands the sovereign remedy for the fatal disease which was consigning them to destruction. They held up the disease and the remedy, and besought men in Christ's stead to be reconciled to God. They were generally not ashamed. Though held in low esteem by the learned and the wealthy, they were wise in turning men to righteousness.

In their preaching to Christians there was, I think, another peculiarity. They were remarkable for what was called experimental preaching. They told much of the exercises of the human soul under the influence of the truth of the gospel. The feelings of a sinner while under the convicting power of the truth ; the various subterfuges to which he resorted when aware of his danger ; the successive applications of truth by which he was driven out of all of them ; the despair of the soul when it found itself wholly without a refuge ; its final submission to God, and simple reliance on Christ ; the joys of the new birth, and the earnestness of the soul to introduce others to the happiness which it has now for the first time experienced ; the trials of the soul when it found itself an object of reproach and persecution among those whom it loved best ; the process of sanctification ; the devices of Satan to lead us into sin ; the mode in which the attacks of the adversary may be resisted ; the danger of backsliding, with its evidences, and means of recovery from it ; the dealings of God with the soul in bereavement and disappointments ; the hidings of his face in order to confirm and strengthen it in holy unwavering trust in Him ; the comforts of religion in sickness, poverty, persecution, and death ; the nearness of Christ to the soul when all earthly aid was withdrawn ; these were some of the staple subjects on which our experimental preachers loved to expatiate. They were obliged to look into their own hearts and the hearts of others for subjects, and these were the subjects they found there. They looked into the Bible, and there they saw all this in abundance. They found a response, when they presented these truths, in every devout soul. Christians, when face thus answered to face, were drawn very near to each other. They conversed on these subjects whenever they met. They even used a term to distinguish real Christians from formalists, founded on the consciousness of these exercises. Thus it was very common to hear a devout man designated as an "*experienced* person," or an "*experienced* Christian," by way of distinction from a mere professor or formalist. The mode in which preaching was designated was derived from these ideas. Men did not speak of a sermon as an intellectual effort, a splendid performance, a beautifully written discourse ; but they said that their souls had been fed by it, they had derived food for many days, they had treasured up the truth for months, they had been delivered from the snare into which they were nearly fallen, they were quickened to new Christian effort. These remarks show the tendency of the class of preachers which seems now to be passing away.

IX.

EFFECTS OF PREACHING ON EXPERIMENTAL RELIGION ON SAINTS AND SINNERS.—DISCRIMINATING PREACHING NECESSARY TO THE SUCCESS OF THE GOSPEL.

It will at once be apparent that peculiar results must have followed from preaching of the character to which I have alluded in my last number.

In the first place, religion was brought home in an especial manner to the business and bosoms of men. The preaching told of the workings of the inner man, and the inner man is always at work. It gave to the Christian matter for reflection in the store, the shop, the field, and hence kept the subject alive in his thoughts. It formed topics of conversation. I remember well the meetings of Christians at the house of my father, then a Baptist deacon. The conversation was almost uniformly on experimental religion. The trials and supports, the hopes and the fears of the Christian soul, were matters of every-day thought, and long evenings were spent in the recital of them.

Again, preaching of this kind revealed a broad distinction between the church of Christ and the world. When the exercises of a Christian soul were unfolded, and every Christian soul responded to them, an impenitent man could not conceal from himself the conviction that here was something of which he knew nothing, and that these disciples of Jesus were living in a world as different from his as light is from darkness. His conscience was kept alive by the consciousness of this difference. He stood before himself as a convicted man, and he could not shake off the conviction. There is in such cases, also, little need of argument on the evidences of revelation. The church of Christ, when in earnest, has the witness in itself. The worldly man sees and feels the *present reality* of religion, and what has a *present reality* must of course have a *foundation*.

This style of preaching had also a great power in arousing those who had settled down in a false hope. Men may believe every thing after the most orthodox creeds, and yet be wholly uninfluenced by the gospel of Christ. Their hurt has been healed slightly, and while they have the form of godliness, they are aliens from the commonwealth of God's spiritual grace. When such persons come under preaching which delineates the workings of piety in the human heart, they see that they have never known any thing of this kind of religion. They see also that if religion be a reality, it must produce just such fruits—fruits of which they are perfectly ignorant. Hence it was very common for us to receive into our churches persons who had for many years been professors of religion, but who never knew the plague of their own hearts until they heard the truth presented in the form that was customary among us.

But it will naturally be said that this sort of preaching must have been distasteful and almost incomprehensible to men of the world, intelligent and irreligious. They would never come to hear sermons on experimental religion, and earnest calls to repentance. To gain these, we must of necessity modify our preaching, and deliver discourses in which both church and congregation will readily sympathize.

This is frequently said, and it certainly seems very reasonable, if we look upon it from the point of view which many good men assume. This plan has to a considerable extent prevailed in all denominations. You hear a sermon from almost any pulpit, and hearken to the comments made on it afterward, and you will find men who do, and men who do not profess religion, criticise it in the very same terms. The language, the plan, the delivery, the imagery, are the matters of conversation; the religion of it is equally acceptable to both parties. But let us look at this a little. Is not religion a serious reality? Does not the Bible always affirm that there is an inconceivable difference between the character of him that feareth God, and him that feareth him not; that the desires and affections, the hopes and fears, and the principles of action of the one are utterly unlike those of the other? Now let us suppose any other assembly to be convened, composed of two parties as different from each other as the New Testament represents believers and unbelievers to be.

Suppose one part of an audience to be men professing to be thoroughly instructed in practical chemistry, and the rest wholly ignorant of the science. What sort of a lecture on chemistry would that be which the ignorant understood just as well as the learned, and of which the one party was just as well able to determine the merits as the other? Common sense would at once decide that those men who professed to be learned chemists, really knew very little about it; and that the lecturer, whatever might be his eloquence, was not likely, by his labors, to advance the knowledge of his science. Or take a still more analogous case. Suppose an audience during our revolution to have been composed of thorough-going royalists and ardent republicans, and that a speaker were to address them on the claims of the Parliament and the rights of the crown. Were he to exhort them in such a manner that both parties liked him equally well, and that both sympathized with him in all his sentiments, what progress would he ever make in bringing back his revolutionary fellow-citizens to obedience, and what reward would he expect from the master who had sent him? But an audience is always composed of the friends and the enemies of God, of the servants of Satan and the servants of Christ. The minister is the messenger of God, sent to bring back to their allegiance the lost children of men. If he deliver his message in such a way that both parties like it equally well, and equally sympathize in all his sentiments, he must talk of generalities that mean nothing, or the trumpet must give an uncertain sound, so that no one will prepare himself for the battle.

But it will be said, Are we then to drive away all but

the children of God? I reply, *Is there any Holy Ghost?* If we preach in such a manner that the disciples of Christ are separate from the world, prayerful, humble, earnest, self-denying, and laboring for the conversion of men, the Spirit of God will be in the midst of them, and souls will be converted. The thing will be noised abroad. There is never an empty house where the Spirit of God is present. You could not keep men away from a church where souls were asking what they should do to be saved, and where converts were uttering the new-born praises of the King of Zion. There are certainly these two views to be taken of this subject. There are two ways of seeking to fill our houses of worship. Which is to be preferred? Which looks most like fidelity to the Master?

X.

BAPTIST VIEWS OF QUALIFICATIONS FOR THE MINISTRY.—WE ARE BOUND BY THE APOSTOLIC RULE.—OUR CIRCUMSTANCES NOT ESSENTIALLY DIFFERENT FROM THOSE OF THE EARLY CHRISTIANS.

SOME of my readers have inquired, What are the Baptist principles in respect to qualifications for the ministry? It has been said, and said truly, that I have not treated this subject with sufficient distinctness. This defect I will endeavor to supply.

The essential principle of Baptist belief is, that in all matters relating to religion, we know no authority but the Bible. In matters respecting the Christian church, we know no authority but the New Testament. We renounce the authority of tradition. We eschew all

48 TRADITION AND CUSTOM RENOUNCED.

worldly policy, and resist the encroachment of precedents which would turn us away from the simplicity of the truth as it is in Jesus. Hence it matters not to us how many centuries have witnessed the baptism of infants. *There is no warrant for it* in the New Testament, and we may not practice it. It matters not to us that baptism by immersion is unpopular, and that so public and marked a renunciation of the world is distasteful to many who would otherwise profess Christ. We cannot help it, we must follow in the footsteps of him on whom the Spirit of God descended like a dove and lighted upon him as he *went up out of the water*. It matters not to us that, at an early period in the history of the church, various orders were introduced into the ministry, from which have arisen popes, cardinals, archbishops, bishops, archdeacons, deans, prebendaries, vicars, etc., etc. Jesus Christ has said, "It shall not be so with you, for *one* is your master, even Christ, and *all* ye are brethren," and, though it may deprive us of the attractiveness which belongs to names, and ranks, and dresses, and ceremonials, we feel obliged TO FOLLOW THE MASTER.

So it is in respect to the ministry. We have no right to establish any rules regulating the ministry, which Christ has not established. No single church, nor all the churches combined, have any authority to bind what he has loosed, nor to loose what he has bound. To his word, then, we must go for our directions on this, as on every other similar subject. What then do we find in the New Testament to guide us in this matter?

What can we learn from the example of Christ in the

CHARACTER OF THE APOSTLES. 49

selection of the apostles and first preachers of Christianity? They were evidently chosen not on account of their intellectual endowment, or scientific acquisition, but on account of their religious character. There was, however, among them considerable intellectual diversity and difference of social position. Of the original twelve, John was probably the most cultivated, and mingled in better society than the others. Of the evangelists, Luke seems to have enjoyed the best, and Mark the least advantages of education. Paul had profited beyond many that were his equals in the learning of the schools. It would seem, then, that our Lord chose as the first preachers of the word, men of all variety of attainment, and of very different grades of intellectual culture.

But we may come nearer to our own circumstances. The apostle Paul, after Christian churches were established and pastors were to be ordained, has on two occasions specified at considerable length, the qualifications of a minister of Jesus Christ. The first of these is 1 Tim. iii. 2–7. To save the trouble of reference I will transcribe the whole passage: "A bishop then must be blameless, the husband of one wife, vigilant, sober, of good behavior, given to hospitality, apt to teach; not given to wine, no striker, not greedy of filthy lucre; but patient, not a brawler, not covetous; one that ruleth well his own house, having his children in subjection with all gravity; (for if a man know not how to rule his own house, how shall he take care of the church of God?) not a novice, lest being lifted up with pride he fall into the condemnation of the devil. Moreover, he must have a good report of them which are without, lest he fall into reproach and the snare of the devil."

So, when Paul directed Titus to ordain elders, he gives the same directions almost to a word: "If any be blameless, the husband of one wife, having faithful children, not accused of riot or unruly. For a bishop must be blameless, as the steward of God; not self-willed, not soon angry, not given to wine, no striker, not given to filthy lucre; but a lover of hospitality, a lover of good men, sober, just, holy, temperate; holding fast the faithful word as he hath been taught, that he may be able by sound doctrine both to exhort and to convince the gainsayers." Titus, i. 6–9.

Such, then, is our constitution. Our laws must conform to it. It would seem from these passages that any disciple of Christ, of blameless manners, and pure character, meek, forbearing, temperate, sober, just, holy, thoroughly attached to the doctrines of the gospel, having a natural gift for teaching, and having had some experience in the Christian life—not a novice—has the qualifications for the ministry which the New Testament requires. These are found to be precisely the qualifications demanded in the missionary field, and the men who possess them are the men found to be preëminently useful.

But it will be said, of course, that our circumstances at the present day are very different from those at the time of the apostles. This is more easily said than proved. The whole world of heathenism was then arrayed against the church of Christ. Never was the cultivation of the intellect and the taste carried to higher perfection. The poets and orators, the historians, sculptors, and architects of this heathen world, are, to the present day, our acknowledged masters. The church of Christ was sent forth to subdue this cultivated and intellectual world, and the masses associated with it. And what was the class of men of whom this church and its leaders were composed? They were stigmatized as unlearned and ignorant. The intellectual difference between them and the men whom they were called to meet, was as great in the times of the apostles as it has ever been since. Yet God chose the weak things of the world to confound the mighty. When men of more disciplined mind were wanting, they were called by the Head of the Church. But even here, the greatest of them all declared that he made no use of excellency of speech, or of wisdom, in declaring the testimony of God; that he determined to know nothing but Jesus Christ and him crucified. There is nothing really in the relative condition of the parties, which would render a rule inapplicable *now*, which was applicable *then*.

But it will be said, if we act upon this rule we shall drive off the learned, and intelligent and wealthy, and render ourselves a by-word to the whole community. We shall have nothing but ignorant and illiterate men to preach the gospel.

Well, if this is the rule of the Master, we can not help it. We know of no lawgiver but Christ, and we must obey him at all hazards. If there is any place in which he has a right to supreme authority, it must certainly be the church which he has purchased with his own blood.

But I would ask, How does this conclusion follow? Is every discreet, sober, temperate, holy, just man gifted with power to instruct others, and fervently attached to the doctrines of the gospel, of necessity mean, illiterate, weak, and intellectually contemptible? Are high attainments in piety confined to imbecile intellects? Is there not as fair an average of piety among the more, as among the less cultivated?

Let us meet the question fairly. The apostolic qualifications for the ministry are confined to the illiterate, or they are not. If they are, then it would be safer, after all, to adhere to the apostle's rule, for grace is before gifts in the view of the Master. But if these qualifications are equally distributed through every range of culture, by adhering to the rule we shall have a large variety of gifts adapted to every situation, and after all, have such men as every Christian must say are best suited to the work of saving souls. Our rule would then seem to be, to require, in all cases, the apostolic qualifications, and consider every man a suitable candidate for the ministry who possesses them, whatever may be his attainments or position in society. If he be *apt to teach*, he will be neither an *imbecile* nor a *pedant*.

XI.

IT IS POSSIBLE TO BELIEVE OUR PRINCIPLES AND ACT AT VARIANCE WITH THEM.—CHANGE IN THIRTY-FIVE YEARS.—THE REASON OF THE SAVIOUR'S RULE.

In my last number I endeavored to show what the New Testament requires in a candidate for the gospel ministry. It is obvious that these requirements relate exclusively to moral character, with one single exception, an aptitude to teach. No specific amount of learning is demanded. Aptness to teach is generally a natural endowment, which learning can not confer. Were it otherwise we should not see so many educated ministers who have evidently mistaken their profession, and who would be more useful in some other field.

Now, if such be the rule of the Master, by what authority do we alter, amend, or abolish it? Is Jesus Christ King in Zion? Is he still the head of the church? Or shall we leave him, to follow the example of other denominations, or a worldly public opinion in our own denomination? Or shall we say that these directions were good enough for the times of the apostles, but that we have now outgrown them? By the very same argument we may establish the authority of infant baptism, baptism by sprinkling, or any other practice which man has introduced into the church of Christ.

But it will be said, We all believe these doctrines. Where are they ever disputed? What is the use, then, of argument, when there is no difference?

I well know that we all yield to them a theoretical assent; but this may easily be done when there exists great practical divergency. In many parts of our country, in a meeting called to consider the wants of the ministry, could a man utter precisely these sentiments without giving grave offense, nay, where he would not be stigmatized as an enemy to ministerial education? In meetings of this kind are not ministers who have not received what is called "a thorough training," treated, in fact, almost as "outsiders," as men who, to be sure, are in the ministry, but have a very questionable right to be there? I do not believe that this is intended unkindly, or probably intended at all, but the fact is, we have been so much in the habit of hearing other denominations talk in this way, that we have fallen into it without being aware of its bearing. When any question comes up respecting the supply of ministers for our Home or Foreign Missions, we are presented with an array of statistics from our Colleges and Theological Seminaries, in order to estimate the number that may be relied on. It is manifestly taken for granted, that from these sources alone our wants are to be supplied. We are urged to endow institutions of learning as the means, if not the only means, by which our ministerial ranks may be filled. It is exceedingly painful to observe how, on occasions such as I have alluded to, the feelings of the large number of our most pious, useful, and faithful ministers must be wounded by the remarks of a small number of those who have enjoyed the advantages of a collegiate or theological diploma, or who have taken this subject under their immediate supervision.

It is surprising to remark how greatly we have changed in this respect within thirty or thirty-five years. About thirty-five years since, a distinguished minister of the Congregational church, in order to show the need of Education Societies, published a report, in which he set forth the destitution of the means of grace in the various States of the Union. In States swarming with Baptists he enumerated but a handful of ministers. When an explanation was requested, it was stated that he only counted *educated* ministers, and that, of course, he left the Baptists not educated out of his estimate. There arose throughout the denomination a storm of indignation, and the case was ably argued in an elaborate review of the report. I have, however, lived to see ground tacitly taken, in many of our educational meetings, which would have fully justified the most offensive features of this very report. Yet this has not been done from unkindness, or arrogance, or intentional swerving from principle, but from an unfortunate disposition which we too often exhibit, to follow the example of other denominations, instead of holding fearlessly to the rule of the Master.

The reason why the Saviour adopted this rule is, I think, obvious. He meant to make it evident that his church stood, not in the wisdom of men, but in the power of God ; that the conversion of men was the work of the Spirit, and that nothing which man could add to the simple manifestation of the truth, was essential to its divine efficiency. Hence, he chose the things which men called weak, to confound the things which men called mighty. Hence, also, the apostle Paul, though a well educated man, preaching in the midst of a most refined and cultivated society, laid aside the "wisdom of words," and preached Christ crucified, though it was "to the Jews a stumbling-block, and to the Greeks foolishness, but unto them that were called, both Jews and Greeks, Christ the power of God and the wisdom of God. Because the foolishness of God is wiser than men, and the weakness of God is stronger than men. That no flesh should glory in his presence."

But it will be asked, May not learned and "thoroughly trained" men be holy, humble, meek, self-denying, and apt to teach? Undoubtedly. They are, by reason of their peculiar advantages, under greater obligations to be such. They may be able to do some part of the work better than others. But I ask, also, may not men, not thoroughly trained, be holy, humble, meek, self-denying, and apt to teach also ? Are they not, then, as highly esteemed by the Master as their brethren, and should they not be as highly esteemed by us ? And is there not work in the vineyard to be done, which they can do better than the others ? Has not the greater part of the work of building up and extending the church of Christ been done by men of whose learning the world at least has never heard ?

And besides. Where the New Testament plan has been adopted, it has been always attended with wonderful success. It was so in our own denomination in former times. When every church had its licentiates in large numbers, when every man who possessed the qualifications demanded by the New Testament was called to the exercise of his gifts, when religious meetings took the place of the amusements which now draw away so many of the unwary, we multiplied beyond all example. So it is now in Germany. The little church of seven members, organized and carried on upon these principles, has spread from Hamburg to the borders of Russia, and now numbers its churches and stations by hundreds, and their converts by thousands ; and this work has been accomplished by the use of such gifts and graces as God gave them, improved as they were able to improve them. The Karen and Burman missions furnish a similar example. For a series of years these missions seemed almost stationary. As soon as we began to call to the ministry and ordain all those who seemed endowed with suitable gifts and Christian graces, the missions arose and burst forth as though revived from the dead, and are at the present moment, so far as I know, the most flourishing of all the missions to the heathen. Brethren, are not these things deserving of serious reflection? May not notions have crept in among us, which require to be examined with Christian independence and deliberate caution?

XII.

BY CARRYING OUT THESE VIEWS WE SHOULD HAVE SUCH A MINISTRY AS CHRIST HAS APPOINTED, A MORE NUMEROUS MINISTRY, A MINISTRY ADAPTED TO THE VARIOUS WANTS OF MEN.—CONSEQUENCES OF THE OPPOSITE VIEW.

But it will be asked, If we adopt these sentiments, what sort of a ministry shall we have?

I answer,

1. We shall, in my opinion, have such a ministry as Christ has appointed. Could we have a better? If he has established the qualifications which he requires in a minister of the gospel, can we improve upon them? Have we a right to modify them, or in any respect to alter them? Who will dare to change the constitution which Christ has given to his church? If we may do it in this case, we may do it in all cases, and we assume the very worst badge of the Papacy.

2. I answer, secondly, we shall have a ministry ten times as numerous as we have at present. The ministerial gifts which Christ has bestowed upon the church are now almost hidden. By imposing restrictions such as Christ has not imposed, we are reducing our minis-

try to the absolute minimum. In large and intelligent churches, embracing men in every department of life, men capable of addressing their fellow-citizens on almost any other topic of interest, we can scarcely find one who will dare to speak publicly on the subject of man's salvation. They universally excuse themselves because they have not had a theological education, and no one opens his mouth for God but the pastor of the church. We can find few only who are willing even to speak in a conference meeting. Were we to propose that they should go into a destitute neighborhood and conduct a religious meeting, they would probably, with great self-complacency, tell us that they never interfered with the duties of the minister. We frequently hear this very notion indirectly encouraged by ministers themselves. We hear preachers tell men of the awful guilt of continuing in their sins, when they have been warned by a *commissioned* ambassador of the Most High; as though every man who knew the grace of God was not under obligation to call every sinner whom he met to repentance.

Now by adopting the apostolic rule, all this would be changed. Every man who had any gifts for the work of speaking to men on the subject of salvation, would be called upon to exercise them. We should have men in all the departments of life ready to speak in public for God. Every church, as in Germany, would have its out-stations, where, in school-houses, and halls, and in private houses the destitute would be called together to hear the word of salvation. These stations would, by the blessing of God, soon grow into churches, and these churches, imbued with the same spirit, would be themselves centers from which a similar influence would go forth to Christianize the region around them. Is not this the true conception of a church of Christ?

3. We should have a ministry adapted to the diversified conditions of men. A congregation composed of scholars would, other things being equal, be more profited by the ministrations of a scholar. But how many in a hundred of our congregations are composed of scholars? Our people are generally composed of substantial men, of considerable variety of culture, but not generally highly educated. And again, we are not placed here merely to hear the gospel and profit by it ourselves, but to labor for those who are wandering far from God, and belong to no congregation whatever. We need men, therefore, of every variety of cultivation, men of good sense, fervent piety, apt to teach, to go abroad everywhere and each one gather in his appropriate portion of the whitening harvest.

But some men will ask us whether we are in favor of intrusting the great truths of religion to illiterate men. Will not such doctrines be degraded by coming from such lips? and will not men be deluded and destroyed by reason of the ignorance of the teacher? I answer, first, the great truths of the gospel were first of all committed to just such men. The priests perceived of Peter and John " that they were unlearned and ignorant men, and they marveled; and they took knowledge of them that they had been with Jesus." Such men did good service then, when " they had been with Jesus;" might they not be useful again? We should, however, remember that we live in an age of universal education. Men, not of classical culture, are very far from being illiterate; they are frequently as well informed and as able to move the minds of other men, as many of those who make much larger pretensions.

But if it be true that no man is capable of explaining the gospel to men, and calling them to repentance, unless he be what is called liberally educated, we must carry out our doctrine to its results. We must add that a man not having enjoyed these advantages, can not understand the gospel himself; for, the precise reason why a man can not explain any thing to another is, that he himself does not understand it. We then come to the conclusion that the Bible is a sealed book to the laity, and that we must have a separate order of men to unfold its mysteries to us. It is not, then, a book given to *man*, but only to the *priesthood*, and we, as Romanists, must receive it as it filters through the stupid brains and corrupt hearts of lazy, licentious, and bloated ecclesiastics.

And more yet. This doctrine must shut up almost every Sabbath-school and Bible-class in the land. The business of every teacher in the Sabbath-school is to explain the Word of God to immortal souls, and urge them to repent and believe. These teachers, however, are scarcely ever liberally educated persons, but are, for the most part, young Christians, generally young women, who labor in this manner for the salvation of souls. And is it found that they are unable to labor successfully for Christ? On the contrary, so far as I know, at present, the Sabbath-school converts far greater numbers than the pulpit. It would seem, then, that those who are unqualified to labor for souls convert them, and those who are qualified do not convert them.

Should we, then, surrender all the labor to the qualified class, who would be converted? We believe, on the contrary—and such from time immemorial has been the belief of Baptists—that the gospel is a message sent to every individual; that every individual to whom it comes can understand it, if he honestly and earnestly and prayerfully seeks to understand it, and that what he understands himself he is bound to make known to his brethren who are ready to perish.

But to conclude. Our population is increasing with a rapidity which it is almost frightful to contemplate. The cry comes to us from every denomination for ministers of the gospel. It is said that we ourselves, at the present moment, need four thousand ministers to supply our vacant churches. We look to our seminaries for aid, and for all this northern and western portion of the United States, and for foreign missions, to say nothing of teachers and officers of colleges, they all together present us with twenty-five or thirty ministers annually. In the name of common sense, "What are these among so many?" Things going on thus, we must soon come to an absolute standstill. We must call upon the Lord of the harvest to send forth laborers into the harvest, and we must employ every laborer whom he has designated, or we must give up the effort to evangelize the world. The whole mass of our people must become instinct with life. Every one must find out, or his brethren must find out for him, what the Master would have him to do, and he must do it, not conferring with flesh and blood. Zion would then arise and shake herself from the dust, and put on her beautiful garments; her walls would be salvation, and her gates praise.

XIII.

OBJECTIONS CONSIDERED.—FREQUENT CHANGES OF MINISTERS.—MINISTERIAL SUPPORT.—OUR CONDITION DEMANDS A MINISTRY THAT CAN IN PART SUPPORT ITSELF.—LABOR WITH THE HANDS DEGRADES NO ONE.—DR. ALEXANDER'S FRIEND MR. SHELBURNE.

Those who have read my last number may possibly ask, How can men, such as I have referred to, be supported? They have not the qualifications requisite to satisfy the wants of an educated congregation, and they can not live by the ministry, except by going from place to place, remaining in each church but for a few years. Would this be a useful ministry?

To this I answer,

First, as to removal from place to place, I have not observed the difference between these two classes of ministers, which is here assumed. Men of all grades of acquisition are, at present, remarkably migratory. Whether the more or less educated are the more migratory, it would not be easy to determine.

Second, the Methodists, from choice, remove their ministers every year or two. They have found it no obstacle to their unprecedented enlargement. It does not then seem that this is, in itself, so great an evil as might at first be supposed. But granting that it has some disadvantages, it must be admitted that it is a powerful aid to the building up of an aggressive denomination.

Third, ministers, such as I have designated, would be supported better than they are now. In the first place, there are many among us, of good gifts, who are able to support themselves, who, attending to their secular business during the week, would spend their Sabbaths most profitably to themselves and others by preaching to the destitute. Such a man was the late Ensign Lincoln, of the house of Lincoln & Edmonds, of Boston, who was the means of thus establishing several of our most flourishing churches in that vicinity.

Fourth, there are others who would be able to support themselves only in part. Such men would labor a part of the time in their secular calling, and the remainder they would devote to the ministry. For the part of their time which they devoted to the ministry they must, in all honesty and fairness, be paid. For the rest, which was spent for their own benefit, they would require no remuneration. Thus the German churches frequently send out, to supply stations, men who are engaged in secular business. For the time which this labor occupies, they pay them the same wages which they would earn in their trades. This is just and equal, and valuable services are thus secured at a very small cost.

There are other men who are required by their position to devote their whole time to the work of the ministry. These, on the same principles, should derive their whole support from their ministerial labor. Such would undoubtedly be the case in large and long-established churches, just as it is at present.

Now it is manifest that just such a ministry as this, is required in every aggressive denomination. Denominations that expect to continue in their present state, or to grow only by hereditary increase, do not so much need it. Yet even these can scarcely exist without it. The late Dr. Arnold, of Rugby, most strenuously urged this course on the established Church of England, declaring that unless a class of ministers were introduced into the church, who could adapt themselves to the wants and habits of thought of the common people, the church would lose all its hold upon the mass of the population. The Episcopal church in this country has taken advantage of this suggestion, and it has commenced admitting to the order of deacons men engaged in secular pursuits. A wiser step it certainly could not have taken.

But with us, who know of no semblance of hereditary membership, who must be subduing the world to Christ, or we become stationary and inevitably decline, such a ministry is absolutely essential. Of the four thousand churches who need pastors, and the other four thousand places where churches should be formed in the villages and hamlets of our rapidly extending settlements, how many are there who are able to pay for the whole time of a minister. How many small churches are there, which could not occupy the whole time of a minister if they were willing, by great sacrifice, to pay for it. Every one must see, at a glance, that the proportion of these is very large. These must have a part of a minister's time, or they can have nothing. Why then should we not, by all means, encourage a class of ministers by which alone our wants can be supplied? Such ministers as these, and *a great number of them*, are absolutely necessary to our progress and success, I had almost said to our existence. From the want of them in many parts of our country, we are stationary. We are making decided progress only where such a ministry is cultivated.

But it will be said, What are these churches to do when they increase and need more cultivated gifts? I answer, If a man possess aptness to teach, he will grow with his people, and will keep pace with their increase and improvement. This was the case with this very class of ministers in the western part of New York, who became our most influential pastors. If, on the other hand, a man showed himself incapable of more extensive labor, he would have still his secular calling to fall back upon, if indeed by the honest exercise of it he had not already procured for himself a competence. Every church would thus have within itself the means of extension, every one would "be a fruit-tree, bearing fruit after its kind, whose seed is in itself," by which the surrounding waste would be reclaimed from barrenness.

But it may be said that in thus doing we degrade the ministry, by associating its professional functions with the labor of men's hands, with mean and servile occupations.

To this we would reply as follows:

1. Who is it in the first instance, appointed labor as the portion of man? and shall we who profess to be his servants, call his appointment degrading, or mean, or servile? Shall a Christian look with disdain upon ninety-nine hundredths of his fellow-men, because they labor with their hands? Shall a minister wasting away with dyspepsia, the result of physical inertia, despise his brother, who by obeying the laws of his Maker is hale, hearty, cheerful and happy? Shall a man who is living at ease, call that labor degrading by which alone the means of his support are provided?

2. If this be degrading, then the church of Christ

and its ministers were degraded by its Founder himself. He chose the apostles, the foundations of his church, from the ranks of fishermen, and we see from several incidents in the Evangelists, that they labored at their calling after they were set apart to their apostolic office. Paul, chosen last of the apostles, supported himself, in part, by tent-making. Unless, then, we repudiate the whole early example of the apostolic church, we must agree that working with a man's hands is no disqualification to a minister of Christ.

We fear that the partial prevalence of the opinion that it is in some sense degrading for a minister of the gospel to labor with his hands, is the cause of much of the ill health which afflicts the ministry. To preach a sermon of half an hour in length two or three times a week, should not certainly break down the health of any man. The want of physical exercise will, however, break down any one. It would be greatly for the advantage of the ministry, both intellectually and spiritually, if we had a greater number of vigorous, healthy men, hard-handed, and accustomed to exposure in the open air. They would find themselves, in consequence of out-door exercise, much better prepared for study, able to endure more earnest and protracted labor in the ministry, and every power which they possess would be worth much more to them and to the church, than it is at present.

I do not know that I can close this paper more appositely, than by inserting a passage in the life of the late Dr. Alexander, of Princeton, one of the most learned and able teachers of theology, and one of the most eloquent preachers, that this country has produced.

"Mr. Yarborough took occasion to inform us that there was a Baptist preacher in his employment as a millwright, who would be at the house as soon as his work was finished. Accordingly about the dusk of the evening, an old man in coarse garb, with leathern apron, and laden with tools, entered the house and took his seat on the stairs. Neither Mr. Grigsby nor I had ever been acquainted with uneducated preachers, and we were struck with astonishment that this carpenter should pretend to preach. When we retired, Mr. Shelburne, such was his name, was put into the same room with us. I felt an avidity to question him respecting his call to the ministry, taking it for granted that the old man was ignorant. I therefore began by asking him what he considered a call to the ministry. Mr. Shelburne perceived the drift of my question, and instead of giving a general answer, proceeded to a narrative of his own experience, and to state the circumstances which led him to suppose that God had called him to be a preacher. The substance of his story was as follows:

"'I was born in one of the lower counties of Virginia, and when young was put to learn the carpenter's trade. Until I was a man grown and had a family, I never heard any preaching but from ministers of the Established Church, and did not even know that there were any others. About this time came into the neighborhood a Presbyterian minister, by the name of Martin, whom I went to hear; and before he was done, I was convinced that I was in a lost and undone condition. He made no stay, and I heard no more of him. But a wound had been left in my conscience which I knew not how to get healed, and no one about me could give any valuable advice as to a cure. I went from day to day under a heavy burden, bewailing my miserable state, till at length my distress became so great that I could neither eat nor sleep with any peace or comfort. My neighbors said I was falling into melancholy or going mad, but not one of them had any knowledge, from experience, of the nature of my distress. Thus I continued mourning over my miserable case for weeks and months. I was led, however, to read constantly in the Bible; but this rather increased than lessened my distress; until one Sunday evening I saw, as clearly as I ever saw any thing, how I could be saved through the death of Christ. I was filled with comfort, and yet sorrow for my sins flowed more copiously than ever. I praised God aloud, and immediately told my wife that I had found salvation; and when any of my neighbors came to see me, I told them of the goodness of God, and what he had done for my soul, and how he had pardoned all my sins. As I spoke freely of the wonderful change I had experienced, it was soon noised abroad, and many came to see me, and to hear an account of the matter from my own mouth.

"'On Sabbath evenings my house would be crowded, and when I had finished my narrative I was accustomed to give them a word of exhortation. And as I could be better heard when standing, I stood and addressed my neighbors, without any thought of preaching. After proceeding for some time in this way, I found that several others began to be awakened by what they heard from me, and appeared to be brought through the new birth much as I had been. This greatly encouraged me to proceed in my work, and God was pleased to bless my humble labors to the conversion of many. All this time I did no more than relate my own experience, and then exhort my neighbors to seek unto the Lord for mercy.

"'Thus was I led on from step to step, until at length I actually became a preacher, without intending it. Exercised persons would frequently come to me for counsel, as I had been the first among them to experience the grace of God ; and that I might be able to answer their questions I was induced to study the Bible continually ; and often while at work particular passages would be opened to my mind ; which encouraged me to hope that the Lord had called me to instruct those that were more ignorant than myself ; and when the people would collect at my house, I explained to them those passages which had been opened to my mind. All this time I had no instruction in spirtual matters from any man, except the sermons which I heard from Mr. Martin. But after a few years there came a Baptist preacher into our neighborhood, and I found that his doctrine agreed substantially with my experience, and with what I had learned out of the Bible. I traveled about with him, and was encouraged by him to go on in the exercise of my gift of public speaking, but was told by him that there was one duty which I was required to perform, which was that I should be baptized according to the command of Christ. And as we rode along we came to a certain water, and I said, See, here is water, what doth hinder me to be baptized ? Upon which we both went down into the water, and he baptized me by immersion in the name of the Father, the Son, and the Holy Ghost. From that time I have continued until this day, testifying to small and great, to white and black, repentance toward God and faith in our Lord Jesus Christ; and not without the pleasure of seeing many sinners forsaking their sins and turning unto God.

" 'Now,' said he, 'you have heard the reasons which induce me to believe that God has called me to preach the gospel to the poor and ignorant. I never consider myself qualified to instruct men of education and learning. I have always felt badly when such have come to hear me. But as for people of my own class, I believed that I could teach them many things which they needed to know; and in regard to such as had become pious, I was able, by study of the Bible and meditation, to go before them, so that to them also I could be in some measure a guide. I lament my want of learning, and am deeply convinced that it is useful to the ministry of the gospel; but it seems to me that there are different gifts now as of old, and one man may be suited to one part of the Lord's work, and another to another part. And I do not know but that poor and ignorant people can understand my coarse and familiar language better than the discourses of the most learned and eloquent men. I know their method of thinking and reasoning, and how to make things plain by illustrations and comparisons adapted to their capacities and their habits.'

" When the old millwright had finished his narrative, I felt much more inclined to doubt my own call to the ministry, than that of James Shelburne. Much of the night was spent in this conversation, while my companion was enjoying his usual repose. We talked freely about the doctrines of religion, and were mutually gratified at finding how exactly our views tallied. From this night James Shelburne became an object of my high regard, and he gave abundant testimony of his esteem for me. Whenever I visited that part of the country, he was wont to ride many miles to hear me preach, and was pleased to declare that he had never heard any of the ministers of his own denomination with whose opinions he could so fully agree as with mine. I had the opportunity of hearing him preach several times, and was pleased not only with the soundness of his doctrine, but the unaffected simplicity of his manner. His discourses consisted of a series of judicious remarks expressed in the plainest language, and in a conversational tone, until he became by degrees warmed by his subject, when he fell into a singing tone, but nothing like what was common with almost all Baptist preachers of the country at that time. As he followed his trade from day to day, I once asked him how he found time to study his sermons; to which he replied, that he could study better at his work, with his hammer in his hand, than if shut up and surrounded with books. When he had passed the seventieth year of his age he gave up work, and devoted himself entirely to preaching. Being a man of firm health, he traveled to a considerable distance and preached nearly every day. On one of these tours, after I was settled in Charlotte county, I saw him for the last time. The old man appeared to be full of zeal and love, and brought the spirit of the gospel into every family which he visited. He was evidently ripening for heaven, and accordingly, not long after, he finished his course with joy."

XIV.

WHAT SHOULD BE DONE TO IMPROVE OUR MINISTRY.—EDUCATION OF OUR CHILDREN.—MINISTERS' DUTY IN THIS MATTER.—HIGHER EDUCATION FOR THOSE DESIGNED FOR IT.—THEOLOGICAL SEMINARIES.—THESE VIEWS EMINENTLY FAVORABLE TO MINISTERIAL EDUCATION.

It will, however, be said, Supposing this to be so, we have nothing to do for ministerial education, and we must leave the ministry in the hands of men who are unable to instruct an intelligent audience. We shall have none but ignorant people to hear us, and the cause of Christ will sink into contempt.

To this objection we reply,

1. It is by no means to be taken for granted that God calls by his grace none but ignorant and imbecile men. He requires the labor of all, learned and unlearned, wise and unwise, and he makes some of all ranks the heirs of salvation. If all men of consistent piety, who were also apt to teach, felt their obligations to labor for God in the ministry, the proportion of able and educated ministers would be greater than it is at present. The ablest and most learned man among us, a most devoted pastor, and an author whose writings take their place among the noblest productions of consecrated genius, whose services have been eagerly sought for by a dozen literary and theological institutions, was called to the ministry from the bar. One of the most distinguished Judges of one of our southern States is also a minister of the gospel, who, when the professional duties of the week are closed, dispenses on the Sabbath the word of eternal life to his perishing fellow-men.

2. We should pay special attention to the education

of our children. If we have but little to give them, it is vastly better to spend that little in intellectual cultivation, than to hoard it up, and leave it to them after our death. The father of Daniel Webster, though a poor man, gave to his son all the advantages of education in his power. The result is known to the world, and a century will elapse before it is forgotten. Suppose he had hoarded up the few hundred dollars which this education cost, and left it to him by will, neither the father nor son might ever have been heard of beyond a limited neighborhood in New Hampshire. We are bound to bring up our children for God, and therefore we are under obligation to confer upon them every advantage which will render them useful in his service.

We should pray not only for their conversion, but for their usefulness in the cause of Christ. It is God who confers gifts, and He it is who confers the disposition to use those gifts for the benefit of his church. We should by precept and example, teach our children the worthlessness of all sublunary honor, of the wealth that perishes, and indeed of every thing else but the favor of God. Were we to do this, we should find them by multitudes pressing into the ministry, and willing to surrender the hope of earthly distinction for the blessing which God bestows upon those who serve him faithfully in the gospel of his Son.

3. Ministers of the gospel have here a special duty to perform. By calling out and cultivating retired and diffident talent, they might turn the attention of multitudes to their duty in this respect. But this is not all. Of those who may, in various degrees, be useful in ministerial labor, but a few may, perhaps, be found, who

have the means or opportunity for entering upon a protracted course of education. Others with decided talent for addressing men, have no disposition or ability for abstract study. They may be driven through it, but they derive from it but very small benefit. The gifts and callings of God are without repentance. When God has designed a man for one kind of work, we can not render him successful in another by any course of training. These plain truths should be always borne in mind, in all the efforts we make for the improvement of others.

But what may a minister do for such persons as he finds endowed with means of usefulness, but who are, for various reasons, unable to pursue a protracted course of study? He may do for them what will be of inestimable value. He may direct them to the reading of the best books. He may spend an hour with them once or twice a week, to ascertain their progress, and aid them in their difficulties. He may teach them how to study the Word of God. He may instruct them in the art of making a sermon. He may teach them how to make a skeleton of a discourse, and criticise their skeletons for them. He may send them to proper preaching places, and go with them to observe their manner of address. He may show them their faults, and teach them the manner in which they may be corrected. He may take them with him to visit the sick and afflicted, to attend funerals, and send them to take the lead in conference meetings. And, while doing this, he may give them the results of his own experience, and the benefits of his own mistakes and failures.

No one can tell the advantage of such a course as this to a young man who has a talent for the ministry, and can avail himself of no other resources. If our ministers had always two or three young men in this sort of training, our ministry would be immeasurably increased in number, and improved in quality. Dr. Stillman, Dr. Baldwin, Dr. Staughton, and Dr. Chaplin, in this manner were the means, before any Institutions were established, of doing immense service to the rising ministry. Nor would the advantage be all on one side. Much of a minister's duty might profitably be devolved on such temporary assistants. He might fill his whole vicinity with Sabbath-schools, Bible-classes, and preaching-places, which would add greatly to the power of his church, and bring home many sons to glory. To assist the studies of others would also add greatly to his own stores of knowledge. He would be stimulated to study more intently himself, and would enrich his own mind fully as much as he would enrich the minds of others. Let our brethren who have enjoyed the advantages of higher education, ask themselves whether they have not a duty of this nature to discharge to their younger brethren. A general effort of this kind would be of invaluable benefit to our churches.

Again, there are others whose tastes, abilities, and opportunities, point to the acquisition of more extended education. When this is granted in the providence of God, a man must have but small knowledge of himself, if he does not improve himself to the utmost. We have Colleges and Theological Schools in abundance, where he may enjoy every advantage for study. These seminaries present opportunities for improvement and cultivation, of which, if he do not avail himself, he must have a reason which will justify himself at the bar of God. But let him remember that these can not make him a minister of Jesus Christ. They confer none of the qualifications which Christ has required. They are merely accessories which may give increased efficiency to the essential qualifications. But if he change the accessory into the principal he may be a good lecturer, an eloquent orator, or a neat essayist, yet he will not be a good minister of Jesus Christ.

I may, perhaps, be permitted to say a word respecting our Theological Seminaries. They are all fashioned after the same model, the Seminary at Andover. This is an excellent institution, but it is no heresy to say, that it is not probably perfect, or if perfect for Congregationalists, that it is not of necessity perfect for Baptists. Our views of the ministry, and the conditions of our denomination, are not those of Congregationalists. Would it not be worth while for some one to take up this whole subject and examine it anew, and show what is needed in order to render these institutions far more effective, by adapting them to our own wants, and our own peculiar exigences? At present, the number of young men whom they educate, in comparison with our needs, is but a drop in the bucket, while the expense to the denomination, of each graduate, is very great. Could they not be popularized? Could they not so arrange their instruction as to render it serviceable to men of different degrees of preparation? Instead of educating eight, ten, or twelve, annually, could they not educate fifty or a hundred? With due attention to learning, could they not also labor to make *preachers*—men of popular address, capable of "*think-*

ing on their legs," and able to move an audience by solemn, earnest, stirring, and persuasive address? Our present means for educating ministers are certainly not so successful as to preclude the inquiry, whether they might not be rendered, with the same expense, vastly more efficient. Is it not worth while to ask two very simple questions, first, What do we, the Baptists of the United States, really need? and secondly, By what means may our needs be best supplied? I shall not pretend to answer these questions, but I say that he who will answer them successfully, will do a great service to the denomination.

If, then, it be said, that these views are opposed to an educated ministry, we reply:

1. Is it opposition to an educated ministry, to affirm that *every man* whom God calls to the ministry should cultivate himself, just so far as God has given him the opportunity? Is it opposition to an educated ministry to urge every minister to labor to improve to the utmost his younger brethren, in whom he perceives gifts for usefulness? Is it opposition to an educated ministry to labor to improve the *hundred* instead of only the *ten?* All that we propose is this, that every one be encouraged to enter upon this work who possesses the qualifications which the New Testament has established, and that every one who enters upon this work be urged and aided to give himself all the means of improvement which the providence of God places in his power.

2. If it be said that the apostle Paul urges Timothy and Titus to give attention to doctrine, or learning, or study, we answer, very good, we do the same. He advises those who have devoted themselves to the min-

istry to improve themselves to the utmost. We urge this as strongly as he has done it. A man would never be apt to teach who did otherwise. This is, however, a very different thing from prescribing any amount of classical learning as *a necessary qualification in a candidate for the ministry.* Horace, Virgil, Homer, Æschylus, and Euclid, were as well known to the apostle as to us. But does he make the study of these authors a prerequisite to admission to the work of preaching the gospel of regeneration? We say, let every one improve himself as far as God gives the opportunity, but we dare not prescribe any qualification for the ministry which inspiration has not prescribed.

3. Which has the appearance of opposition to an educated ministry, an effort to educate the whole ministry, so far as it is practicable, or an effort to educate some twenty or thirty a year, and leave the thousand unprovided with any means of cultivation? Do not the multitude, whose advantages have been small, need our aid in this respect more than those who have already received the advantages of a liberal education? While we provide for the one class, shall the larger class be wholly neglected? If education is good for a part, is it not good for the whole ministry?

4. But in this respect, there need be no controversy or unkindness. If some consider it their duty to labor for the good of the *few,* they surely can not be grieved with us, if we desire to labor for the *many.* If some men labor for colleges, they surely would not disparage the motives of those who labor for common schools and academies, without which colleges themselves could not exist. So while some are laboring for seminaries, as it

is said, "of a high order," they will, of course, look kindly on those who desire to introduce to the ministry every one whom God has called, and to give to every one all the advantages which God has placed in our power.

XV.

UNIVERSAL OBLIGATION RESTING ON ALL THE DISCIPLES OF CHRIST TO LABOR PERSONALLY FOR HIM.—SUNDAY SCHOOLS.—COLPORTEURS.— GENERAL INEFFICIENCY OF PROFESSORS OF RELIGION.

I HAVE already extended these notes on the subject of the ministry very far beyond my intention. It is time to bring them to a close.

To sum up what we have said, in a few words. We believe that every individual whom God has called by his grace is under the most solemn and imperative obligations to labor not only indirectly but directly, for the extension of the cause of Christ. No man can be religious, unless he be a religionist. To this work he must consecrate his whole being, and this work he can not delegate to another.

In this work there are various departments of service, each one having his own gift, one after this manner, and another after that. To suppose Christ to call a man to be his servant, and have nothing for him to do, is absurd. Among these gifts is *aptness to teach*, or a power bestowed, in different degrees, to address men on the subject of their souls' salvation. On some men this gift is bestowed so largely that they are called to devote their whole time to this service. On others it is less largely bestowed, and these may very properly combine labor in the ministry with some secular pursuit. It is surely sufficiently common for a man to begin with the ministry and end by uniting it with a secular calling; why may not a man, with equal propriety, commence with a secular calling, and end by combining with it the work of the ministry?

That this is the apostolic plan, is, I think, evident to any one who will candidly read the New Testament. That this view of the ministry is according to the mind of the Spirit, is, I think, evident from the success that has attended it wherever it has been adopted, whether in heathen or in Christian lands. It is in vain to say that to adopt these views is to place ourselves in opposition to the public opinion of the world, and of the various denominations of Protestant Christianity. The opinions and practice of Protestant Christianity are by no means as sure a guide as the precepts and examples of the New Testament. It can scarcely be denied that, at the present moment, Christianity is everywhere losing its hold upon the masses of the population, Our ministry and our houses of worship are becoming the ministry and the houses of worship of the rich and the educated, while the whole body of the people is uncared for and forgotten. Jesus Christ taught us that one of the evidences of his divine mission was, that to the *poor* the gospel was preached. If we do not preach to the poor as well as to the rich, we lose this badge of discipleship. Shall we then follow the example of a declining Christianity, or shall we tread in the footsteps of the Master?

The fact is, if we must speak the truth, almost all our denominations are sinking down into the belief that all the direct work for the conversion of the world is to be done by the ministry; thus making a broad distinction between the clergy and the laity (I use these terms, not because I approve of them, but because they are so much in vogue). We are coming to think the minister is to do the work of the Lord, and the business of the private brother is simply to pay him for it. I say we are *coming* to this belief, *we* have not yet *exactly arrived at it*. Our Sabbath-schools form an exception. It is still held that the *uncommissioned* messengers of Christ may, and ought to labor *here*. But these are conducted mainly by the young, especially, as I have before remarked, by young women. Had it not been for Richard Raikes, I do not see what employment could have been found for our young disciples. But, as it is, as a Christian advances in age he gradually leaves even this service, and thus this work really finds employment for but a small portion of the Lord's host.

Another exception is in the case of colportage. It is strange that we are governed so much by names. The introduction of a French word has here wrought almost a miracle. A colporteur is generally a man, as our Episcopalian brethren would say, not in *holy orders*, who travels from town to town, and goes from house to house to distribute tracts, converse with families, hold religious meetings, and by every means but *formally* taking a text and pronouncing the benediction, does precisely the work of a minister. He is to all intents and purposes a *lay preacher*. Yet, call him a lay preacher, and thousands would tremble for the respectability of the ministry. Call him a colporteur, and every one subscribes to sustain him, and all acknowledge that his agency is of vital importance to the church of Christ.

Yet this work is confined to young men, frequently to illiterate men, to foreigners, and in general to those whose time can be purchased at the cheapest rate. What would our merchants and lawyers and men of property and worldly standing think if we should urge them to undertake this same labor? What would they say if we should ask them to spend their vacations and intervals of leisure in the summer months in doing substantially the labor of a colporteur, or to use the offensive term, of a lay preacher? They would tell us they will give their money. Yes, but God requires not your *money* but *yourselves.* And how much of your money do you give? Why, two or three men worth some hundreds of thousands apiece, will unite in supporting one such laborer, when they might each one support ten or twenty, by denying themselves of some expenditure for useless and soul-destroying luxury.

The fact is that our most intelligent, able, middle-aged, private brethren *have little to do, and they do little.* This broad distinction which has grown up between them and the ministry, has reduced their effort for the cause of Christ to its minimum. Our lawyers, merchants, men of business in the several departments of active life, our teachers and professors have no spiritual work before them beyond caring for their own souls. Hence their piety languishes, they become entangled in the world, they follow its customs, they adopt its maxims, they share in its amusements, simply because they have no spiritual work to do by which their religious principles may be invigorated. Let any one look over one of our churches at a communion season, especially over an old and wealthy, and, as it is called, a most respectable church, and say whether in what I have said I have overstated the facts. Monopoly is a curse, either in state or church. This growing monopoly must be broken up, or the whole church will sink into fatal worldliness.

The private brethren of the church have *rights*. Jesus Christ has called them to be his servants, and he has conferred on every one the privilege of working in his vineyard, and has promised to each laborer a rich reward. He has given to each servant some particular gift, and permitted him to use that gift for him. Of this right no man, or body of men, or ecclesiastical authority may deprive him. Every Christian is Christ's freeman, and he has a right to labor for Christ in any place where his Master opens a door, and he is to seek diligently to ascertain where the door is opened for him.

If the private brethren of our churches have *rights*, then it follows that they have also *duties*. If Christ has given them the right to labor for him, then he has imposed upon them the corresponding duty. It is the imperative duty of every brother who has any power of public address to use it for Christ. You say that you have not this gift. Did you ever try? When you was first converted you had it, and was willing at all times to tell men of the excellency of Christ. Had you continued to do so, like James Shelburne, you would now have become a Christian of a very different character from what we now behold. You have so long buried your talent in the earth that you do not know where to find it, and your whole spiritual nature is suffering on account of it. Let me ask you a plain question. Do you believe that Christ called you that you might go forth and bear fruit, or that you might be a branch that beareth no fruit, whose end is to be burned ? Do you believe that Christ called you by his grace, that you might be a very respectable, influential citizen, a kind and worthy neighbor, willing to attend church twice on Sunday, pay your pew tax, and subscribe to beautify your house of worship, and give perhaps the interest of your income to advance his cause, and has nothing more for you to do ? And are you to excuse yourself for your disobedience to Christ, by pleading that you pay your minister for laboring for souls, and that you are not in " *holy orders ?*"

Brethren, beloved in the Lord, excuse my plainness in this matter. I write not to please you, but to do you good. I humbly hope that "the love of Christ constraineth me." Look abroad upon Zion ; consider her desolations. Iniquity abounds. The love of many waxes cold. Our youth are growing up without any regard for religion, and are yielding themselves up to all the allurements of a soul-destroying world. The masses of our people are not under the influence of the institutions of religion. Multitudes among us, even at our own doors, are pressing on to the judgment day, as ignorant of the way of salvation as the heathen in India or in Africa. Foreigners by hundreds of thousands are landing upon our shores, the decided and avowed enemies of the cross of Christ. The governments of the world acknowledging the name are enemies to the power of the religion of Jesus. And at such a time as this, are we all to sit down quietly and satisfy ourselves with doing nothing for Christ, because we pay the minister's salary that he may do it for us? No! the cause, at this emergency, requires the most active employment of every talent of every true disciple. The masses of the church must be aroused, or the enemy will come in like a flood, and there will be neither faith nor power to raise up a standard against him.

But, while we do this, we must rely on something infinitely better than an arm of flesh. Let us meditate over these things, and ask the Master to show us our duty. Let us with one heart pray for a universal descent of the Holy Spirit upon all his churches. Should the dayspring from on high visit us once more, we could not remain in our present condition. We should be constrained to arise and make sacrifices for God. Then the feeblest among us would be as the house of David, and the house of David as the angel of the Lord.

XVI.

BAPTISTS ACKNOWLEDGE THE SOLE AUTHORITY OF THE NEW TESTAMENT IN OPPOSITION TO TRADITION AND DECREES OF COUNCILS.—BAPTISM: THE MODE OF ADMINISTERING THIS ORDINANCE WHICH WE CONSIDER OBLIGATORY.

I HAVE, for the present at least, concluded my remarks on the subject of the Baptist ministry. I proceed to some other of our distinguishing tenets.

The fundamental principle on which our difference from other evangelical denominations depends, is this: we profess to take for our guide, in all matters of religious belief and practice, the *New Testament*, the *whole* New Testament, and *nothing but* the New Testament. Whatever we find there we esteem binding upon the conscience. What is not there commanded, is not binding. No matter by what reverence for antiquity, by what tradition, by what councils, by what consent of any branches of the church, or of the whole church, at any particular period, an opinion or practice may be sustained, if it be not sustained by the command or the example of Christ, or of his apostles, we value it only as an opinion or a precept of man, and we treat it accordingly. We disavow the authority of man to add to, or take from the teachings of inspiration as they are found in the New Testament. Hence, to a Baptist, all appeals to the Fathers, or to antiquity, or general practice in the early centuries, or in later times, are irrelevant and frivolous. He asks for *divine* authority as his guide in all matters of religion, and if this be not produced, his answer is, "in vain do ye worship me, teaching for doctrines the commandments of men."

It is from adherence to this principle that our divergency from other denominations of Christians originates. We do not make this assertion in any invidious sense. Other Christians may *believe* as firmly as we, that they also adhere to this principle ; and, in fact, did they not claim such to be their belief, they would cease to be Protestants. We fully concede these to be their sentiments, and therefore we love and honor them. We can not, however, divest ourselves of the opinion, that we have escaped some of the errors which crept into the church at the time of the Reformation, and in this respect, how much soever we may fail in other respects, that we are nearer to the New Testament than many of our Christian brethren, whom we love as heirs with us of the glory which shall be revealed.

As I have before remarked, we agree in holding the general doctrines of the plan of salvation with the other evangelical denominations in this country, and throughout the world. The Westminster Confession of Faith probably expresses our sentiments on these subjects as nearly as almost any other document. With the thirty-nine Articles of the Episcopal church, we should find but little at which we could take exception. With the Orthodox Friends we are, on most points, closely in harmony. From the Methodists we differ principally in our views of the sovereignty of God, and the doctrine of election. The Congregationalists of the North, in their general teachings, express our sentiments in all important particulars. With all these Christian brethren we delight to take sweet counsel, and walk to the house of God in company. We rejoice in their success. We grieve in their affliction, and we gladly coöperate with them in every good work, just so far as we can do it without compromising our fidelity to conscience.

The difference which separates us from other denominations of Christians arises, mainly, from our views of the ordinance of baptism; and from the results which naturally flow from that difference. What our views are on this subject, it will be proper for me here briefly to explain.

First, then, as to the *mode* of baptism.

We believe that the ordinance of baptism is to be administered by the immersion of the body in water; baptizing the candidate " *into* the name of the Father, the Son, and the Holy Ghost." We much prefer the simple formula as given in the Evangelists, though of late, some of our ministers have here and there added a phrase or two to it, after the example of other denominations, or in explanation of their own views of the subject.

We prefer the preposition *into* to *in*, in the apostolic formula. *Into* is the proper translation of the original word. This is a sufficient reason for our preference. Nor is this all. It expresses, as we believe, the meaning of the ordinance, which the other word does not. *In the name* of any one means merely *by the authority of*, and nothing more. The word *name* here, however, has a totally different signification. The *name* "of the Father, Son, and Holy Ghost" is only the Hebrew mode of signifying "the Father, Son, and Holy Ghost." Thus, "we will trust in the *name* of the Lord our God." "Hallowed be thy *name;*" that is, we will trust in the Lord our God. Hallowed be our Father in heaven, etc. The idea of the formula of baptism is, then, baptizing into the Father, the Son, and the Holy Ghost. Thus, says Robinson, "to baptize, or to be baptized *into* any one is, into a profession of faith of any one, and sincere obedience to him." (See Robinson on this word.) So the children of Israel were "baptized *into* Moses," that is, into discipleship to him. They thus took him for their leader and lawgiver, promising to obey and follow him. Precisely thus do we understand the formula of baptism. The person baptized abjures the world, and enters into covenant with God. He *was* an enemy to God by wicked works, he *is* now a child of God through faith in his Son ; he was *dead in sin*, he is now *alive to God;* the Spirit of God dwells in his heart, and to that Spirit he professes to subject every thought and purpose, every motive and action. This is what we suppose is meant to be symbolized in the ordinance of baptism, and hence the meaning of the expression, baptized *into the name of*, or *into the Father, and the Son, and the Holy Ghost.* The difference between the two expressions is thus clearly manifest. We could baptize any thing *in* the name of the Father, Son, and Holy Ghost. The Episcopalian service uses this expression (we think very improperly) in the ceremony of marriage. The Romanists baptize bells, standards, or any thing whatever in the name of, etc. We can not, however, baptize *into* the Father, Son, and Holy Ghost, any thing but a *rational* being, a sinner repenting of his sins, and now entering into covenant with the Father of his spirit.

In the administration of this ordinance we immerse the whole body in water, instead of merely sprinkling water upon the face. The reason for this is briefly stated. We believe this to be the meaning of our Saviour's command, when he directs us to go forth to baptize the nations. In this belief we are confirmed by the testimony of all antiquity, by the practice of the Greek church, by all the indirect allusions to the ordinance of baptism in the New Testament, and by the almost universal consent of scholars, from the revival of letters in Europe to Conybeare and Howson of the present day.

We know it is said, Suppose this be so, yet any precept of this kind is to be modified according to the customs of the age and country in which we live. To this we reply, that *we do not feel at liberty* to institute such changes, in a matter which Christ has commanded. Besides, were this so, our brethren who differ from us should abide by their principle. Among Greeks, among Orientals, and Mohammedans, where bathing the whole body is a matter of daily practice, they should certainly follow the apostolic example. The manner of obedience to the command of Christ, would thus become a matter of climate and of public opinion. We do not feel at liberty to adopt such principles of interpretation.

But it is said again, The manner is of no consequence, every thing depends upon the spiritual act, the state of mind of the candidate. If he renounces sin, and submits himself to God, this is the *essence* of the act, and all else is "mint, anise and cummin." Here, however, it seems to us that our brethren who differ from us relieve themselves of one difficulty by plunging into a greater. If the *manner* be nothing, and the *state of mind* every thing; if baptism be *essentially* the profession of faith in the Lord Jesus Christ, how can that be baptism which is administered to unconscious infants, who are absolutely incapable of these spiritual exercises. We well remember to have seen the father of exegetical study in this country sorely embarrassed in the lecture-room by a question of this kind. Nor have we ever been able to perceive how these two views can possibly exist together.

It may, however, be said, that a public profession by an act in itself so noticeable, is a severe trial to persons of delicacy and refinement. It is a cross which they will not take up, and if we adhere to what is here supposed to be a command of Christ, we shall keep many of the most intelligent and influential persons out of the church of Christ.

Of all this we are perfectly aware, and yet it does not move us. Men and women living in sin, are perfectly willing in the most open and noticeable way to profess their allegiance to the enemy of souls. They do not go to theaters or operas by stealth, but glory in the service which they have chosen. They do not shrink from performing dances, at which modesty must blush, in the presence of a whole assembly. And when they put off all these things, renounce the service of Satan, and assume the livery of Christ, is it not proper that this should be done by the performance of a public and noticeable act? If they have denied Christ before men, is it not right that they should also confess him before men? Is it not meet, that at the commencement of the Christian's life, he should take up his cross in the presence of those who by his example may have been led into sin? Would not a disciple in a right state of mind do this from choice, and insist upon doing it?

But this is not all. If we believe that Christ has commanded any thing, be it ever so small, it is morally dangerous to decline the doing of it, because we choose to call it a little thing. This principle once admitted, where shall it end? Why shall we not repeat this plea, as often as it suits our convenience, until every precept which we wish to escape seems a little one, and therefore we may be at liberty to ignore it? With these views, whatever be the consequences, we prefer to obey the simple command of the Saviour.

Few things are more impressive than the act of Christian baptism. In the sight of the whole world, the candidate is buried with Christ, with him renouncing allegiance to the world which he formerly served. He rises from the water as Christ rose from the dead, to live a new life, the life of which Christ is the author and finisher. The act may be an offense to the world, but it is glorious in the sight of God, of angels in heaven, and of saints on earth.

I do not, however, propose to enter into this controversy. My object is merely to set forth the views which we entertain on this subject. The correctness of our opinions on the apostolic mode of baptism is now so generally conceded, that argument in its favor is almost a work of supererogation.

NOTE.—In this and a following number, the New Testament is referred to as our only guide in matters of religious faith and practice. It was intended by this assertion, as the context will show, to exclude the authority of tradition and of all uninspired men claiming the power to legislate for the church of Christ. Several writers, in commenting on these remarks, have thought it their duty to state that the author denies the divine inspiration of the Old Testament. To such an imputation he does not think himself called on to reply. He, however, believes the New Testament to be the standard by which the precepts and teachings of the former revelation are to be judged, and that, thus, it is our only *rule* of faith and practice. Its relation to the Old Testament is very different from its relation to the doctrines and traditions of men. In the one case it is the relation of the meridian sun to the preceding twilight, in the other, the relation of the meridian sun to perfect darkness. It is my intention to discuss this subject at large, as soon as previous engagements will permit.

XVII.

SUBJECTS OF BAPTISM.—REASON WHY BAPTISTS DO NOT BAPTIZE INFANTS.—WE ARE NOT CONVINCED BY THE VIEWS GIVEN IN FAVOR OF INFANT BAPTISM.—ITS EFFECT UPON THE CHURCH.

IN my last paper, I referred to the *mode* of baptism, as a distinguishing feature of the religious practice of Baptists. We also differ from other denominations of Christians, in respect to the *subjects* of this ordinance.

1. The rule which we adopt in our interpretation of religious duty, governs us in this case also. We baptize by immersion, simply because this mode was, as we believe, commanded by Christ, and practiced by his apostles. So, on the other hand, we decline to baptize children, because we can find no command on this subject in the teachings of Christ, and we find neither precept nor example of such baptism in the history of the apostles. Here we rest; and until such precept or such example can be produced, we must continue to believe such baptism to be without scriptural authority. To this authority we hope that we shall always willingly submit, but to nothing else can we bow in the matter of religion, without doing violence to our conscience, and being unfaithful to our Master.

2. But we go further. We conceive that if the baptism of infants had been the practice of the apostolic age, it could not possibly have escaped mention either in the Acts of the Apostles or the Epistles. But it is never in a single instance alluded to. We hear of believers being baptized, *both men and women*, but we hear not a word of children. It is true, that in some

two or three cases the baptism of households is recorded; but, even here, the Holy Spirit has seemed to take peculiar pains to prevent misconception, by informing us in some way or other that these *households were believers*.

3. To the same effect is the command of our ascending Saviour, Go ye therefore and teach all nations, baptizing them into the name of the Father, and of the Son, and of the Holy Ghost. Baptism is evidently meant to be restricted to those who are taught, or made disciples. We can therefore baptize no one who is incapable of being thus taught or made a disciple.

4. All the allusions to the ordinance of baptism in the New Testament, refer to the baptized as regenerate persons, who have been buried with Christ and are risen with him, who have put off the filth of the flesh, etc., etc. This could not certainly be said of unconscious infants, who could have no spiritual exercises, and who could by no possibility make them known.

For these reasons, we feel ourselves bound to decline all semblance of infant baptism, and to bear our testimony against it soberly but firmly, as an innovation upon the doctrines and example of Christ and his apostles.

If it be said that this is intended as a consecration of the child to God, a manifest duty of pious parents; we reply, it is undoubtedly the duty of every pious parent to consecrate himself, his children, and all that he has to God. This is well; but what has this to do with baptism? Suppose this done, what should prevent the person so baptized as an act of his parents, from being afterward baptized, if ever he professed faith as an act of his own? The two acts are essentially different in character, and surely, without a special command, the one should never be substituted for the other. Suppose, then, this were the ground for the baptism of infants, it has no connection whatever with the baptism of adults. And yet more, we ask who has required this at our hands? Where, in the Scriptures, is this consecration, a general duty applying to every thing as well as children, in any manner associated with the ordinance of baptism? The formula is, I baptize thee into the name of the Father, the Son, and the Holy Ghost. This is understood by all evangelical Christians to mean, in the case of adults, just what we understand by it. But in the case of children, our brethren of other denominations understand it to mean, I consecrate this child to God, as I do every thing else that God has given me. Can the same words be intended by the Holy Spirit to mean ideas so essentially different? Were there two distinct ordinances, would there not have been two different formulas of baptism?

But we are told that we ought to baptize our children, because baptism came in the room of circumcision.

To this, again we reply, We do not find this asserted anywhere in the New Testament. We see no ground for even an inference that this is the case. And even were there ground for an inference, we dare not, on our inference, command as a precept of Christ what he has never commanded. The worst corruptions of the Romish church are founded on precisely such inferences. We, as Protestants, hold this to be a sufficient reason why we can not conform to the opinions and practice of our brethren of other denominations in this matter.

But we go further. If baptism took the place of

circumcision, it must have taken that place either in a *physical* or *spiritual* sense. If in a *physical* sense, it must follow the same law, and be attended by the same consequences. Thus, every Hebrew was commanded to circumcise his children, and every Christian parent, it is said, in the same manner is commanded to baptize his children. But the child thus circumcised was at once a member of the Jewish church, entitled to all its ordinances. The church of the Old Testament was an hereditary church, it followed directly in the line of blood. If in this sense baptism came in the room of circumcision, then the church of Christ is an hereditary church, and all the children of the members of a church and their descendants forever, are members of the church of Christ, just as Jews are at the present day by descent members of the Jewish church.

If it be said that baptism takes the place of the Abrahamic covenant, we reply in the same manner. If it is governed by the same law, then not only a Christian's children, but all the males in his family, must be baptized; and they and their posterity are, by natural descent, members of the church of Christ. If, however, it be said, that baptism takes the place of circumcision in a *spiritual* sense, then hereditary descent is thrown out of the question. Abraham is the type of a believer. Every true *believer* is a *child* of Abraham, and is, *for this cause*, entitled to baptism. If ye be of faith, then are ye Abraham's children according to the promise. To this doctrine we do not object. It is what we believe, though we suppose ourselves to have a much more direct way of arriving at the same conclusion.

If it be urged upon us that infant baptism is spoken

of by the writers of the second or third century, we are willing to grant all on this subject that can be legitimately proved; but we can not fail to observe, that among the early writers, it rests not on the command of Christ, but on the doctrine of the necessity of baptism to salvation. We reject the foundation and the superstructure that is built upon it. Besides, what error is there, either in doctrine or practice, that can not be supported on the same authority? If we go beyond the New Testament for our authority in matters of faith or practice, where shall we stop short of all the errors of Romanism? The ground on which the argument for infant baptism is frequently founded is, as it seems to us, large enough to sustain the doctrine of extreme unction, the various orders of the priesthood, auricular confession, and the most corrupt errors of the Catholic church.

And finally, we seriously believe that the general tendency to hereditary membership has been the great curse of the Christian church. This has laid the foundation of established and national churches, and its universal result must be, in a few generations, to break down all distinction between the church and the world. If the principles on which infant baptism is founded be carried to their true result, they must inevitably end here. *We* believe in a spiritual church, and we would exclude from it every thing that does not worship God in spirit and in truth. The reason why infant baptism, in this country, does not work out these results is, in our opinion, that the principles on which the practice is founded, are not carried to their legitimate consequences. We think our brethren are in these respects inconsistent with themselves. We rejoice that they are so, for it is infinitely better to be inconsistent in doing right, than consistent in doing wrong.

Such are some of our reasons for differing from our brethren of other denominations on the subject of baptism. We baptize by immersion, because we believe it was so commanded. We do not baptize infants, because we find for such an ordinance neither example nor command in the New Testament. And still further in the case of infants, as neither the manner of the act, nor the spiritual exercises essential to the act, as we understand it, are present, we do not perceive how we can recognize such an act as the baptism of the New Testament.

For this reason we were formerly designated Anabaptists. We baptize those who have been sprinkled in infancy, because we do not consider them to have been baptized.. We consider ourselves not to *baptize again,* but to baptize those who have never yet submitted themselves to this ordinance. So with respect to restricted communion, the doctrine held by most Baptists in this country. We, with most other denominations, believe that a person must be baptized before he is admitted to the ordinance of the Supper. If, then, we do not admit to the table of the Lord those whom we do not belive to be baptized, we do precisely the same as our brethren who differ from us. The question may yet be raised among us all, whether this is the true limit to communion; but as we hold it in common with our brethren of other Christian denominations, it is a general question, in which we are no more interested than others.

These remarks are not made in the spirit of controversy. Inasmuch as inquiry is frequently made respecting our views on these subjects, it has seemed proper, in a plain manner, thus to set forth what we believe is commonly received among us. As we differ from the greater part of the Christian world in these respects, it is well that the reasons of this difference should be distinctly seen. We believe that we act conscientiously. We freely concede the same belief to others. We will coöperate with them in all that does not compromise fidelity to the Master. We can go no further, nor should they require it of us. We are by no means particularly anxious to propagate our sentiments. We freely and frankly bear our testimony to what we believe to be the truth, referring those who differ from us to the teachings of Christ and his apostles for our justification. We believe the points of difference to be important in themselves, but vastly more important on account of the principles which they involve. To us they seem to hold a place among the corner-stones of Protestantism.

XVIII.

MODE OF ADMISSION TO THE MINISTRY BY THE CHURCH.—NO BETTER METHOD.—BUT CHURCHES MUST DO THEIR DUTY IN THIS MATTER.—ENTERING THE MINISTRY MERELY AS AN AGREEABLE PROFESSION.

I INTENDED, at an earlier period, to have offered some suggestions on the subject of the licensure and ordination of ministers. What I should perhaps have done before, I will endeavor to do now.

I have often heard our mode of licensing ministers

spoken of with marked disrespect. It has been said, How can we have any improvement in the ministry while the authority of licensing ministers is held by the church ? What do common, uneducated brethren know about the fitness of a man to preach the gospel ? I do not say that other men have heard such questions, I only say I have heard them myself.

Now with this whole course of remark I have not the remotest sympathy. I believe that our mode is not only as good as any other, but further than this, that it is, more nearly than any other, conformed to the principles of the New Testament. Let our churches, then, never surrender this authority to single ministers, or to councils, or to any other organization whatever. I believe that Christ has placed it in their hands, and they have no right to delegate it. Let them use it in the manner required by the Master, and it can be placed in no safer hands.

In the Episcopal Church the candidate is admitted to the ministry by the Bishop. In the Lutheran Church, I believe, substantially in the same manner. In the Presbyterian Church, it is done by Presbyteries. Have these means been successful in keeping the ministry pure in doctrine and holy in practice ? How is it in the Established Church of England ? How is it in the Lutheran churches in Germany, of whose tender mercies our own brother Oncken has had so large an experience ? How is it with the old Presbyterian Church of Scotland ? Of the former condition of this church we may inform ourselves by reading " Witherspoon's Characteristics." How much they have improved of late years, the secession of the Free Church might possibly inform us. But to bring this matter to a test, would we exchange our ministry, just as it is, for the ministry of either of these churches at the present day? Or, take our own country, where freedom of opinion, and the watchfulness of other denominations has had a powerful influence over these churches in matters of admission to the ministry, and look at the result. The object of a church of Christ is to subdue the world to God. Which mode of admitting men to the ministry has here been most successful in this respect? For a long time after the settlement of the colonies, Baptist sentiments were confined almost exclusively to Rhode Island. Some of our Rhode Island ministers were whipped and imprisoned for holding a private religious meeting in Lynn, Massachusetts. The Revolution, however, abolished, for the most part, the power of the established orders, and our sentiments began to extend. At this period we were few and feeble. The men have but recently died who remembered when our whole denomination embraced but two or three associations. The land was filled with Congregational, Presbyterian, and Episcopalian churches. We now, I presume, outnumber them all, and we should have outnumbered them to a vastly greater extent, had we not swerved from our original practices and principles for the sake of imitating those of our neighbors. We need not certainly speak lightly of a ministry, or of a mode of introducing men to the ministry, which has led to such remarkable results.

We want no change in our mode of licensing candidates. We do, however, need that the subject should receive more attention, and that in this, as in every thing connected with the church of Christ, we should specially act in the fear of God. If a church will act in this matter, with conscientious desire to please the Master, we know of no better hands into which we could intrust the power of admission to the ministry. Some twenty-five years since, I knew a church refuse a license to two young men, to whom, I presume, it would have been readily granted by almost any Bishop or Presbytery. Both were graduates of college; one was among the first scholars in his class, but his delivery was so exceedingly dull that he could by no possibility interest an audience. He was refused a license because the brethren could obtain no evidence that he was called to the work, inasmuch as he had *no aptness to teach*. He, however, persevered, obtained a license from some church less scrupulous, and if I mistake not, went through a Theological Seminary, and received what is called a thorough training, but I think he was never called to be the pastor of any church, and so far as I know, never entered upon the work of the ministry. The other was the case of a young man of brilliant powers of elocution, and very respectable scholarship, but of erratic and eccentric character. The same church refused to license him, because they deemed him wanting in the sobriety of character and consistency of example which are required in a minister of Jesus Christ. Subsequent events proved that they did not act without good reason. If all our churches would act in this manner, we should want to go no further to find a safe depository of the power of admitting men to the ministry. If, on the other hand, we are false to ourselves, and treat this subject as a matter of form, to be acted upon without thought or consideration, it is not our principles but ourselves that are in fault. Any system that man could devise would make mischief, if it were treated with the thoughtlessness which I fear is fast overspreading many of our churches.

Let us, then, look for a moment upon this subject as our churches profess to understand it. We believe that there is such a thing as a call to the ministry ; that is, that a man is moved to enter upon this work by the Holy Spirit. This call is manifested in two ways ; first, in his own heart, and secondly, in the hearts of his brethren. So far as he himself is concerned, it appears in the form of a solemn conviction of duty resting upon him with such weight that he believes it impossible for him to please Christ in any other way than in preaching the gospel. He dares not enter upon any other pursuit until he has made every effort in his power to be admitted to this work. I beg these remarks to be remembered. They may be considered by many as obsolete and behind the age. It may be so, and yet the age may be wrong. There is a word of prophecy surer than this age or than any age. I know it is common to hear men, even among Baptists, talk of the choice of a profession, and of balancing in their minds whether they should be lawyers, ministers, teachers, or physicians. They will say, perhaps, they dislike the turmoil of politics, the hard and irregular labor of a physician, the monotony of teaching ; they are fond of study, of writing, and of quiet mental improvement ; and besides, they can enter the ministry, be married and settled so much earlier and so much more easily than would be possible in any other profession, that they, on the whole, prefer it. Now I would always dissuade such a man from entering the ministry at all. If he could, with just as clear a conscience, be a lawyer as a minister, let him be a lawyer by all means. The church of Christ can do without him. He proposes to enter the ministry of reconciliation from merely selfish motives, and the Saviour has no occasion for his services. He makes a convenience of the ministry of the word; he uses it to promote his own objects; he is a hireling whose own the sheep are not. If he begins in this way, in this way he will, unless the grace of God prevent, so continue. He will soon tire of the work and leave it for something else, or he will continue in it to shed around him on every side the example of well-educated, cold, worldly-minded selfishness.

And here, at the risk of being considered a Puritan of the deepest dye, I must hazard another remark. This notion of considering the ministry in the same light as any other profession, to be preferred merely on the ground of personal advantage, is working very grave evils in the church of Christ. I rejoice, however, to declare that I believe these views to be much less prevalent among Baptists than among other denominations. A young man preparing for the ministry with these views, feels himself much in the condition of any other professional student. He takes frequently a pride in sinking every thing that smacks of the cloth. He is anxious to appear a man of the world. He will talk over fashionable insipidity and personal gossip, with the most amusing volubility. He converses about his sermons as a young lawyer would about his pleas or political harangues. He is more at home at the evening party than at the bed-side of the dying, and is oftener seen at the concert than the prayer-meeting If any one should suggest that such a life was not quite consistent with the character of a young evangelist, he would probably ask, with most amusing innocence, What is the harm of all this? He means to discharge his professional duties, and this being done, why should he not indulge his tastes and love of society just as well as any other professional man? The apostle James seemed to think his question unanswerable, when he asked, "Doth a fountain send forth at the same place sweet water and bitter? Can a fig-tree, my brethren, bear olive berries, either a vine figs? So can no fountain both yield salt water and fresh." Many of our young evangelists, however, have found out the way in which this can be done. The same lips can discuss the insipidities of fashion during the week, and the solemn truths of repentance toward God and the eternal judgment, on the Sabbath. Brethren, these things ought not so to be.

Suppose such a man enters the ministry and assumes the care of souls. He is continually comparing himself with men of other professions. *They* strive to advance themselves, why should *he* not do the same? His object is not to convert souls, but to distinguish himself as a writer or speaker, and thus to secure some more eligible professional situation, a church in a city, a splendid edifice, a congregation of the rich, the fashionable, and the well-conditioned. Or, he may desire the fame of a lecturer, or may seek for any other form of distinction and notoriety to which success in the pulpit may conduct him. If the ministry of the gospel is like other professions, why should he not? But if the Holy Ghost has called him to follow in the footseps of Christ, and has committed immortal souls to his charge, and if he will be called to account for the proof which he has given of the ministry; in a word, if religion be a reality and no sham, if the crown of glory be bestowed only on those who fight the good fight, if only those who turn sinners to righteousness shall shine as the stars forever—why, then, it is a very different matter.

XIX.

EVIDENCES OF A CALL TO THE MINISTRY OUR OWN CONSCIOUSNESS AND THE CONSCIOUSNESS OF OUR BRETHREN.—DUTY OF A CHURCH TO A CANDIDATE.—MISTAKES IN THIS MATTER.

In my last paper, I referred to the conviction in a man's own mind of his duty to preach the gospel, as one of the evidences of a call to the ministry. I endeavored to show that this was essential. If a man has no other feeling than a desire to enter the ministry because he thinks it a more agreeable calling than law or medicine, he had better not enter it. His motive is wholly selfish. His desire is simply to please himself. He will never labor in earnest, for his motive is low, worldly, and sinful; for it is surely sinful to profess to undertake the work of God, from a desire to please ourselves. And besides, the same motive which led a man into the ministry would as easily lead him out of it. If he found that the ministry was a very different thing from what he had supposed, if he found that it would not elevate him to the position after which he aspired, what is there to prevent him from abandoning it altogether and seeking some more congenial occupation? Is not this the reason why, at the present time, so many are leaving the ministry, and engaging in secular or semi-secular pursuits.

But suppose a man convinced that he is called of God to preach. He could not turn a deaf ear to this impression without doing violence to his conscience, and, in his own view, disobeying God. He feels that a woe would rest upon him if he did not preach the gospel, and that a curse would rest upon all his endeavors if he left this duty unfulfilled. Here, then, is one evidence of his call.

But this is not enough. We may frequently mistake our motives. We may overrate our capacity. We may thus run before we are sent. Hence we frequently see men in the ministry who have manifestly mistaken their calling, who are useless as preachers, while they might have been very useful in some other situation. What then, in addition, is needed, in order to assure a man that he has not mistaken the voice of God in this matter?

I answer, he in the next place lays his convictions before his brethren, who know his walk and conversation. He asks them to tell him, in the fear of God, whether or not their convictions correspond with his own, whether or not they in truth believe that he is called to undertake this work. They are bound to take up this subject with solemn deliberation. They do wrong, if they do not employ all the means in their power to come to a right decision. They must hear him preach, until they are able to form an opinion of his gifts, his knowledge of the Scriptures, and his aptness to teach. If, after a sufficient trial, they can not be convinced that the brother possesses ministerial gifts, they must honestly tell him so. He may then conclude that he has mistaken his duty, and that with a good conscience he may devote himself to some other calling. It was well that it was in his heart to build the temple of the Lord, and he shall have his reward, though the Master sees fit to commit the work to another. If, on the other hand, his brethren are convinced by their knowledge of his Christian character, aptness to teach, and acquaintance with the Scriptures, that he is called to the ministry, this union and harmony of *his* convictions with *theirs* may assure him that he has not mistaken the voice speaking within him, but that it is his duty to devote himself, either wholly or in part, to the ministration of the word.

It is not improbable that to some of my readers all this may seem nothing better than fanaticism, mysticism, and, as they may possibly call it, humbug. They will ask how a church meeting can judge of the qualifications of a man who has spent half of his life in studies of which they know nothing, and may intimate that this notion of the interference of God, for the sake of enabling men to decide such a question, is childish and impertinent. I am prepared to meet all this. There are truths which some men can never see, but they may be truths notwithstanding. The natural mind understandeth not the things of the Spirit, neither can he understand them, for they are spiritually discerned. To all such objections I reply by asking the simple question, Is there any Holy Ghost? In the face of all this ridicule, I maintain that he who has ascended on high, at the present moment confers gifts upon his disciples for the building up of his church; and that he reveals the presence of these gifts by the conviction which he awakens in the mind of the individual, and in the minds of his brethren concerning him. I know of no better way than this by which a man may be introduced to the work of serving Christ in the gospel of regeneration. If any man knows of any better, let him propose it. It is not sufficient that he think lightly of this way. This is not enough. Let him propose *his* more excellent way. Let him do it openly, plainly, without disguise, and make no higgling about it. Let us have both ways plainly set before us; let the people of God place them side by side, and determine which is according to the teachings of the New Testament.

It will be seen, from what I have said, that the act of a church in licensing a candidate, is one requiring grave and serious consideration.

It is a matter of great consequence, both to the candidate and to the church of Christ. To him it involves frequently a change in his whole course of life, and a new direction to all his energies. If he enter upon a calling for which he has no aptitude, his life is, for the most part, thrown away. When a Christian brother asks our advice on a subject of so much magnitude, we are surely bound to give him the soundest and most deliberate opinion in our power. To the church of Christ it is a matter of moment. To advise a brother to leave his present field of usefulness and enter upon another, for which he has no adaptation, is to throw away an important helper, and burden the ministry with a brother who, in that situation, can render it no service.

But this is not all. The brother asks for *our conviction* as to his call to the work of the ministry. When we vote to grant him a license, we deliberately say that we, in the fear of God, believe him to be called by the Holy Spirit to this work. We can not say this in truth, unless we have taken means to ascertain his qualifications. We can not say it in truth, unless, having taken means to ascertain the facts, we have arrived at this deliberate conclusion. If we have arrived at the conclusion, we shall with pleasure make it known to our brother. If we have not arrived at it, we can not say that we have, without incurring the guilt of falsehood. It may give us pain to disappoint the expectations of a brother. This, to be sure, we would gladly avoid, but we can not make a lie about it. We can not say that we believe one thing, when, in our hearts, we believe the opposite.

Such seems to me to be the nature of the obligation under which we are placed in the act of licensing a candidate for the ministry. I fear, however, that we have become very thoughtless on this subject. It is frequently said, if the brother wants to preach, let him preach, and on this ground a license is voted. Now this is manifestly wrong. If he wants to preach, he can preach without our sanction, if he can find any one to hear him, and if he preach no heresy we can not prevent him by any ecclesiastical proceeding. This is not what he wants. He desires to know whether his brethren recognize in him the gifts which will render him useful in this peculiar field of labor, and this is the question which, in the fear of God, they are called upon to answer. Again: I have seen license granted without any inquiry, on the ground that the license is only for a year. This is merely trifling with a brother. He asks us for our conviction, and we give him what is no conviction at all, because the license is only for a limited time. Sometimes the fear of offending friends and relations, urges a church to the same result. All this is bad. It is acting falsehoods. We are asked to answer one question, and we answer another, when truth and the love of Christ would clearly teach us to speak in simplicity and godly sincerity.

Another error on this subject is creeping into our churches, of a mischievous character. A young man, perhaps even a boy, gives evidence of piety and joins a church. He, with the natural fervor of youth, exhorts his companions in a conference meeting, or he may have distinguished himself in school as a promising pupil. It is at once suggested that he should study for the ministry. The Education Society is ready to receive him, if he can present a testimonial from the church. He is too young to furnish any evidence of adaptedness to the ministry. To *license* such a person would be absurd. The following course is adopted : the church certifies that they believe him to have talents, which, with proper education, will fit him for the ministry ; that is, they do not believe him now to possess ministerial gifts, but that education will either furnish or develop them. With this certificate he is admitted a beneficiary, and it is certain that, unless some gross immorality prevent, he will become a minister. In the course of six or eight years he presents himself for a license. He has learned to write a religious discourse. At the recommendation of the church, he has spent a large part of his life in a preparation which has, to a great extent, disqualified him for any other calling. They seem to have no choice, and a license is a matter of course.

The evil here is alarming. The mere youth is placed in a course which decides his calling for life ; a calling which he can not leave without seeming to have apostatized, and he must go through it or be disgraced. Young persons are not unfrequently placed in this course at an age when no judicious parent would allow a son to choose for himself irrevocably a secular profession. And yet we urge young persons, under these circumstances, to pledge themselves to the ministry. Of their course of life while pursuing their education, the church knows nothing. Whether they have been thoughtful or thoughtless, industrious or idle, earnest Christians or mere formal professors, but few ever make any inquiry. The license is granted, and the young man is, by their authority, a candidate for ordination. Can this be the way to build up a spiritual and earnest ministry ?

Of the temptations which beset a young man when pursuing a course of education, few persons are aware; and it requires deeper piety, and a more matured character, to resist them, than is commonly supposed. The beneficiaries of Education Societies possess, in general, the same moral and religious standing as other young men in college who profess personal piety. Now, suppose twenty young men, professors of religion, to enter college, and pursue their course to the close. It will be well if five of these twenty maintain a consistent religious character, attending meetings for prayer with constancy, on every occasion standing up fearlessly for what they know to be right, and bearing testimony everywhere in favor of religion. Of the remainder, a part would rank among the timidly conscientious, willing to be on the side of right, where there was nothing to lose. Some would become Christians only in name, known to profess Christ only by their presence at the communion table; some would be seen equally active for Christ and for the world, and a few would be known as the worst enemies of religion, taking part with the irreligious and profane, and furnishing by their participation in it, an excuse to others for every form of ill-doing. I do not think that in this statement I exaggerate the facts. In specially favored localities it may be otherwise, but I think, after some consideration, that I have made the supposition no more unfavorable than the reality. Now, is it safe to take these twenty together, and place them under circumstances in which they will all, if they choose, enter the ministry; nay, where they must enter it, or lose character among their friends? Does not a system of this kind require some modification? Can we thus fill the ministry with such laborers as the Lord will bless? Are we not expecting from education what education can never do, nay, what it is very liable to undo? Would it not be better to wait a little longer, and try our candidates further, before we place them in such a course? Are we not in danger of laying our hands upon novices, and thus doing an irreparable injury both to them and to the church of Christ?

I write these things with pain. I am, however, dealing with facts, and facts which should be in the possession of every one who is called to form a judgment in this matter.

XX.

ORDINATION.—ITS NATURE.—IMPORTANCE OF EXAMINATION OF THE CANDIDATE.—IN NO OTHER MANNER CAN THE MINISTRY BE IMPROVED.

In my last number I alluded to the manner in which the Baptist churches grant licenses to preach the gospel. It may not be amiss to add a few words on the subject of ordination.

The license is generally given at first with limitation in respect to time. It is renewable every year, and expresses merely, that the church of which the candidate is a member, approves of his design to preach whenever an opportunity may be offerred. By ordination, a licentiate is admitted *permanently* to the pastoral office, and it is generally understood that he is to make this the great work of his life. A single church does not ordain. It calls a council, generally representing the churches in the vicinity, who are present by their minister and such private brethren as they may select. At the time appointed, these delegates meet and organize themselves by the choice of a Moderator and Clerk. The doings of the church calling the council are read. The candidate gives a narration of his conversion, views of the ministry, and of his call to the ministerial office, and presents a brief synopsis of the doctrines which he believes, and purposes to preach. If these are satisfactory to his brethren, they resolve to proceed to his ordination. The various services are assigned to the several brethren composing the council. The candidate is set apart by prayer and laying on of hands. The minutes of the council are recorded in the church books, and thus the service is completed.

MODIFICATIONS SUGGESTED. 115

So far as the theory is concerned, we seem, in this matter, to need no change. The churches in the vicinity may be considered as the representatives of all the Baptist churches. The churches represented appear, as is proper, by ministers and private members. They obtain such evidence as satisfies them that the candidate is called, not merely to preach, but to devote himself to the work of preaching, and they set him apart to this work accordingly. I do not perceive how our custom, in this respect, could be improved. Were I to suggest any alteration, it would be in the ordination service. Following more and more closely in the footsteps of Congregationalists and Presbyterians, we have made it much longer and more complicated than formerly. And besides, it seems to be taken for granted, that a *part*, as it is called, must be assigned to every member of the council. This seems a little puerile, and might properly be corrected.

It will be at once apprehended that the act of a council in this matter is one of no ordinary solemnity. The candidate has previously asked the church, whether, in their opinion, the Holy Ghost has called him to publish the good news of salvation, wherever he may have opportunity. They have decided in the affirmative. After a sufficient time for trial, in the presence of the churches, a council of elders and private brethren is assembled, and of them he inquires, whether, in their judgment he is called of God to devote his life to the work of an evangelist or a pastor. It is natural to suppose that, before answering this question, the council would take pains to ascertain the facts on which their opinion must be founded; that they would inquire into the Christian walk and conversation of the candidate; his manner of life since he contemplated entering the ministry; his character as a man of piety in the academy, college, or seminary, in which, if he have been a student, the last few years of his life have been passed; the impression which he has made on the churches among whom he has labored; and, besides all this, that they would hear him themselves, in order to be able to judge from his gifts whether he be called to the work. Besides, it would be expected that a company of grave and solid men would desire to ascertain the knowledge possessed by the candidate of the way of salvation, and that they would minutely and carefully examine him in some of the cardinal doctrines of revelation. The strictness of this examination would depend much on the advantages of the candidate. The greater his advantages, the stricter should be the examination. No precise amount of knowledge should be specified as absolutely necessary, but the fact should be determined, that the candidate was a sober and earnest inquirer into the truth of the New Testament, and that, besides knowing what was necessary to his own salvation, he was able to teach others also. It is natural to expect that an ordination would be a season of moral thoughtfulness, solemn deliberation, and earnest prayer for divine direction; that the elder brethren would point out any thing defective in their younger brother, and unite in an effort, as far as was in their power, to render him a faithful minister of Jesus Christ. Would not such a course do much to improve the character of the ministry? Where is there a minister of Jesus Christ who would not now thank God, if such a course had been pursued when he was entering upon his work? It is somewhat strange that, while so much is said at present about raising the standard of ministerial qualifications, so little attention is paid to this subject. The Methodists carry out very thoroughly a system of examination for all their licentiates, and this is one reason of their unparalleled success.

I fear, however, that these important considerations are frequently neglected. The council ordinarily convenes on the day that has been publicly announced for the ordination. They have no time for any such inquiries as I have suggested, and they are, therefore, never made. It frequently happens that not a member of the council has ever heard the candidate preach, or has the means of knowing any thing of importance respecting his qualifications. The statement of the candidate's call to the ministry, and of his views of doctrine, have almost passed into a stereotype form. An ordination, in short, is in danger of being considered merely a pleasant meeting of ministers—the private brethren in attendance being very few—to transact a matter of form, to be kindly entertained, and attend the ordination service in the afternoon. Is this the nature of ordination as it is set before us in the New Testament? Is this the answer of a good conscience, when a brother solemnly inquires of us whether we believe that God has set him apart for the pastoral office?

To illustrate what I mean on this subject, allow me to refer to an ordination which I attended but a few years since, in New England. The candidate was a young man of good education and religious standing, and he had preached as a candidate for the church that called him to ordination, for a reasonable length of time. Letters were sent out inviting a council, composed of delegates from the neighboring churches, and as usual, the parts were assigned to the several members in advance. The council was to meet in the morning, and the ordination services were appointed for the afternoon. At the time specified but few members appeared, but they dropped in one by one, on the arrival of the cars. A considerable period had elapsed, after the hour of meeting, before the council was called to order. When the church was called on to state to the council its action in the premises, hardly any member was present; the clerk had not yet arrived; he could not be found; and there were really no documents on which the council could properly proceed. It was determined to commence without them, and read them as soon as they could be produced. When the candidate was called upon, it appeared that he was not a member of the church over which he was to be ordained, his letter of dismission from the church in the town where he had been residing, not having yet come to hand. There was, therefore, no documentary evidence that he was a member of any church at all. After giving an account of his conversion, and the usual statement of his call to the ministry, and a very general view of the doctrines which he believed, the council was invited to ask the candidate any questions they thought fit. After a short pause, an elderly minister who happened to be present, began to question the candidate on some of the fundamental doctrines of the New Testament. The questions were such as any person who had studied the **word of God** carefully, should be able to answer on the instant, and yet I heard them spoken of as constituting a very searching examination. They had, however, been continued but a short time, when it was evident that the business would not be completed in season for dinner, if they were much longer protracted. The question came up for admitting the candidate to ordination. The records of the church had, in the mean time, been produced, and found to be satisfactory. Several members testified that, to the best of their knowledge and belief, the brother was a member in good standing, and it was resolved unanimously to proceed with the ordination. It seemed to be taken for granted that the act of the council was merely a matter of form. This is, I presume, very much like a large portion of the ordinations among us, in many parts of this country. I ought, perhaps, to add, that I was not a member of the council, but being present, was politely invited to a seat.

My brethren, we hear frequent complaint of a deterioration of the ministry; that our young ministers are not as grave, devout, and as well acquainted with the Scriptures as formerly. I ask at whose door shall the blame be laid. If we make the licensing and ordaining of ministers a mere matter of form; if the churches turn this duty over to the Committees of the Education Societies, and the Education Societies neglect it because it is the duty of the churches; and if councils meet merely to record what has been theoretically done, but practically left undone by both churches and Education Societies, what is to become of the ministry? In whatever business we are engaged, if any thing is going wrong, it is always wise to ask first of all, What part of the blame rests upon ourselves? Whatever deficiencies there are in the ministry, it is in the power of the churches to correct, and the power exists nowhere else on earth. If we agree to admit every one who chooses into the ministry, why should we turn about and complain that every one who chooses is admitted? We must all begin at home, if we would see the evils of which we complain corrected.

Here, as I have had occasion so often to observe, we have been led astray by following the example of other denominations. We believe that a man is moved by the Holy Ghost to enter the ministry, and that when he is thus moved, the mind of the Spirit is made manifest to him and to his brethren. A great part of our Pedobaptist brethren consider the ministry merely as a profession, which any church member of sufficient education may enter. The two views are entirely dissimilar. They have constructed their system of preparation for and entrance to the ministry on their own views. We, while holding radically dissimilar opinions, have, I had almost said, servilely adopted their system in almost all of its parts. Hence our doctrine and our practice are at variance with each other, and there is danger lest our practice undermine and subvert our doctrine altogether. Would it not be better to reverse this order, and conform our practice to what we believe to be according to the mind of the Spirit?

In conclusion, let me ask, First, would it not be better for no church to grant a license, or semblance of a license, until they have taken all reasonable means to ascertain that the applicant was designed by the Master to be a preacher of the gospel?

2. Is it not incumbent on a council, in a corresponding manner, to satisfy themselves that the candidate possesses the qualifications required in the New Testament for the office of a pastor or an evangelist?

3. Ought ordinations ever to be held on the day of the meeting of the council?

4. Should not the council, besides fully examining the candidate, hear him preach themselves, at least so often that they may be able to form a judgment concerning his qualifications for the work?

5. Would it not be well to render ordinations and meetings of councils, seasons of solemn and united prayer for the blessing of God on the candidate and the church?

This, it is said, will take much time. I have, however, found that the *very shortest time in which it is possible to do any thing, is just so much time as is necessary to do it well.*

XXI.

THE POINTS IN WHICH WE DIFFER FROM OTHER SECTS IMPORTANT.— THE MANNER IN WHICH WE HAVE ESCAPED THE ERRORS INTO WHICH OTHERS HAVE FALLEN.

I HAVE, on several occasions, alluded to the fact that we have suffered loss, as Baptists, by following the examples of other denominations. It would almost seem to an observer that we were ashamed of our own peculiar sentiments, and took pleasure in testifying that between us and other sects there were no real points of difference. I think the points of difference are important, and that our whole history is, in the highest degree, honorable to us as a Christian sect. If any sect "has occasion to glory, we more." If any man among us does not feel a manly pride in the sentiments which have distinguished us, and in the manner in which we have maintained them, there must exist something peculiar either in his head or his heart.

The nature of the difference which distinguishes us from others, is on this wise: it is evident that all disciples of Christ must hold essentially the same belief respecting the character of God, the obligations and character of man, and the way of salvation through the merits and atonement of the Redeemer. But it is also evident that, holding these truths, men may adopt sentiments at practical variance with them. These sentiments, in process of time, may encroach upon and undermine the truth, so that it becomes more and more inoperative, until, at last, a church once spiritual and heavenly-minded becomes formal, ritual, and worldly. Of course we are to judge of any denomination not merely by what it believes, but also by the contradictory elements which it has associated with its belief, and which, in the long run, may cause it to swerve from the simplicity of the truth as it is in Jesus. This, we think, has been the misfortune of many of our Christian brethren, whose belief, according to their formularies, agrees quite closely with our own.

We, on the other hand, think that, by the grace of God, we have been enabled to exclude from our belief many of those principles which have exerted a deleterious influence on some of our brethren. In a word, we hope that we have followed more closely in the steps of the Master, excluding the errors derived from the traditions of the fathers, the decisions of councils, and the enactments of state, and cleaving more firmly to the simple teachings of Christ and his apostles. We utter this in no spirit of arrogance or self-esteem, but in devout thankfulness to the Great Teacher, who, we believe, has condescended to make known to us the truth more perfectly.

But it will be said, How can you ascribe this more perfect knowledge of the word of God to yourselves? You have not numbered among you profound philosophers, learned philologists, acute logicians, or any of those gigantic intellects to whom we look up as the lights of the advancing ages. I answer, we have arrived at a clearer knowledge of divine truth, for the very reason that we have had no such guides to follow. Our fathers were, for the most part, plain, unlearned men. Having nowhere else to look, they looked up in humility to the Holy Spirit to teach them the meaning of the word of God. They had no learned authorities to lead them astray. They mingled in no aristocratic circles, whose overwhelming public sentiment might crush the first buddings of earnest and honest inquiry. As little children they took up the Bible, supposing it to mean just what it said, and willing to practice whatever it taught. Thus they arrived at truth which escaped the notice of the learned and the intellectually mighty.

This is just what we might have expected. The New Testament was given as a revelation, not to the learned or the philosophically wise, but to every one born of woman. In it, God speaks to *every individual* of our race, as much as though that individual was the only being whom it addressed. Such a communication must evidently be made as plain and simple as language could make it. In the New Testament, Infinite Wisdom has put forth its power to render the truth by which we must be saved easy to be understood. Such being the nature of the revelation, it is manifest that the best of all interpreters must be a humble and childlike disposition. The mind which is most thoroughly purified from every desire to conform the word of God to its preconceived opinions or biases, will be, of all others, the most likely to discover the truth which the Spirit intended to convey. Such is clearly the teaching of our Saviour on this subject. "I thank thee, O Father, Lord of heaven and earth, because thou hast hidden these things from the wise and prudent, and hast revealed them unto babes. Even so, Father, for so it seemed good in thy sight." I hope I have all due respect for learning, and especially for philological learning. I trust I am not wanting in reverence for the wise and good of our own and of preceding ages. But I would ask, in that age of robust scholars, which of them had so deep and thorough an understanding of the mind of the Spirit in the New Testament as John Bunyan? Shut up for twelve years in Bedford jail for the testimony of Jesus, his soul wrung with anguish by the tears of his starving wife and helpless babes, with no book but the Bible, a ray of light from the throne of God shone down on the sacred oracles, as he looked upon them, and revealed to him mysteries which the learned could not see, and which he has unfolded to the admiring gaze of all the coming ages. Take another case of a different character. Neander was learned in philosophy, and in the history of the church, beyond any man of this age, perhaps of any age. Take up now his Commentary on John's First Epistle, the best of his works, of this character, with which I am acquainted. The excellency of this exposition is not at all owing to his marvelous learning, but to the childlike and loving temper which places him in so delightful harmony of spirit with the beloved apostle. If such be the law of the divine dispensation, it is not remarkable that the truth which was hidden from the wise and prudent has been revealed unto babes. And that this nas been so, would seem to be evident, from the fact that the sentiments which we have maintained for generations, amid obloquy and contempt, are now admitted to be truths by the profoundest thinkers and the most learned Christian philosophers of the present age; by men of the logical acumen of a Whately, and the philological and historical learning of a Bunsen and a Neander.

XXII.

HEREDITARY MEMBERSHIP AT VARIANCE WITH THE IDEA OF THE SPIRITUALITY OF THE CHURCH.—TENDENCY OF INFANT BAPTISM TO ESTABLISH HEREDITARY MEMBERSHIP.

IN my last paper I stated, in general, the reasons why a Baptist should be thankful to God for the past history of his denomination. It may be expected that I should present the case more in detail. I trust I am prepared to do so, and will illustrate my meaning by examples.

In common with other evangelical denominations, we hold the doctrines of the depravity of man, the necessity of piety to church membership, and the necessity of regeneration, in order to render a man fit for the kingdom of God in heaven, or the church of Christ on earth. That is, we believe that the heart of man is estranged entirely from God, and is, therefore, in its natural state, incapable of holy affections, or of any act which fulfills the requirements of the law; that the church of Christ is made up, not of those who are members by profession, but only of those who are changed in their affections, who love God with a filial temper, and submit themselves in all things to the precepts and example of Christ, relying wholly on his merits for salvation. This change of heart is called, in the Scriptures, regeneration, and hence our belief is, that the church of Christ is made up wholly of regenerated persons. To the truth of these doctrines we have always borne testimony, and we have always intended to reject every practice and ordinance at variance with them. On these doctrines rests the superstructure of a spiritual church, of that church whose members are "a royal priesthood, a holy nation, a peculiar people." Suffer them, for any cause, to be obscured or undermined, and the dividing line between the church and the world is removed, and what was once a church of Christ in reality, becomes such only in name. I do not say that such will be the result within a single generation, but such is the tendency, and as surely as things follow their tendencies, they must sooner or later arrive at this termination.

For instance, suppose a church of Christ, holding

the doctrines I have referred to above, also admits the practice of infant baptism. It is granted that there is no precept commanding, or example sanctioning this rite in the New Testament. It must, therefore, if a duty, be such in consequence of some other truth which necessitates the obligation to perform it. What, then, are the doctrines on which this obligation rests? Is it the covenant with Abraham? But all the children of Abraham, and the servants born in his house, were members of the patriarchal church. Why, then, should they not be members also of the Christian church, if it be formed on the same model? Or, is the ground of infant baptism the rite of circumcision, under the Mosaic law? Every male, by this rite, and every female without it, became a member of the Hebrew church, entitled to eat the Passover, and enjoy all the immunities belonging to the theocratic commonwealth. If this be our model, why should not corresponding privileges be accorded to the children baptized under the New Testament dispensation? Here the door is at once opened to hereditary membership. The practice and the principles of Christians holding these beliefs are at variance, and, in such cases, it commonly happens that the practice encroaches on the principle. This occurred in the time of President Edwards. In the first place, the children of those who were not church members were admitted to baptism. Then persons who had been baptized, and were of moral life, who professed a desire to be converted, were admitted to the church. And thus it came to pass that, at one period, every respectable householder of the town was expected to be a member of the church. Thus, at the same time, in the Reformed Dutch churches in this country, Mrs. Grant tells us that every young man, at the age of twenty-one, was married and joined the church, as a matter of course. In the Established Church of Enland, confirmation, by which a person is admitted to communion, is expected of every one on arriving at a suitable age. In the Lutheran churches the custom is universal. Thus the doctrine of the spirituality of the church is, in the end, subverted by the doctrine of hereditary membership, introduced by the principle on which infant baptism is supported.

A striking illustration of the result of the admission of the doctrine of hereditary membership is seen in the history of the Friends, or Quakers. They had arrived at remarkably clear ideas of the religion of the New Testament, and of the obligations which it imposed. They, however, rejected ordinances altogether, observing that they had become merely a matter of form. Yet they adopted the principle of hereditary membership. In a few generations, the societies of these disciples, who, at the first, proclaimed the truth of the spirituality of the church, were filled with hereditary members destitute of the grace of God. Then ensued a division, by which the formal and the spiritual were separated from each other. But the spiritual, adhering to the doctrine of hereditary membership, were soon again overwhelmed by merely worldly professors. Other divisions ensued. Thus, in spite of the purity and beauty of their original principles, they have been continually diminishing; and, it is to be feared, will before long cease to be a distinct denomination of Christians. We can not but believe that a high honor has been conferred on us by the Master, in that we have been taught to bear testimony at all times, against what we believe to be an error so subversive of the doctrine of the spirituality of the church of Christ.

But take the other grounds on which the baptism of infants is enforced. It is said by some that baptism purifies the child from original sin. If it be thus purified, and its nature made holy, why should it not at once be admitted to a holy church ? Or, is the doctrine of baptismal regeneration entertained, and is it said before baptism that "none can enter into the kingdom of God, except he be regenerated and born anew ;" and after baptism, "thanks are rendered to God that he has been pleased to regenerate this infant with his Holy Spirit, to receive him for his own child by adoption, and incorporate him into his holy church," why should he not be admitted to all the privileges of the church of Christ ? But it is practically found that no moral change follows this ordinance, and hence the church is filled with worldly men, and the doctrine of the spirituality of the kingdom of Christ is virtually ignored.

Or, is it said, that setting aside all these views, we found the obligation of infant baptism on the traditions of the church, and its practice in the latter part of the second, and the beginning of the third centuries ? We then concede the principle, that the acts of men of that period had power to bind the conscience, and we are obliged to receive as truth whatever they taught, and to follow their example in whatever they put in practice. Here, then, we abandon Protestantism, and adopt almost all the errors of the church of Rome.

Against these errors, as we conceive them, and the

principles on which they are founded, we have had the honor of ever bearing our earnest and decided testimony.

XXIII.

OTHER TRUTHS TO WHICH BAPTISTS HAVE BORNE TESTIMONY.—THE SPIRITUALITY OF THE CHURCH OF CHRIST.—THE RIGHT OF PRIVATE JUDGMENT.—THE SUFFICIENCY OF THE NEW TESTAMENT AS OUR RULE OF FAITH AND PRACTICE.—THE SEPARATION OF THE CHURCH FROM THE STATE.

IN my last paper I took occasion to observe that while the Baptists, with other evangelical denominations, held the doctrine of the exclusive spirituality of the church of Christ, to them belonged the honor of holding this fundamental truth in its purity and simplicity, and of rejecting every principle and practice at variance with it. I also alluded to the fact that infant baptism can not be maintained without involving some belief opposed to this fundamental article of vital Christianity. We may at various times have become lax in our discipline, and have failed to carry out in practice the principles which we believe. In such cases, all we need is to seek out the old paths and walk therein, to act, in a word, according to our established belief, and "we are ourselves again." On the contrary, those who hold to practices founded on beliefs at variance with this doctrine, can not be thus rectified. Their principles are contradictory, and to carry them all out to their legitimate results, must lead either to inextricable confusion, or else to the subversion of some fundamental doctrine of the gospel.

But this is not the only tenet by which our denomination has been always distinguished.

1. As a natural and inspired consequence of the doctrine of the spirituality of the church, we have ever held to that of the universal priesthood of believers. We have always proclaimed that every child of God has the right, in his own person, of drawing near to God through the intercession of the one only Mediator and High Priest. Hence we reject all notions of the necessity of human mediators, and with it, all belief in the holiness of a priesthood, and in general of an ecclesiastical caste. While we believe that men are to be set apart for the duties of the ministry in whom we see the evidence of ministerial gifts, yet, that it is the church itself—by which I mean not the clergy, but the whole body of Christians—which sets them apart; and that when thus appointed to this work, they are, by this act, rendered no better or holier than their brethren. They are not thus made lords over God's heritage, but servants of the church, appointed to minister in spiritual things. They have no authority, either individually or collectively, to legislate for their brethren, but are, in all respects, just as any other believers, subject to the law of Christ. This, in a country like our own, where the press is free and the church can not wield the arm of the state, may seem a matter of secondary moment. But let any one cast his eyes over the past history of Christianity, and observe the universal tendency of teachers of religion to constitute themselves into a priesthood, to assert dominion over the conscience, and to use the power which they have usurped for their own advantage, and to the extinction of piety, and he will, I

think, come to a very different conclusion. No more fatal error has, in all ages, dogged the footsteps of the church of Christ, than the belief in the official holiness of the teacher of religion, and the necessity of a human mediator, in some sort, to appear on our behalf before God. From this belief have been developed those various forms of ecclesiastical hierarchy, which now, with their appalling weight, press down the masses of Europe, and hold them bound in the fetters of spiritual ignorance and sin.

Another truth which has always been inscribed on our banner is, the absolute right of private judgment in all matters of religion. We have always believed that the New Testament was not given by God to a priesthood, to be by them diluted, compounded, and adulterated, and then retailed by the pennyworth to the people; but, on the contrary, that the whole revelation in its totality, in all its abundance of blessing, with all its solemn warnings, and its exceeding great and precious promises, is a communication from God to every individual of the human race. It is given to the minister in no higher, or better, or different sense, than it is given to every one who reads it. Every one to whom it comes is bound to study it for himself, and govern his life by it. The wisdom of Omniscience has tasked itself to render this communication plain, so that he that runs may read, and that a wayfaring man, though a fool, need not err therein. The Holy Spirit has, moreover, been sent to assist every one who will, with an humble and devout heart, seek to understand it. With such a revelation, and such spiritual aid, every man is required to determine for himself what is the will of God. Seeking to know his duty in this manner, he will not fail to discern it. He has, therefore, no excuse for disobedience. He can not plead before God that he could not know his will. He can not excuse himself before his Judge on the ground that his ministers deceived him. The revelation was made to the man himself, and the means were provided for his understanding of it. "Every one of us must give account for *himself* unto God." Such are the views which we have always entertained.

Allied to this is another like unto it. As I have before remarked, we have always held to the perfect sufficiency of the Scriptures to teach us in all matters pertaining to religion. We, moreover, believe that the New Testament, the word spoken by the Son of God from heaven, and by the apostles whom he himself inspired, was given not to one nation, but to the whole human race for all coming time, and that by this word we are to decide upon the obligatoriness of every part of the older revelation. It is, therefore, in this sense, our only *rule* of faith and practice. To every precept of it we bow implicitly as God's last, best, and final revelation of his will to mankind. We judge the Fathers, as they are called, by the New Testament. We judge tradition and the rites and usages of men by the same law. We appeal "to the Word and the testimony, and if they speak not according to this word, it is because there is no light in them." Hence we are delivered from the yoke of antiquity, tradition, and ecclesiastical usurpation, and rejoice in the liberty wherewith Christ has made us free.

We hear much at present, which indicates the dissatisfaction of honest and able men with the Christian church as it now exists in Europe, and to some extent in this country. It is surely not without foundation. We hear of various projects for a reformation of Christianity. None of these projects can, however, reach the evil. It will never be reached, and the world will never be reformed, until Christians prune off all the beliefs and usages which have been ingrafted on the church, as it was left by the apostles, and in simplicity and truth adopt for their only and sufficient rule, the New Testament, as it was committed to them by our Lord and Saviour.

Another article of our belief, and the last that I will mention, is that the church of Christ is distinct from every other association of men, and is wholly and absolutely independent of the civil power. The authority we plead for this belief is found in the reply of Peter and John to the Jewish Sanhedrim: "Whether it be right in the sight of God to hearken unto you more than unto God, judge ye, for we can not but speak the things which we have seen and heard." We accordingly have ever believed that the state has no authority to legislate in matters pertaining to the conscience. When man violates the rights of man, the state may interfere, and prevent or punish the wrong. But, in matters which concern our relations to God, the state has no jurisdiction. It has no right to take cognizance of our duties to God. Hence it is guilty of wrong, if it prohibit or annoy any form of religion, if it favor one more than another, if it restrict the exercise of any form of devotion, either public or private, or in any manner whatever interfere in the matter of religious belief or practice. Such was the view taken of this subject by Roger Williams, and hence, when he established a commonwealth, its fundamental principle was perfect freedom in religious concernments; or, as he so well designated it, "SOUL LIBERTY." No man of his age had so clear conceptions of the rights of conscience as the founder of Rhode Island, and no one had ever carried them so honestly to their legitimate conclusions. I go further: no one has yet been able either to take from or add to the principles of religious liberty which he so simply and powerfully set forth. They stand as imperishable monuments to his fame, like the obelisks of Luxor, on which the chiseling of every figure is now just as sharply defined as when, three thousand years since, they were left by the hand of their designer.

These sentiments we have held, as I have said, unalloyed by any opinions or practices at variance with them. Hence it is evident that we must, on various occasions, have differed in practice from those who, though agreeing with us in the main, have adopted practices and usages derived from other sources than the Scriptures. It is to our honor that we have borne testimony to these great truths through evil and through good report, amid obloquy, scorn, contumely, and persecution even unto death.

That the Protestant leaders, at the time of the Reformation, did not perceive the evil and the wrong of the alliance between the Church and the State, is one of the most inscrutable of the hidden things of the Almighty. They rejected many of the errors of Romanism, but retained this, which gave to them their power over the nations. They claimed for themselves the right of private judgment, but as soon as they obtained the power, they denied it to those who with themselves had been fellow-sufferers for conscience' sake. Hence their anxiety everywhere to gain the adherence to their sentiments of Electors, Princes, Counts, Barons, and civil rulers of every rank and description. And hence, as in various countries, Protestants of different names came into power, Baptists suffered from them all intolerance and persecution. Nor was this persecution a matter of ephemeral passion. It has been continued even to the present day in most of the countries of Europe. The sufferings of our brethren under the house of Stuart can not be read without a shudder. Even at the present day, though they are favored with *gracious toleration*, yet the unrepealed laws of England, if put into execution, would sadly interfere with the acknowledged rights of conscience. In Germany, our brother Oncken has suffered months of imprisonment for preaching Christ, and the members of our churches are now subjected to punishment by the civil magistrate for not bringing their children to the Lutheran priest for baptism.

In our own country, under the Puritans, the case was no better. The Puritans were noble men. The world owes them a debt which can never be canceled. I would not detract from the honor which they deserve. I respect a man who will suffer the loss of all things rather than submit to injustice, and confess himself to be a slave. The Puritans were ready to die, rather than bow their consciences to the will of man. But they sought for liberty of conscience only for *themselves*. They failed to generalize their principles, and yield to others what they claimed as their own inalienable birthright. Hence persecution was soon as rife on this side of the Atlantic as on the other. Every one knows the treatment received at their hands by Roger Williams. Several of our brethren from Rhode Island were fined and whipped for preaching the gospel at Lynn. And this spirit has not been allayed until within the memory of men now living. I have myself conversed with men who, in two of the New England States, have suffered the loss of goods and even imprisonment, because they would not pay taxes for the support of Congregationalism, or, as it was then called, " the standing order."

Here, then, is the peculiar glory of the Baptists. While they have suffered persecution at the hands of almost all the dominant sects that emerged from the Reformation, their garments have never been defiled by any violation of the rights of conscience. What Roger Williams claimed for himself, he as freely granted to others. He tells us: " I desire not that liberty to myself which I would not freely and impartially weigh out to all the consciences of the world beside." " All these consciences, yea, the very consciences of the Papists, Jews, etc., ought freely and impartially to be permitted their several worships, their ministers of worships, and what way of maintaining them they freely choose." And this, be it remembered, was said, and a government was established in conformity to it, at a time when, out of the little colony of Rhode Island and Providence Plantations, there was not a foot of the habitable earth where a Baptist could, without molestation, worship God according to the dictates of his own conscience. And at a later day, when there was not a colony in America in which the charter of a Baptist college could have been obtained, Brown University was incorporated. True to their principles, our fathers inserted a provision in the charter of this institution, by which the various sects in Rhode Island; Baptists, Episcopalians, Congregationalists and Quakers, in proportion to their then population, should forever constitute the government of the college. Such has ever been the constitution of this seat of learning.

Of the unspeakable importance of the principles to which I have thus alluded, there can now be no controversy. The doctrines of the spirituality of the church, the right of private judgment, the perfect sufficiency of the Scriptures as a rule of faith and practice, and the absolute separation of Church and State, are admitted to be the articles by which the church of Christ must either stand or fall. The truths which Roger Williams first exemplified in his own little colony, are now the glory of this great republic; and they are at this moment agitating the millions of every nation of Europe. They must ere long make the circuit of the earth. And these other doctrines are now disturbing the repose of ritual and formal Christianity everywhere, and the churches can never "shake themselves from the dust, and put on their beautiful garments," until they are universally adopted.

The Baptists may then lay claim, to say the least, to as high moral distinction as can be awarded to any sect in Christendom. They have borne testimony to the most important doctrines of revelation, in their unadulterated purity and simplicity. From each sect in turn, they have, for bearing this testimony, suffered scorn, contumely, reproach, and persecution. When they have obtained the power to persecute in turn, they used that power only to return good for evil, by granting to their persecutors every right which they claimed for themselves. When any sect can lay claim to higher or more honorable distinction, we will bow before them, and cheerfully yield them Christian precedence.

Such being the facts known to all the world, have we any reason to be ashamed of our fathers? When the very principles for which they suffered are now acknowledged to lie at the foundation, not only of pure Christianity, but of all civil and religious liberty, shall we hide our light under a bushel, and blush to bear testimony to eternal truth? After having so long stood in the vanguard of that noble host who have contended for apostolic Christianity and the inalienable rights of conscience, now that the victory is half achieved, and our principles are arousing the nations, shall we lay down our arms, furl our banners, and retire ingloriously from the combat? I know not what may be your answer, but I know what would have been the answer of Roger Williams.

XXIV.

APPROXIMATION OF OTHER SECTS TO THE PRINCIPLES HELD BY BAPTISTS.—THE SPIRITUALITY OF THE CHURCH.—THE SUFFICIENCY OF THE NEW TESTAMENT AS OUR RULE OF FAITH.—LIBERTY OF CONSCIENCE.

In my last number, I referred to some of the principles always held by the Baptists, and for our testimony to which, we had suffered persecution from almost all of the dominant sects in Christendom. I also stated the fact, that when the power had been in our hands we had never abused it, but advocated in its widest extent, SOUL LIBERTY; we had always accorded to our brethren—nay, to all men of what belief soever—the same privileges which we have ever claimed for ourselves. We acknowledge with thankfulness the grace that was thus bestowed on our fathers. We consider it an honor to walk in their footsteps. They have done nothing for which we should blush, and much in which we may glory. We stand in need of no patronage. We ask the loan of no old and worn-out garments to hide their mantle which has fallen upon us. Without arrogance we may take our place in the front rank of those who have exemplified and suffered for the truth as it is in Jesus.

A correspondent of *The Examiner*, in Illinois, has requested me to exhibit the relative positions of the Baptists and Pedobaptists, and the reciprocal influence which they have exerted upon each other. The subject is important, and this is, perhaps, the proper place in which to consider it. I will, therefore, in compliance with the request of my brother, offer a few suggestions which have occurred to me since the reading of his communication. In matters of minor detail I may sometimes err, for I have not at hand the means of verifying all my opinions. As to "the general scope and tenor," as the old ministers used to have it, I think my views may be relied on. I shall offer them without much attempt at arrangement, as they may present themselves to me on brief reflection.

I remark, in the first place, that in many of the most

essential points of Christian belief, our brethren of other denominations have, within the last fifty years approximated more nearly to the views which we have always entertained. For instance, the doctrine of the spirituality of the church of Christ, that is, that every member of the church of Christ must be "regenerated" or "renewed in the spirit of his mind," is much more distinctly understood, and more firmly believed, than it was half a century ago.

This is very apparent in Great Britain, and it would be so to a much greater extent, were it not for the connection between the church and the state. The laws of the realm oblige a minister of the establishment to admit to the ordinances of the church, every British subject who has been baptized in infancy, and who is not of publicly immoral life. This is, however, felt by a daily increasing number to be an intolerable grievance. It is not defended as right, but mourned over as a necessity imposed by law, for which there is no relief. The better portion of the evangelical clergy, at the present day, hold forth the doctrine of the necessity of regeneration with as much plainness and power as any preachers living. There are daily issued from the press volumes of sermons on the most vital doctrines of Christianity, which in the days of Toplady and Romaine would have subjected their authors to unmingled and almost universal scorn. These volumes are read and appreciated by thousands in the establishment, who, though they do not coöperate with other denominations, are laboring and praying for a reformation in their own. Such men were the Thorntons, Wilberforce, and the saints who, within the present century, tabernacled on Clapham Common. I do not, however, suppose that this change in the religious character of Great Britain is in any appreciable degree to be ascribed to the testimony of Baptists. It was owing, no doubt, mainly to the rise of Whitfield and Wesley, Scott and Simeon, and some other excellent men within the pale of the establishment.

In our own country the change has also been manifest. The Puritans held that every voter, or freeman, as he was called, must be a member of the church. The result was, as might have been anticipated, every voter, and especially every candidate for office, became a church member. President Edwards's sermons on Justification, and his treatise on the Affections created a great sensation in his time, because they insisted on qualifications for admission to the church which were at variance with the common belief of New England. But few of the leading ministers in our large towns would admit Whitfield into their pulpits. At the present day, Edwards is the standard author among all evangelical Congregationalists, and he would now be a rare man who did not number Whitfield among the most wonderful pulpit orators that any age has produced. Contemporary with Edwards, and in the generation preceding him, there were clergymen of decided talent, who were considered as belonging to the lights of their age. Who, however, now reads their sermons except the antiquarian? Who quotes them as authority? The inaccuracy and mistiness of their views on the subject to which we are now referring, have done much to consign them to oblivion, while the works of the great American metaphysician have steadily increased in the estimation of theologians, until, at the present day, if a clergyman has twenty religious books, you may be sure that one of them will be a volume of Edwards.

The effect of Edwards's writings was deep and widely extended, though it failed to reach the mass of Congregationalists. A large portion still continued to hold the sentiments of the older divines. Hence, every church, in the course of time, was divided against itself, a part holding to the great doctrines of spiritual religion, and the others, commonly the larger party, believing in an almost hereditary membership. At last, the great Unitarian disruption ensued; the churches throughout Massachusetts were divided, the Orthodox party forming churches by themselves, and the others professing Unitarianism. The Orthodox boldly affirmed the spirituality of the church, and the necessity of regeneration; and the others, merely changing their belief concerning the personal nature of the Deity, retained their former sentiments. The Orthodox Congregational church then shook herself from the dust. Revivals were multiplied throughout New England, and the foundations were laid of those benevolent enterprises which are now the glory of our country.

In this change of sentiment in the churches of our New England brethren, the influence of the Baptists may be distinctly observed. Our preachers went everywhere, and in barns, in school-houses, and in private dwellings, preached with simplicity and godly sincerity the great truths of spiritual religion. They were generally opposed as interlopers, who were interfering with the privileges of the "standing order." The more they were preached against, the greater numbers attended their ministry. In some cases, good men who at first opposed, were led subsequently to imitate them, and preaching more fervently the doctrines of the cross, their own churches were revived. In other cases, members of churches who attended a formal ministry were converted and formed a little band of earnest, prayerful men, by whom the surrounding mass was to a greater or less extent leavened.

The city of Boston presents an illustration of this influence which it is well to remember. Early in the present century, the great doctrines of grace had there been almost wholly supplanted by what may, for the sake of distinction, be denominated hereditary Christianity. At this time a glorious revival commenced under the preaching of Dr. Baldwin, and extended to the neighboring church of Dr. Stillman. It continued for between one and two years. The meeting-houses of these excellent men were thronged, multitudes were converted, and among them many members of the Congregational churches. These men became, of course, dissatisfied with the ministry on which they had regularly attended, but as a kind Providence ordered it, they did not become Baptists. In a few years they united and formed Park-street church, which was, for a while, the only Orthodox Congregational church in Boston. To this beginning may be traced the present prosperous condition of Orthodox opinions in that city. In referring to these facts, I am only repeating what has often been minutely related to me by men who were themselves parties to all the transactions. The same influence, under other forms, has been exerted in many of the towns and villages of New England.

The doctrine of the absolute sufficiency of the New Testament, as our only rule of faith and practice, has also been much more widely and definitely maintained than formerly. This has been, doubtless, a result of the greater mental independence of the age, though it may in part, also, be owing to the uniform testimony of Baptists on the subject. From whatever cause it has arisen, the fact must, I think, be apparent, that in all religious controversy, the parties (Puseyites excepted) refer much more exclusively to the teachings of the New Testament than formerly. We hear much less about the fathers than we once did. It has been found that the opinions of the best of them were, in many respects, radically erroneous; that many of them were weak and puerile in intellect; that they were, in fact, just like the men of this or any other age, and that their teachings are utterly valueless, only in so far as they are in harmony with the Scriptures. Men are beginning to find out that an opinion gains nothing, either in truth or power, by being buried for one or even two thousand years, and that like the opinions of our contemporaries, it is to be judged solely by its conformity to the word of God.

From the combined action of these two beliefs, it has come to pass that the practice of infant baptism is growing into desuetude. It is now the universal complaint of our Congregational and Presbyterian brethren, that their members do not bring their children for baptism. This would naturally arise from the facts to which I have alluded. The more prominent our belief in the spirituality of the church, the greater must be our difficulty in reconciling it with infant baptism; and the more decided the impression that nothing is binding on the conscience which is not found in the Scriptures, the more readily would men doubt the authority of an ordinance for which the Bible furnishes neither precept nor example.

The right of private judgment has been so generally advocated by Protestants, that it does not require any special notice. The doctrine of perfect liberty of conscience, and the entire separation of church from state may, however, deserve a passing remark. It is too well known that in no country of Europe is this doctrine practically acknowledged. In our own country its progress was steady and irresistible, though it is only within a few years that its last vestiges have been erased from the soil of New England. It is strange to observe how deeply the notion becomes engraved on the mind of a dominant sect that religion can not be supported unless it be sustained by the civil arm. When this question was agitated in the Convention that formed the present Constitution of Massachusetts, as late, I think, as 1820, almost all the Orthodox clergy were in favor of the provision by which every citizen was obliged to support Congregationalism, unless he could produce a certificate that he paid taxes to some other sect. In the most distinguished seat of theological learning in New England, every professor but one favored this opinion.

The effect of Baptist theory and practice in correcting the opinions of the public on this most important question, can not, I think, be doubted. They, in Virginia, in Massachusetts, in Connecticut, protested against all civil differences on account of religious belief, and boldly asserted that this was a subject which did not come under the jurisdiction of the magistrate. They have at last prevailed, and the principles of Roger Williams now bear undisputed sway from the St. Lawrence to the Gulf of Mexico, and from the Atlantic to the Pacific.

These are some of the points in which the progress of opinion, in other denominations, has tended to the beliefs which we have always held. In how far our precept and practice has tended to this result, we are willing to leave to the judgment of others. If any one desires to see this whole subject treated with great fullness of research, and with singular fairness and ability, I would refer him to Professor Curtis's work on the " Progress of Baptist Sentiments," lately published by Gould & Lincoln, of Boston.

XXV.

POINTS IN WHICH WE HAVE ERRED BY IMITATION OF OTHERS.—CHURCH MUSIC.

FROM several of the previous numbers it will be perceived that I believe the Baptists to hold a distinct position among other Protestant sects; that they entertain sentiments, which, if carried into practice, must render them somewhat peculiar, and that they are perfectly capable of establishing their own usages, and of adapting their modes of worship and rules of discipline to the principles which they believe. They need borrow from no one. They have no occasion to hide their sentiments, or blush for the results to which they lead. Their very peculiarities are their titles to distinction, because they are founded on principles which are essential to the permanent spirituality of the church of Christ. It must, therefore, be a great error to obscure the distinctness of our testimony, by adopting usages which spring from principles directly at variance with those which we have always cherished.

In my last paper I referred to several important respects in which our brethren of other denominations have approximated more nearly to us. Whether we have had any agency in the production of these changes is a matter of inferior moment. We rejoice in the fact, as an indication of important progress in the whole body of Christian disciples.

On the other hand, however, within the last fifty years, we have, in various particulars, conformed to our brethren of other denominations. Whether these changes have been for good or for evil, there may be a difference of opinion. In many cases it must, I think, be observed that we have fallen into practices by no means in harmony with the doctrines which we hold. Some of these I will here take occasion to state. How general the usages are, to which I will refer, I am unable to say. From a somewhat singular disposition to adopt the practices of those around us, it must follow that we are, in various respects, not only inconsistent with our principles, but also at variance with each other. I shall mention only such as have either come under my own observation, or been stated to me as facts, by my brethren, in the course of ordinary conversation.

One of our essential beliefs is that of the spirituality of the church, that is, that the church of Christ is composed exclusively of spiritual or regenerated persons. As God is a spirit, and those that worship him must worship him in spirit and in truth, we have always believed that the real worship of God was performed only by believers. To us, worship, either in public or private, is the offering up to God of holy and devout affections. Hence we believe that no one can be a minister of the sanctuary, unless he be a devout and regenerate man. Hence we believe that to sing the praises of God without really lifting up the heart to him, is in no sense Christian worship, and is, in fact, no acceptable service. Hence our belief always has been that singing is a part of worship which belongs, in a peculiar manner, to the disciples of the Saviour. In this service they, with one voice, utter the confessions of penitence, the triumphs of faith, the confidence of hope, and bow down together with one feeling of holy adoration. Hence our singing was a service of the church, in which others united with them only in so far as they could sympathize with them in the sentiments which they uttered. These are, if I mistake not, our beliefs on this subject, and to it our practice, until lately, conformed. A member of the church selected the tunes, led the singing, and the whole church, and the devout portion of the congregation, united with him in this part of religious worship. Their design was *to make melody in their hearts to the Lord.*

For these reasons, Baptists formerly were universally opposed to the introduction of musical instruments into the house of God. They asked, How can senseless things speak the praises of God? In this, they may or may not have erred. I do not deny that something of this sort may be useful to harmonize the voices of a congregation. I leave the decision of this question to the judgment of others, yet I can not but remark, in passing, that I have rarely met a Christian person who did not prefer the singing in a vestry-room below, where nothing was heard but the voices of the congregation, to the music of the choir, aided by the organ in the meeting-house above. Hence the singing in Baptist churches was formerly what is now denominated congregational. We had neither choirs nor organs. Nothing but the voices of worshipers was heard in hymning the praises of God, and in this service every devout worshiper was expected to unite.

I do not pretend that in this singing there was any artistic excellence. This is never needed in popular music, or that music which is intended to move a multitude of people. All national airs are simple, and they strike upon those chords which vibrate equally in the bosom of the common man and the amateur. When you hear a thousand Englishmen unite in the chorus of "Rule Britannia," or as many Americans join in singing "Hail Columbia," you forget every thing about chords and discords, but you are deeply moved by the common feeling, and can hardly refrain from leaping and shouting from deep emotion. So in religious music. The tunes employed were perfectly adapted to religious sentiment, and blended the whole audience in one consciousness of solemn worship. To use the language of Burns—surely a competent authority—

> "They chant their artless notes in simple guise,
> They tune their hearts, by far the noblest aim:
> Perhaps *Dundee's* wild warbling notes arise,
> Or plaintive *Martyrs*, worthy of the name;
> Or noble *Elgin* fans the heavenward flame,
> The sweetest far of Scotia's holy lays.
> Compared with these, Italian trills are tame;
> The tickled ears no heartfelt raptures raise,
> No unison have they with our Creator's praise."

But a change has come over us. The Episcopal church always have approved of organs, and the music of choirs. The Congregationalists imitated the Episcopalians, and we, of course, imitate the Congregationalists. We have organs in all our city churches at the North, and they are now deemed essential in our small towns and villages, and even in the country. The organ requires an organist. The organist requires a leader and several other professional singers to constitute an appropriate choir. This involves a heavy expense. These singers have a professional character at stake. They must perform in such a manner as to promote their own reputation. They select their own music—music in which the congregation can not unite. The congregation listens in silence to a mere musical performance, precisely as the audience at a concert or an opera. The performers are not unfrequently the very persons who amuse the theater on the evenings of the week, and the church of God on the Sabbath. I have known cases in which they had so little of the common respect for religion, that they have left the house of God as soon as their performance was ended.

I know of a case in which the leader of a choir had conducted this part of what is intended to be the worship of God for several years, but who, during this whole period, as he confessed on his death-bed, had never once heard a sermon. We believe in spirituality of worship. We believe that God requires us to worship him in spirit and in truth. In how far such a service corresponds with our principles, let every Christian judge.

This great change has come over us somewhat gradually. We were partly overcome by the declamation of men who professed great knowledge of music, and who ridiculed what they were pleased to call our want of taste. The strongest argument was, however, addressed to our love of imitation. It was said, other denominations employ professional musicians, and we must do it also, or we shall be behind the times, and lose our congregations. Pious men and women doubted. They were not convinced, but they distrusted their own judgments, and were unwilling to oppose any thing which seemed to promise an advantage to the cause of Christ. They have, therefore, borne it all in silence, and rejoice that there is one place left, the humble vestry, in which they can unite together in singing with one voice the praises of their Redeemer.

I hope, however, that a reaction in this matter has commenced. Men of piety have begun to feel that it is wicked to substitute a mere musical diversion for the solemn worship of God. Men of correct taste, at least, acknowledge that congregational singing, and solemn and devout music, are alone appropriate to the service of the sanctuary. Whenever a return to the old customs has been tried, it has met with unexpected success. May the reform be universal throughout our Baptist churches.

XXVI.

CHANGE IN OPINION RESPECTING CHURCH MUSIC.—CHURCH ARCHITECTURE.

In my last paper, I endeavored to show that we have erred by imitating the examples of others in the matter of church music. I alluded, also, to the fact that the best writers on this subject are now beginning to advocate the very principles which we, too thoughtlessly, discarded. The highest authorities on sacred music now admit that the singing of the house of God should be congregational, and forsaking the *"Italian trills,"* to use the words of Burns, are falling back on a style of music adapted to the utterance of devotion; that is, they are reviving the very airs which were once scouted as old-fashioned. It is now granted by all reasonable men, that music may be good for one purpose and yet very bad for another; that, for instance, an air may be very well suited to an opera or a march, very well adapted for a charge on the field of battle, and yet very ill adapted to the devotions of an assembly uniting in the worship of God.

We hope that this return to a more correct taste will have its perfect work. In the mean time, it may be well for us to remember that a practice is not, of necessity, either wise or in good taste, because other denominations adopt it. And still more, we may learn from this experience that the sober sentiments of religious men are worth something, even in determining a matter of taste. After surrendering our own principles for the sake of imitation, we find those whom we have imitated coming round to the very principles which we had deserted. Would it not have been as well for us to have adhered steadfastly to what we believed to be right?

A similar mistake, from the same cause, may be observed, if I do not greatly mistake, on the subject of church architecture.

Our fathers, it is well known, built very unsightly and inconvenient churches, in by-ways and hedges, frequently in the outskirts of towns, and in places difficult of access. It is very easy to smile at this, and to ridicule their want of taste, and their selection of such strange localities. But let us pause and ask, Was there no other reason for all this, except an ignorance of the beautiful, and a passion for discomfort? Let it be remembered that the builders of these houses were poor men destitute of influence, a sect everywhere spoken against. In multitudes of cases, they were unable to purchase more eligible sites, or if they had offered the full value of a lot, it would not have been sold to them for the erection of a Baptist meeting-house. They preferred worship in a meeting-house inconveniently situated, to a worship of which they conscientiously disapproved. They had no agents to scour the country and raise funds with which to erect a "commanding edifice." They could not afford to pay architects for plans of building. They had not learned to run in debt for churches. They labored on their building with their own hands, and, in the result, though we may not take their buildings for our models, we may surely respect the manly independence which governed their construction.

That we should imitate their models when we are able to do better, would be absurd. But in avoiding this, we have, by following other examples, verged very far toward the opposite error, and thus come in conflict with our own established principles.

For instance, we have no belief in holy places, or places in which God may especially be acceptably worshiped. We do not profess to build a shrine, which, standing in a holy place, shall address the eye, and overcome us by its magnificence. We have no *priesthood* who wait upon the altar, and offer up, in our behalf, our sacrifices to God. Our view on this subject is summed up in few words. We meet for worship, relying simply on the promise of Christ, " Wherever two or three are gathered together in my name, *there am I in the midst of them.*" We assemble to offer spiritual sacrifice. We meet to *hear* the word of God explained and brought home to our consciences and our hearts, and to bring under the sound of the gospel as many as we are able. Christ came to preach the gospel to the poor, and to the end of time, the evidence of the truth of his religion is, that " to the poor the gospel is preached." Hence we need a neat, convenient *audience-room*, well ventilated, well warmed, and also perfectly adapted to the wants of both speaker and hearer. We want this to be provided at as small expense as possible, for two reasons: first, we wish to bring the gospel within the reach of the poor, and of those of moderate means ; and, secondly, we need a great many such houses, because, if we are faithful to Christ, we expect an abundant increase.

I regret, however, to say, that in the building of meeting-houses, we have acted at variance with all these principles. In this matter, we have followed the example of our Episcopalian brethren. At the Reformation, they entered into the possession of the Catholic cathedrals and churches of the middle ages, and of course adopted this style of architecture. It is peculiarly unfitted for the purpose of an *audience* room. Who would think of erecting a Gothic building for a court-house, a legislative hall, a lecture-room, or for any purpose (except a church), when the object was to enable a large number of persons to *hear a speaker*. The Gothic is an enormously expensive style, and must, from its costliness, exclude from the sanctuary all but the rich. It may be endured where a denomination is small in numbers, and abundant in wealth, but for a denomination made up mainly of the middling classes, and the poor (according to the apostolic model), nothing could be more inappropriate.

In spite of all this, however, that style is coming into vogue among us. In our cities we have our Gothic temples, instead of Baptist meeting-houses. The fashion is spreading from the cities to the towns and the country, and our brethren are everywhere beginning to rejoice in naves, and transepts, and chancels, and altars, and oriel windows, and stained glass, shedding abroad, as they tell us, "a dim *religious* light." I have lately seen a Baptist meeting-house, the windows of which were emblazoned with a strange variety of mystical symbols that must have amused the children by their grotesqueness, and sorely puzzled any plain man like myself, not deeply learned in the researches of the Ecclesiological Society.

Now in all this, it seems to me that we underrate ourselves, and do injustice to our principles. We are sacrificing our principles to architects, as in the former case, we sacrificed them to musicians. We are following examples at which the sound common sense of good men everywhere is beginning to revolt. We are certainly able to know what we want in a meeting-house. We are able to devise, or to cause to be de-devised for us, some chaste, simple, pleasing, and well proportioned form, which, at a very moderate expense, shall furnish us with all that can be desired in a Christian place of worship. We should show more respect for ourselves, by carrying out our principles to their practical result, than by imitating examples emanating from principles which we have ever repudiated. If we could all unite upon some plain, neat, convenient and economical model for a meeting-house, which might be used in city and in country, for large houses and for small, so that every one would know a Baptist meeting-house as soon as he saw it, we might build two churches where we now build one, and attract to the worship of God thousands and tens of thousands whom the present prices of pews and pew-rent exclude from any place in the sanctuary. Can any reason be assigned why we should sacrifice these advantages for the sake of imitating the gorgeous structures of the Catholic church, with which are associated bigotry, persecution unto death, and the most soul-destroying perversion of the doctrines of the cross ?

We have an architect,[*] one of our own brethren, at the head of his profession in this country, who could not more effectually serve the cause of Christ, than by publishing a set of drawings and specifications, by the aid of which we might all be enabled to construct church edifices on the principles which I have suggested. Such a consecration of his eminent abilities to the service of his brethren, would confer the most important benefit that architecture has ever rendered to the cause of Christianity. Architecture, has thus far shown its power in diminishing the number of worshipers; by this means it would indefinitely increase it. We want a model of a Baptist meeting-house which, in future, we all may adopt; so that we may have convenient, economical, and pleasing houses of worship, AND A GREAT MANY OF THEM.

XXVII.

SABBATH SERVICES.—POSTURE IN PRAYER.—READING NOTICES.—FORMULA IN BAPTISM.—SERVICES AT WEDDINGS AND FUNERALS.

IN my last paper I endeavored to show that we, from our love of imitation, had violated good taste, and compromised our principles in the matter of church architecture. We certainly are as able to determine what we want, as others are to determine it for us. We are as competent to select a style of architecture suited to our wants, as others are to select it for us. Let us then have respect for ourselves, and carry our principles into practice.

[*] T. U. Walter, Esq., of Washington.

There are, besides these, several other minor particulars, in themselves of small moment, but which derive importance from the *tendency* which they cultivate. To some of these I will now allude. I shall here refer chiefly to our usages in conducting public worship.

Our services in the house of God have suffered no change. They consist of (generally) a prayer of invocation, singing, reading the Scriptures, prayer, singing, sermon, prayer, benediction. In some of our churches we sing twice, in others three times, and in others, the prayer at the opening of the service is omitted.

According to our former custom, we stood in prayer, and sat in singing. Of late, we have adopted, in part, the practice of our Episcopalian brethren, by standing in singing, and sitting in prayer. I say in part, for the prayer-book directs the congregation to kneel during prayer, and their pews are generally adapted to this posture. If, however, they do not kneel, they bend reverently forward, and shutting out external objects, remain in this position to the close of the supplications. We do not profess to kneel, and the result is that our congregations sit, too commonly, gazing about irreverently, while the minister is offering up solemn petitions and adoration. In this respect we have, certainly, suffered loss. The solemnity of our service is diminished. The imitation is, at least, unsuccessful. To kneel in prayer is exceedingly appropriate, and I wish it could be universally adopted. To stand is expressive of reverence, when we approach into the presence of God. To sit listlessly gazing around, when we profess to be offering up our supplications to God, can surely be justified neither by religion or good taste. I must, therefore, consider our change in this respect to be a failure. It would have been better had we remained as we were. Our love for imitation has overstepped itself, and excluded what was good, both in our own usage and that of others.

Again, our notion of worship is simply this. We meet together on the Sabbath to offer up to God, each one for himself, the sacrifice of prayer and praise, and to cultivate holy affections by the reading and explanation of the word of God, and by applying its truth to our own souls. The preacher has a particular portion of the Scriptures to which he directs our attention. It is his design to *unfold the mind of the Spirit*, as it is made known in this part of revelation. To this end he selects his hymns, and the portion of Scripture which he reads, desiring, so far as possible, to have every part of the service aid in producing a definite moral effect. From beginning to end it is one act of *worship*, from which every thing irreverent, or even irrelevant, is to be, from the nature of the case, excluded. Nothing should divert the mind from the great moral object for which the assembly has convened. This idea was formerly carried out among us. No notices were read, or announcements made, except they pertained to the religious meetings of the church, and lest these should distract the attention of the audience, they were given at the close of the last singing, just before the congregation was dismissed.

The Episcopalian theory of service is somewhat different. With them, the reading of the liturgy is the essential portion of worship, and the sermon is merely an addition. Hence, they have adopted the practice of reading notices, publishing bans, etc., at the close of the liturgy, just before the commencement of the sermon. They, however, have been always careful of the nature of their announcements, and nothing secular, or disconnected from the services of the church, is ever heard from their pulpits.

In this respect we have fallen into a strange variety of practice. Some of our brethren imitate the Episcopalians, and read notices, etc., and take collections immediately before the sermon. Others choose for this purpose the time immediately following the prayer for the presence and blessing of the Holy Spirit. Others have no rule, but take sometimes one time, and sometimes another. Nor is this all. We not unfrequently hear notices for all sorts of meetings, lectures, etc., read from the pulpit, breaking up the continuity of the worship, and distracting the attention of an audience. I have known the worship of God interrupted to inform the congregation that some itinerant showman would admit Sabbath-school scholars to visit his panorama, on a certain day, at half-price, A multitude of cases of this sort will, I doubt not, occur to the recollection of most of my readers.

Here again, by our facility of imitation, we have acted at variance with our principles, and introduced a variety of practice leading to disorder. Nor is this all. We have, as it seems to me, detracted from the solemnity of the house of God, and materially affected for the worse the character of our service. The great idea of worship is in danger of passing away, through our various and changeful innovations. We desire to impress a congregation with the idea that they come up to the sanctuary to converse with God—that they are in the immediate presence of Christ. How can they believe us, when we are ever ready to interrupt our service in the most solemn moments, to publish notices, to take collections, or perform any miscellaneous business in itself alien from the idea of worship. Suppose we were visiting at the house of a friend, and were uniting with him in family devotion. How strangely would it strike us, if after reading the Scriptures, before he engaged in prayer, he gave to his household their various directions for the labors of the day. It would be still more strange, if he gave as a reason for his practice, that they were there all assembled, and that his directions would be better remembered, if he gave them in the midst of his devotional exercises.

I ask, then, what have we gained by the change in this respect? Would it not have been better had we adhered to the old usage? Would it not be better now to return to it? Would not the solemnity of our service be increased, by allowing nothing to be read from the pulpit which could interfere with the solemnity of worship, and that the necessary announcements be made after the last singing, or after the whole worship was closed?

Other minor divergences from our common usages may deserve a passing notice. For instance, our usual formula of baptism is simply, "I baptize thee," etc. Some of our brethren adopt the Episcopalian form, prefixing the Christian name of the candidate, John, James, Elizabeth, etc. If our object is to designate the individual, we should give the whole name, for merely the Christian name designates no one. If it designates nothing, I see no reason for adopting it, except that of following the example of another sect, who always use this mode of baptizing children. In fact, the common belief is, that it is this act which gives the child its name.

Our principles lead us to entire simplicity in every form of religious service. We naturally shrink from every thing ritual which has not been commanded, even in indifferent things, because we wish to bear testimony against all human additions to the precepts of the New Testament. Hence in the performance of the marriage ceremony, and in funeral services, we have always avoided every thing but simply religious service. Notwithstanding this, however, I learn that some of our brethren are introducing the ceremony of giving a ring in marriage, and that others at funerals are in the habit of using a large part of the Episcopal service, and even some of the ceremonies of that denomination. How extensively these changes have been adopted, I am unable to affirm, but I think I do not err in saying that cases of this kind have occurred, and I think the tendency is at present decidedly in this direction.

I know it will be said, that in these remarks I am interfering with the Baptist doctrine of the *independence of ministers*. I reply, I did not know that the *independence of ministers* was ever a Baptist doctrine, though it is the doctrine of some other sects. Independence of *churches is* a Baptist doctrine, and this I think would teach us that no minister has any right to introduce any usage not common to us, without the direction, or at least the consent of the church of which he is the pastor. These two ideas are very dissimilar, and I regret to perceive that they are in danger of being confounded. The distinction is of great moment, and is worthy of serious consideration.

If a church sees fit to forsake our own usages and adopt those of other sects, I do not doubt the right, but I may certainly be allowed to question the expediency.

1. I ask, Are not our Baptist usages as good as any other? I ask again, as they are illustrative of our own essential principles, are they not *for us* better than any other?

2. Does it not show more self-respect to continue a usage common to us and to our brethren, than to forsake *them*, and borrow usages from the other sects with whom we chance to associate? Are we so chameleon-like, that we must of necessity take the tinge of every object with which we come in contact?

3. If we adopt this principle of conformity to others, what must be the result? Our children will be led to believe that not only our usages, but the principles which govern them, are matters of no consequence; that we sink them as far as we are able, and are only waiting for an opportunity to forsake them altogether. If we put them in the road leading to other communions, what wonder is it if they follow it to the end?

I know it may be said that these are all trifles, wholly unworthy of public remark. To this I reply, If they are such trifles, why should we, for the sake of trifles, destroy the visible unity of our own people? I reply again, whatever affects the unity of our churches is no trifle. These little things indicate tendencies, and great things as well as small, follow their tendencies. Small aberrations lead to wide deviations. The greatest mass becomes powerless when broken into fragments and pulverized into atoms. A cockade is a very little thing, but a cockade has changed the destinies of empires.

XXVIII.

RELATIONS BETWEEN THE CHURCH AND THE CONGREGATION.—GRADUAL CHANGE IN THIS RESPECT.—UNFORTUNATE POSITION OF A MINISTER.

IN my last paper, I alluded to various cases in which, by thoughtless imitation of others, we had been led into usage, neither for our advantage nor in conformity with our principles. I turn now to some other practices, in which, from the same cause, we have diverged from our former beliefs.

The first point which I shall consider, is the relation subsisting between the church and the congregation.

What our legitimate views on this subject are, may be easily inferred from our belief in the spirituality of the church. We, as I have said, understand the church to be a company of spiritual persons, who, from being dead in trespasses and sins, are made alive in Christ Jesus. Hence, upon such persons devolves the whole responsibility of directing the affairs of the church, that is, in fact, of directing their own affairs in all that concerns their religious association. They admit to their fellowship such, and such only, as they believe to be regenerate; they establish under Christ their own rules of order and discipline; they call their own pastor; they provide for his support; they erect their own house of worship, and assume the whole management of their own ecclesiastical affairs, both spiritual and secular. If others choose to worship with them, they welcome them with all gladness. If others are willing to contribute to the support of the gospel, they receive it with all thankfulness. We rejoice to see them in the sanctuary, listening to the proclamation of the gospel. We will put ourselves to any inconvenience for the sake of accommodating them there. We will labor and pray for their salvation, but we will give them no authority to interfere with any thing which relates to the kingdom of Christ, until they themselves enter into it. Such are the views which harmonize with our principles.

Nor in this is there any thing, as we suppose, either arrogant or unreasonable. We stand to the unregenerate in the relation of spiritual advisers. If we are what we profess to be, we know better what is for their spiritual benefit than they do themselves. They so consider it. If they need advice or instruction respecting their soul's salvation, they do not go to one who is with them simply a member of the congregation, but to the clergyman, or, perhaps, quite as frequently, to some member of the church, to the most devout and godly man of their acquaintance. They thus admit that we have a knowledge of spiritual things of which they are destitute, and are thus capable of advising them in matters of which they confess themselves ignorant; nay, they frequently and justly complain of us because we do not more earnestly and solemnly warn them of their danger, and point out to them the way of eternal life. Now the uniting with us for the support of worship neither alters these facts nor changes this relation. If we know better than they what is for their spiritual good, it is for their benefit that we should provide for them spiritual instruction. The case is in many respects analogous to that of professional advice. He who pays a physician, does not by any means acquire the right of directing his own medical treatment. The physician here must act simply for the recovery of the patient. He can not obey him to his injury. The patient may, if he chooses, select another physician, or he may prescribe for himself; but he may not control the treatment which his medical adviser conscientiously prescribes.

These were favorite ideas with our older Baptists. Perhaps they even carried them to excess. They were frequently unwilling even to be incorporated by a legislative act, lest they should thus, in some manner, lose their Christian liberty. If they were incorporated, they preferred to be incorporated as a church, and not as a society. The church thus held and controlled whatever property might be appropriated to the purposes of worship. In the calling and dismission of a pastor, they acknowledged no authority but their own; considering every thing that belonged to the church of Christ to be a purely religious concern. These principles were, to the best of my knowledge, always conceded to them; and on this basis our meeting-houses were formerly erected. They greatly feared committing themselves to any arrangement by which those who were not by profession religious men, should acquire a control over religious things.

In this respect, we were unlike most of the leading sects in New England. Some of these allow baptized pewholders to vote on all church questions, and admit them as members of conventions, covocations, and other ecclesiastical bodies, thus merging the church and the congregation in the same society. Other sects make out of a company of worshipers two separate organizations, called the "*church*" and the "*society*." The church consists, in this case, of the communicants, of whom the pastor is the chairman; the society consists of the pewholders, who form their own rules, elect their own chairman, and keep their own records. These two organizations have coördinate jurisdiction on most questions affecting the interests of the whole. For instance, in the settlement of a pastor, the church makes out the call, but it is not considered valid unless it is concurred in by the society. The church, it is true, calls the minister, but the society votes the salary; so that the society has always a negative on the acts of the church, and without their concurrence, the act of the church is of no value. When the members of the church form the large majority of the pewholders, so that the same persons act in these two capacities, this plan would work with entire harmony. If, however, it were otherwise, and a majority of the pewholders were merely members of the congregation, it is easy to see that the pastor might be chosen, in fact, by persons really not members of the church.

In this respect we have followed the latter of these examples. When it was considered necessary to erect houses of worship at an expense far beyond the pecuniary ability of the church, it seemed indispensable to follow the course adopted by our brethren of other denominations, and make larger concessions to the pewholders. Hence, in New England, and in those States in which New England opinions prevail, the company of Baptist worshipers is divided into two organizations, in the manner to which I have just referred. The church calls the minister, the society concurs or not in the call, and by the power of voting the salary, determines whether or not the call shall be accepted. The influence of the society has gradually increased among us with the increase in our expensiveness of worship. I have known a case in which the society called a clergyman to ministerial service on their own motion, and sent their vote to the church for their concurrence. I am far from affirming that this arrangement is without its apparent advantages. By this means we are enabled to build larger and more magnificent meeting-houses, and sustain a far more costly worship, at a much less expense to the members of the church ; but whether the spiritual benefits correspond may be a matter of doubt.

The position of the minister of the gospel is by this arrangement manifestly changed. The gospel recognizes in him but one character, that of *pastor of the church of Christ*. As our assemblies are at present constituted, he is also a lecturer on religion to the congregation, who are supposed to have appointed him for this purpose, and who are, in fact, the persons responsible for his support. These two parties, as I have said, may be the same persons, acting in different capacities. But suppose it not to be so. Suppose the church small and poor, and " the society" large and wealthy. Suppose, also, that the expenses of public worship are greater by far than the church is able to bear, and that, unless the house is filled and the pews all rented, the society will fall hopelessly in debt. This combination of circumstances—by no means, I think, an unusual one—places a minister of the gospel under temptations too great for ordinary human virtue. Suppose still further, that the preacher is an educated man, addicted to books and literature, and of cultivated taste; that his *church* is composed, for the most part, of plain men and women, in moderate circumstances, and that the society numbers among its members many families of opulence, refinement, and social position. The latter are well pleased to attend upon a religious service on the Sabbath; they admire a classical style, an eloquent delivery, and serious, though not too serious, reflection. They are really attached to their clergyman as a well-educated, accomplished, and highly-esteemed friend. The echo of a "successful effort" comes back to him from a hundred tongues:

> "Praise from the shriveled lips of toothless, bald
> Decrepitude, and in the looks of lean
> And craving poverty, and in the bow
> Respectful of the smutched artificer,
> Is oft too welcome, and may much disturb
> The bias of the purpose. How much more,
> Poured forth by beauty, splendid and polite,
> In language soft as adulation breathes."

Can it be expected that the "bias of a man's purpose" will remain undisturbed under such a pressure? But to this let me add another circumstance. Suppose that the pulse of religion beats feebly in the heart of the church itself. Suppose that a portion of them also are wealthy, and that they indulge in the same forms of luxury, frequent the same amusements, and are as anxious to be known among the leaders of fashion as the members of the "society" who make no pretensions to religion. Suppose, still more, that the professors of religion are as greedy of gain, as tortuous in trade, as other men, and that in the eyes of the community many of them hold a place decidedly inferior to that of some of their fellow-worshipers who cherish no hope of salvation. Suppose the minister to know that if he urged sinners to be renewed in the spirit of their minds, it would at once awaken the response, "We should be very sorry to be renewed after the model of those whom you set before us as examples." What condition on earth can be more trying than that of such a minister? What shall he do? How shall he preach? Are there any such congregations and ministers among us? Do not such facts as these explain the reason why we sometimes fail to hear from orthodox pulpits the doctrines of human depravity, the certain condemnation of the wicked, the necessity of regeneration, its nature and evidences, and the broad moral distinctions, so frequently repeated in the Scriptures, between the characters of the righteous and the wicked?

XXIX.

PREACHING TO BUILD UP A SOCIETY.—VESTRY SERVICES.—CHURCH DISCIPLINE.—AMUSEMENTS.—HONESTY IN MERCANTILE DEALING.

In my last paper I stated briefly some of the temptations which beset the path of the minister of a fashionable congregation. What human virtue can be expected to resist such insidious and continued pressure? We complain that ministers are not faithful, and yet we surround them with conditions that would render faithfulness almost a miracle. I hesitate not to say, that a man who would welcome the fagot or the scaffold rather than deny his Lord, might succumb under the moral trials of many a city pastorate.

When I say succumb, I beg to be understood. I do not mean that a good man, under such circumstances, would deny the faith, or become vicious in character, or preach any thing which he did not believe to be true. It would, however, be strange if his life did not witness a ceaseless struggle between his conscience and his practice. He knows that if he should preach the gospel in its simplicity, and tell men their duty and their danger with all plainness, the congregation would be amazed, and either he would, by the grace of God, change them, or they would very soon change their minister. He would generally resort to a middle course, and preach, not *to convert souls*, but to *build up his society*. He would preach religious truth, but preach it in so general a manner, unfolding the doctrine, but applying it to no one, that the whole congregation would believe it, but scarcely an individual would ever turn it to any practical moral purpose. His sermons would be addressed, in reality, to neither saints nor sinners, but to some imaginary class of moral agents, belonging neither to the one class nor the other. No one is converted by his preaching; in fact, it is not to be expected that any one will be. The additions to the church are made from the Sabbath-school and the Bible-class, where a few men and women, unknown to the world, and, it may be, unknown to the *leading members* of the church and society, in simplicity and godly sincerity prayerfully press home the claims of the gospel upon the minds of the young. So far as his Sabbath services are concerned, the minister sinks down into settled hopelessness, and consoles himself with reflections upon the importance of the pulpit to the general condition of the community, its conservative influence in politics, its value in the support of our liberties, and in the preservation of our republican institutions. He believes that he is doing good in this way, and this seems all that he can expect to accomplish.

But beset as is the pastor by these discouragements, there is yet one place toward which he looks with hope. It is the plain, humble vestry, where, on the evening of some week day, he meets his brethren and sisters, who are praying and waiting for the salvation of Israel. Here no organ distracts the attention, nor performs for the congregation the worship of God. Here no architectural magnificence frowns down upon the humble and poor disciple of Jesus of Nazareth. Hither, while their fellow Sabbath worshipers are preparing for the concert, the assembly, the opera, or the theater, the saints resort to hold communion with their Saviour. Here the minister of Christ can breathe freely. Here he can pour out his heart in supplications with which he knows that every hearer sympathizes. Here he can speak the language of Canaan, and he feels that every hearer understands it. Here, with his whole soul, in the exercise of a lively faith, he can urge men to repent and believe, for he knows that those still unregenerate, who come within this circle, are inquiring what they must do to be saved. Here, then, is real worship.

This is the real Sabbath of the soul. Here the piety of saints is fed with manna from above. Here the lamp of Christian piety is fed with the oil from the sanctuary. It is thus that religion is kept alive in our magnificent churches. Were it not for this, they would all sink, and be engulfed in formalism and worldliness. O why could not the vestry be removed to the audience-room above?

There has been also, as might be supposed, a great change in our discipline, while these other changes have been in progress. Holding firmly to the doctrine of the spirituality of the church, our fathers conceived that there must, of necessity, be a vast difference between them and the world. They knew that if they were true to their principles, they must, of necessity, be a peculiar people. They took it for granted that they would be out of sight of the gay, the thoughtless, and the pleasure-loving. They cultivated plainness of dress. The Methodists and the Baptists might once be known by the simplicity of their attire. Hence our brethren were never met with in places of public amusement. You would as soon have found a Baptist in jail as at a ball, an opera, or a theater. To be found in such a company would have incurred the censure of the church. They would have entered into no metaphysical disquisition on the question, How far a disciple of Christ may go in conformity to the world? they would only have asked, How can a spiritual mind take delight in "the lusts of the eye, the lusts of the flesh, and the pride of life?"

In all the transactions of ordinary business, they were watchful over the character of each other. They were not in haste to be rich, and hence they escaped many "foolish and hurtful lusts which drown men in destruction and perdition." Public opinion, I think, had less weight with them than now, hence they did not dare to seek a morally doubtful advantage, because it was customary with men of the world. They might, like other men, be unfortunate in business, but I think it was considered the duty of the church, in such a case, to look into a brother's affairs, and ascertain for themselves that he had been guilty of no dishonesty. I once knew a case of this kind. A most exemplary man, a deacon of a Baptist church, failed in business, in a time of extreme financial pressure. He did not act as an officer of the church, and I am not sure that he partook of the communion, until a committee had investigated his affairs, and the church was satisfied that his conduct had been unexceptionable. The purity and honor of his character were soon made manifest to the world. His estate paid every creditor, with interest, met all the expenses of insolvency, and left him a handsome amount as a remainder. A failure of this kind was no dishonor to the cause of Christ, but it is spoken of, even to this day, as a memorable example of Christian integrity.

In these respects, there has a change come over us. I fear that in attendance upon places of amusement, and in participation in social luxury, our practice is different from that of our fathers. In the matter of mercantile integrity, I do not know that there is any thing now to distinguish us from others. The church discipline, which was formerly universal, could not now be carried into effect. The tide of worldliness, the love of gain, and the ambition of expense, which has been, for some years, flowing over the Christian world, has overwhelmed us also.

In how far, in these respects, we have suffered by following the example of others, need not here be considered. Whatever be the amount of our blameworthiness, it rests, after all, exclusively on ourselves. Nay, more, it is evident that in this matter, if we have sinned, we are exceedingly sinful. When a denomination does not hold distinctly and clearly the doctrine of the spirituality of the church, it is especially liable to the irruption of worldliness. Those who were admitted to communion for the sake of making them better, only make the others worse, and thus the standard of piety in a church is reduced. The worldly example of one professor of religion is taken as a rule for others who desire an excuse for seeking pleasure rather than seeking God. Thus the infection spreads from member to member, from church to church, and from denomination to denomination, because there is no recognized and established principle to resist it. We, however, have no such excuse. It has pleased God to reveal to us clearly the doctrine of the spirituality of the church, and he has taught us to avoid all beliefs and rites at variance with it. On us there was devolved the momentous duty of exemplifying this doctrine, in all its moral beauty, to the whole Christian world. Had we been true to our Master and to our own principles, what blessings might we not have conferred upon the church of Christ? The wave of worldliness that has been rising so fearfully, would have beat harmlessly at our feet, and our example might have strengthened our brethren of other denominations to check its destructive progress. Is it yet too late? May we not yet arise from the dust, and put on our beautiful garments? Is it too much to hope that God will yet honor us as the harbingers of an era of more elevated piety in the history of the church. Good men of all denominations are becoming greatly alarmed at the present tendencies. The vast discrepancy between Christianity as it now appears, and the Christianity taught and exemplified by Christ and his apostles, is mournfully apparent. Poets, satirists, and journalists, scoff at it, and jeer at it, and hold it up to stinging and universal ridicule. Merchants declare that they consider an account against a professor of religion worth no more than that against any other man. Ought not every denomination of Christians, then, to awake out of sleep, and does it not become us to be the first to set them the example?

XXX.

INDEPENDENCE OF THE CHURCHES.—CAN A CHURCH PROPERLY BE REPRESENTED?

BEFORE closing my remarks on the dangers to which we are exposed from following the examples of other denominations, I desire to offer a few remarks on our ecclesiastical organization. We are liable in this respect to swerve from our principles, and of this liability it is well to be aware.

The Baptists have ever believed in the entire and absolute independence of the churches. By this, we mean that every church of Christ, that is, every company of believers united together according to the laws of Christ, is wholly independent of every other; that every church is perfectly capable of self-government; and that, therefore, no one acknowledges any higher authority, under Christ, than itself; that with the church all ecclesiastical action commences, and with it it terminates, and hence, that the ecclesiastical relations proper, of every member, are limited to the church to which he belongs. If it be said that a member may thus be exposed to the tyranny of a majority, and suffer censure when it is undeserved, without hope of redress; to this I reply, the principles of independence, carried consisten ly to their results, furnish a remedy for this form of injustice. A church owes courtesy to every other church, but is under no obligation to take part with it in wrong-doing. The injured person may, therefore, apply to any other church for admission. It is perfectly competent for them to examine the case for themselves, and if, in their opinion, the member has been guilty of no wrong, they may rightfully receive him. In such a case, however, it would probably be the preferable course to call a council of disinterested brethren who might examine the facts, and give the aggrieved members, and the church with which they proposed to unite, the benefit of their advice. This seems to provide a sufficient remedy against ecclesiastical tyranny, and this is the result to which the doctrine of the independence of the churches necessarily leads.

The doctrine of the independence of the churches rests upon a few plain and well-established principles. Some of these I take to be the following:

1. Religion is a matter which concerns exclusively

the relations between an individual man and his Maker. It teaches us how we may so serve God as to secure his favor, both here and hereafter.

2. The manner in which we may acceptably serve God must be made known to us by God himself. The moral history of man teaches us that we are wholly incapable of determining this question.

3. In the New Testament, God has therefore in mercy furnished us with a perfect rule of duty. From this source we may learn our obligations to God, to our fellow-men in general, and to our Christian brethren in particular.

4. This revelation being a communication from God to every individual, every individual is under obligation to understand it for himself. Aid, sufficient to guide every candid inquirer, is promised to all who will ask for it. By the light thus obtained, every man is under the highest conceivable obligations to govern his conduct, though it be in opposition to every created authority.

5. Men who, by such an examination of the New Testament, arrive at the same conclusions respecting its requirements, unite together in churches for the sake of promoting holiness in each other, and subduing the world to obedience to Christ. In doing this, however, they neither assume on the one hand, nor concede on the other, any power of original legislation over each other. Christ is the head of the church in general, and of every individual church in particular. The members all profess obedience to his laws, and by his laws they submit, at all times, to be judged. Whatever the New Testament teaches, either by precept or through ex-

ample, the church may require of its members; and the individual members may require of the church. Whatever passes beyond this rule, must be left to the judgment and conscience of the individual, it being without the limit of church authority.

6. Such being the nature of a Christian church, I do not see how it can possibly be *represented*. Representation always supposes that there are certain rights, duties, obligations, etc., in which the individual agrees to be governed by the majority. The various constituencies unite in sending certain persons of their own number, who represent their sentiments in these respects, and they agree to obey such laws as these representatives, when assembled together, shall enact. Thus, in this country, we agree to submit to the decision of Congress all questions relating to peace and war, imports, currency, etc. There are, however, other questions, as for instance, those relating to the rights of conscience, which we have never submitted to their authority. Whatever laws they enact, therefore, in respect to all matters which we have placed under their jurisdiction, we adopt as rules of our conduct, unless they be in violation of our duties to God.

7. Such being the nature of representation, I ask how can a church of Christ be *represented?* The matters which could be committed to representatives are clearly but two: First, those which Christ has *not* commanded, but which are properly left to the decision of individual conscience; and secondly, those which *have been commanded* by Christ or his apostles. Concerning the first class, these, not being commanded, but being left to the decision of individual conscience, are already

without the jurisdiction of the church, and, of course, the church can commit jurisdiction concerning them to no representation. It can not transfer to another a power which by concession it does not possess. But take the other class of duties, or obligations, those commanded by Christ. Can it commit the commands of Christ to any human tribunal? Can a church, or can churches commit the precepts of Jesus to a representation, thus acknowledging their power to add to, to abolish, or to modify what the Master has enacted? Or again: can it concede to any representation the right *to interpret for* us the precepts of Christ? This would be to abolish the right of private judgment, and convert us into Romanists. Nor, lastly, can we commit the *execution* of these laws to representatives, since the power to enforce the laws of Christ rests with each church itself.

It would seem, from these simple principles, impossible that a church of Christ can be *in any proper and legitimate sense represented*. We have nothing to submit to representatives. We have no representatives to whom any thing is to be submitted. I will go further, and add, that what can not be done properly and legitimately must not be done improperly and illegitimately. It is as truly a violation of the independence of the churches, and the right of private judgment, when several hundred brethren meet in some public convention, and manufacture public opinion, and adopt courses which their brethren are called upon to follow, on pain of the displeasure of the majority, as when they establish a formal representation, to whose decisions all the constituency must submit.

These have always been favorite ideas with our Baptist churches. In this we differ essentially from our Presbyterian brethren. With them, every church is represented formally, and legally, in its Presbytery, by which its acts may be reviewed and reversed. The Presbytery is, in like manner, represented in the Synod, and also in the court of final ecclesiastical appeal, the General Assembly. This form of church government, as it is called, appears well enough, if we look upon a church of Christ as a civil organization. We, however, take very different views of the theory of the church of Christ, and in practice, we have never seen any thing in the representative form to recommend it. If any of our Christian brethren like it, we are glad to have them adopt it. We, however, have ever looked with great disfavor upon any practice which, in the remotest degree, violates the great principle of the independence of the churches.

Jesus Christ left his church without any general organization. Throughout the New Testament we can discover not a trace of organization beyond the establishment of individual churches. Their bond of union was sympathy with him through the indwelling of the Holy Spirit in each individual. Is it not probable that as he left it, so he intended that it should continue to the end of time ? The object of the church of Christ on earth is very simple : it is the conversion of souls. This object, it seems to me, can be accomplished without the use of the complicated, cumbrous, and frequently soul-destroying machinery, with which his disciples have for so many ages been burdened. Under the old dispensation there was an established and formal organization, and every thing respecting it was definitely prescribed, even to the minutest particular. As, in the New Testament, no trace of this kind can be discovered, is it not reasonable to suppose that nothing of this kind was intended, but that the Master chose that it should remain just as he left it? Moses was commanded, saying, "See that thou make all things according to the pattern showed thee in the mount." As Jesus Christ has showed us no "pattern," is it desirable for us to make one for ourselves?

XXXI.

ATTEMPTS TO FORM A BAPTIST REPRESENTATION HAVE FAILED.—BAPTIST GENERAL CONVENTION.—MISSIONARY UNION.—NO ONE OF ALL OUR BENEVOLENT ASSOCIATIONS REPRESENT THE BAPTIST DENOMINATION.

I HAVE referred to the doctrine of the independence of the churches, and the grounds on which we suppose it to rest. It is a belief to which the vast majority of our brethren have adhered with a most commendable and consistent tenacity.

Notwithstanding this, attempts have been made, at sundry times, among us, to establish some kind of informal representation. They have never met with favor, and have obtained influence among us only through ignorance of their real character. To some of these I will briefly allude.

When State Conventions were first proposed, it was by many believed—and of these I freely confess myself to have been one—that through them we might establish a general Baptist organization. If the churches sent delegates to the Association, the Association sent delegates to the State Convention, and the State Convention sent delegates to the General Convention of the Baptists in the United States, or to the Triennial Convention then existing, it would seem that all this might easily have been accomplished. I now rejoice exceedingly that the whole plan failed, and that it failed through the sturdy common sense of the masses of our brethren. The churches were from the first unwilling to confer this power on the Associations. The Associations took very little interest in it, and frequently sent no delegates to the State Conventions. The churches did not greatly favor them, and hence they never seemed to take root naturally among us. They are now, in fact, merely Domestic Missionary Associations, and as such have been very useful. But I believe that their usefulness would be increased, and that they would associate themselves more intimately with our churches, by adopting a name more strictly indicative of their character, and calling themselves what they are—Home Mission Societies of the States to which they belong.

The Triennial Convention was really a representative assembly, composed, however, not of representatives of *churches* as such, but of representatives chosen by the contributors to Foreign Missions. These contributors were sometimes individuals, sometimes Mission Societies, sometimes churches, sometimes Associations, and sometimes State Conventions. Any Baptist organization whatever, which contributed a given amount annually to the funds of the Convention, had a right to send its representative. Hence it was a very common thing, at its meetings, to hear members tell about their *con-*

stituents. An attempt was made, pretty early in the history of this organization, to give it the control over all our benevolent efforts. It was proposed to merge in it our Education Societies, Tract Societies, Home Mission Societies, and our Foreign Mission Societies, so that one central Board should have the management of all our churches, so far as their efforts to extend the kingdom of Christ were concerned. After a protracted debate, this measure was negatived by so decided a majority that the attempt was never repeated, and this danger was averted. We look back, at the present day, with astonishment that such an idea was ever entertained.

Though the Triennial Convention was thus restricted to its appropriate object, the work of Foreign Missions, its representative character remained. It was, by the community at large, considered to be the grand meeting of the Baptist denomination in the United States, a sort of General Assembly, to which all our affairs were brought for decision. Hence, if for any cause it was deemed desirable to commit the whole Baptist membership to any course of action, this was considered the proper place in which to make the attempt. I well remember that, on one occasion, a series of resolutions was introduced, of which the only object was to express our approbation of General Jackson's measures for the removal of the Cherokees. Hence, though missions were the ostensible object for which we assembled, missions were frequently the last thing thought of. Propositions for amendments to the Constitution, of course, occupied a considerable part of the session. Then the attempts of brethren from the East or West, the North or the South, to procure an expression of the denomination in favor of this matter or that, totally unconnected with missions, must be disposed of. When any of these exciting questions were discussed, the house would be filled to overflowing; but when *nothing but missions* was under consideration there was room enough, and to spare. A large part of the time of the meeting was thus wasted in angry altercation. Hence this attempt at representation, intended to unite us all as one denomination, proved the source of manifold alienation, and, I fear, injured the very cause of missions which it was its avowed object to promote.

I shall not soon forget the remarks made by a beloved brother from Ohio, at one of the last meetings of the Triennial Convention which I ever attended. After the meeting had been for several days in session, he obtained an opportunity to address it, and spoke to the following effect: " My brethren, I have ever been deeply interested in the cause of missions, and once hoped that I might myself be permitted to labor in the foreign field. My health, however, failed, and the providence of God forbade me to prosecute my purpose. I have never before attended a meeting of the Convention, much as I have desired it. For some time I have denied myself many conveniences, that I might secure the means for making this journey. I expected here to meet the fathers and brethren of the Baptist denomination, and hear from them much concerning the progress of the Redeemer's kingdom, and the plans which were to be adopted for its further increase. In a word, I expected to hear about missions, but we have been now in session for several days, and the subject of missions has hardly been introduced. I have thus far heard nothing but the contentions of brethren. There seems really less interest in missions here, among brethren who are considered leaders in the missionary enterprise, than in the forests of the West. Brethren, I shall return home sad at heart." The words thrilled through the assembly, and there was not a man there who did not confess that every word was true, and that the reproof was richly merited.

Things had arrived at that point, that every member who loved the cause of missions, or even the peace of our Zion, looked forward to the meetings of the Convention with fear and apprehension. Our best men were becoming glad of an opportunity to be absent from its meetings. When the separation between the North and the South took place, every one saw that a totally different organization had become absolutely indispensable. The Constitution of the present Missionary Union, which is formed on entirely different principles, was unanimously adopted. This was the end of the only representative organization ever attempted among us. The result showed it to be utterly alien from all our principles, and calculated to work nothing but division and dissension among us.

The Constitution of the "Union" excluded all semblance of representation. It was originally composed entirely of life-members, who became such by the payment of $100, though this feature has since been slightly modified. The life-members elect a Board, who hold office for three years, one third being elected every year. The Board elect an Executive Committee for the special management of the concerns of missions. Here, then, every man speaks for himself, and for himself alone.

He can throw the blame of his actions on no constituents, but must stand up and answer to the public for himself. This has been a great advantage, and has tended to save us from many a useless, angry, and partisan discussion. The membership is also much more permanent, and so much time is not occupied by brethren, who, for the first time, have attended a general missionary meeting, and are wholly ignorant of the subject of missions.

Still it is ever to be borne in mind that the Missionary Union, together with the various Associations that frequently meet at the same place, and nearly at the same time, is no *representation* of the *Baptist denomination*, that is, of the Baptist churches, which are in truth the denomination. This is so important a fact, that it deserves a word or two in explanation.

In point of numbers, the members of our Societies, meeting at any one time, are a very inconsiderable fragment of the denomination. Or take the whole membership of these Societies together—and they are, in fact, generally the same persons over again—and they would amount not to a twentieth, probably not to a fiftieth, of our whole number. But whether many or few, they come not as representatives of churches, for the churches have never sent them nor commissioned them; they come together on their own motion, merely as members of the Union, or of the Home Mission, or Bible, or any other Society. The limits of their action are fixed by the Constitution of the Society to which they belong. When they have cared for its interests, they have nothing further to do, and have no more right, at such a time, to act *for the denomination*, than they would have, if by chance they happened, each one in the pursuit of his own business, to meet at the central terminus of several railroads. They are members of these Societies, and nothing more, and directly, or indirectly, to assume to be any thing else, is by just so much to violate the principle of the independence of the churches.

But suppose, it may be said, that every member of a Baptist church was a member of these Societies for Christian benevolence, would not the delegations sent by the churches to the meetings of these Societies, represent the churches? I reply, by no means. The constitution and laws of the church are found in the New Testament. What we find there enjoined, we may enforce, and nothing more. Much remains, however, which the church may not enforce, but which is left to individual duty. What is thus done, though done by every member of the church, is not done by the church, and the church has no right to exercise any control over it; nor have those who do it any right to enforce it upon the church. I will take the plain and obvious case of foreign missions. No church has any right to oblige any member to *give* to foreign missions, any more than to *go upon a foreign mission*. The same may be said of a Bible Society, a Home Mission, or any other Society. A church may demand of every member the consecration of himself and his property to Christ, and may very properly exclude him for covetousness, just as it would for lying, profanity, lewdness, or any other sin. But as to the *manner* in which the individual shall exercise his liberality, the church can not direct. He may give his money and his labor to missions, home or foreign, or to the distribution of tracts or Bibles, or to the assistance and improvement of the poor in his own vicinity, and it is all out of their jurisdiction. This is done out of the church, on the individual's responsibility to his Master. Suppose individuals engaged in these various good designs unite together in advancing them, they form their own laws, adopt their own arrangements, but they are not the church, they can not control or represent the church, nor can the church represent them, or control them, unless they violate the precepts of Jesus.

XXXII.

LOVE TO THE SAVIOUR THE BOND WHICH MUST UNITE BAPTISTS TO EACH OTHER.—ERRORS TO BE AVOIDED IN CONDUCTING BENEVOLENT ASSOCIATIONS.—THE SPECIAL OBJECT OF A CHURCH MUST NOT BE TRANSCENDED.—INFANT DEDICATION.—CONCLUDING REFLECTIONS.

Those who agree with me in the suggestions which occupy some of my last numbers, will readily see that the representation of churches, in any legitimate sense, is at variance with the first principles to which we have always adhered, that all the attempts to establish any thing of this kind have been eminently unsuccessful, and that they have been, and ever must be, productive of dissension and strife, instead of unity and peace. The more steadfastly we hold to the independence of the churches, and abjure every thing in the form of a denominational corporation, the more truly shall we be united, and the greater will be our prosperity. If it be asked, What is there then to unite us? I answer, love to Christ and adherence to principle. When these fail, we shall sink with them. Destitute of these, we ought to sink. If we die, why should we not be buried? If the piety and zeal of the Baptist churches become extinct, the denomination will be absorbed into other sects and be no more known. This is to me one of the strongest evidences that we are on the true foundation. A church organized after the manner of a civil commonwealth may retain its form long after the last vestige of piety has vanished, and continue for ages an enemy to Christ and a persecutor of the saints. The soil of Christendom, at the present day, is covered with the festering carcasses of churches, from which the Spirit has for generations departed. The moral atmosphere is rendered pestilential by their presence, and neither piety nor humanity can breathe it and survive.

Let us, then, ever bear it in mind that the Baptist denomination, that is, the Baptist churches, is one thing, and the benevolent associations formed or sustained by individual Baptists are another and a very different thing. Individual members of our churches have a right to form such associations, not at variance with the precepts of the Master, as they choose. All who wish to unite in the promotion of such on object, of course join with them. This, however, imposes no obligation on those who are not like-minded. They are just as free to let it alone as to unite in it. They may be as good Baptists in letting it alone as in joining it. "A brother or sister is not under bondage in such cases." We give and receive freely in such matters the right of private judgment. It pertains to the church to which I belong to see that I am not wanting in

Christian benevolence, and to exclude me if need be for covetousness, but the direction which my benevolence shall take must be left to myself.

And where such associations are formed, they have each one its appropriate office, whether it be foreign or domestic missions, the circulation of Bibles, or tracts, or any other good design. This object is exclusive. It may not properly be transcended or mingled with any other. No one, not of this Society, has any right to interfere with its management, nor has it a right to interfere in the management of any other Society. There are two ways in which this important rule may be violated.

In the first place, we may use one Society to advance the interests of another. For instance, I am a member of a Mission Society. I am bound in this relation to consider simply the interests of missions. My brother is a member of a Bible Society; he is, in this relation, to consider simply the circulation of the Scriptures. But I am also a member of the Bible Society. I have no right to enter that Society and seek to make it subservient to the Mission Society, nor has any brother a right to render the Mission Society subservient to the Bible Society. I have no right to elect officers of the Bible Society who favor my missionary views, nor he to elect officers of the Mission Society who favor his Bible views. Neither has he a right to take measures in another Society for the purpose, as it would seem, of committing the denomination to the Society which he considers it his duty especially to favor. Let each stand separately on its own merits, and gain the favor of the whole, not by partisan management, but by good works.

The latter course leads to harmony, independence, and mutual love ; the other to intrigue, dissension, tyranny, and disaffection. Unless these principles be observed, our general associations will prove a curse rather than a blessing, and a voluntary association which is found to be a curse, will soon cease to exist.

Again, we may interfere with each other in a different manner. One Society may be engaged in a work which is especially blessed of God and finds general favor with the brethren. Another Society, formed for a different purpose, finds less favor with the churches ; its object is not believed to be of vital importance ; its field of labor is, from necessity, circumscribed, and it spends so large a part of its collections in agencies, that it languishes and is liable to perish. Such a Society may, for a time, be revived, by undertaking a part of the labor of the more fortunate associations, and thus, instead of doing the work for which it was constituted, do the work appropriate to an entirely different organization. Then we have two Societies with their separate rooms, officers, and agents, at a very large expense, doing the same work, each going through the churches making collections for the same object, and neither succeeding but at the expense of the other. It is for this, among other reasons, that the business of agencies is so shockingly overdone among us. The very name of an agent is by no means a favorable introduction to any of our churches. The congregation is always small when it is known that an agent is to occupy the pulpit. A feeling so general cannot be wholly without foundation. If we wish our general benevolent associations to prosper, they must confine themselves to their legitimate and constitutional objects; and if they can not stand on this foundation, they had better be abandoned.

I have spoken above of the distinctive character of the church of Christ. On this subject let me add a single word. I think we should be careful to bear this in mind in all our arrangements. For instance, I have known a church form itself into a Temperance Society, and oblige every member on entering it to take the Temperance pledge. Now, God forbid that I should say a word against temperance, but still, a church is not a Temperance *Society*. A church may very properly, nay, it *must of necessity*, require of every member that whether he eat or drink, he must do it to the glory of God. It may enforce the direct precepts of the New Testament, and the indirect precept of the apostle Paul, in respect to causing a brother to offend; and it may inform every member that this is required of him, and will be enforced accordingly. Nay, further, if a brother has ever been liable to this sin, it may require of him specifically total abstinence on account of his peculiar temptation. But I think that it can go no further. The difference here is important. In the one case, it is a promise of a moral duty made to man, in the other, it is submission to the revealed will of God. The value of this difference must be evident to every one.

So I have known churches to take the Sabbath-school under their care, as it is called, and constitute themselves, in fact, a Sunday-school Society. I do not see how this can be, unless every member is required to teach in a Sabbath-school. No one, however, would believe this to be correct. Under this view, the Sabbath-school scholars are sometimes called " children of the church." I always supposed that the church had none but regenerate children ; for if she have unregenerate children of one age, why not of another ? Would it not be more in accordance with our principles to consider the Sabbath-school an association of Christians uniting for this purpose under their own laws, and subject to their own arrangements ?

These may seem matters of small moment. They may not be great in themselves, but they are of importance if we consider the principles which they involve. If brethren united in church fellowship have the right to take matters not strictly belonging to the church under their legislation, what is there that may not be taken under the cognizance of the church ? Where shall the line be drawn ? and when a member joins a Baptist church how shall he know to how many things, not commanded by Christ, he commits himself ? Many of the worst corruptions of the Catholic church were introduced by requiring as a *universal duty*, what was properly left to *individual conscience*. It may be very suitable for a burdened conscience to unbosom itself to a minister or Christian friend before coming to the table of the Lord. Left precisely in this form, as a matter to be decided by the individual himself, nothing could be more innocent. Require it to be done as a *command of Christ*, and we have the practice of auricular confession, one of the most terrific engines ever devised by Satan for enslaving the conscience, and bringing the soul of man under the unlimited power of the priesthood. This is not fancy, but fact. It was thus that auricular confession was introduced into the Romish church.

INFANT DEDICATION.

A Welsh Baptist desires me to say a word on the subject of Infant Dedication. In complying with his request, I would remark, that I never before heard that such a practice obtained in the Principality. I see no allusion to it in Christmas Evans's Sermons, nor in any other Welsh writers with whom I am acquainted. In my youth, I knew several able and eminent Welsh Baptist ministers, such as John Williams, John Stevens, and others, but never did I hear from them a word of any such practice. They certainly never introduced it into this country.

I never have heard of the practice of infant dedication until within a few years. I learned, some time since, that some of our missionaries at the East were in the habit of holding a prayer-meeting shortly after the birth of a child, to ask for it the blessing of the Saviour, and in a special manner to consecrate it to God. It was purely a voluntary service, and was merely a meeting of the particular friends of the family for prayer for a particular object. The missionaries, however, found that it was liable to be mistaken, by the converts from heathenism, for an appointment of Christ, and they wisely, on their own motion, abandoned it.

It is, I perceive, asserted that a practice of this sort is in use among some of the churches in Germany. Of this I know no more than I have seen in the newspapers. I never heard Mr. Oncken allude to it.

The above exhausts my knowledge on the subject. To my Welsh brother I would, therefore, reply, "We have no such custom, neither the churches of God."

In concluding this part of my subject, I would remark, that our position is, in one respect, remarkable. The unexampled facilities for the acquisition of wealth have stimulated the love of gain and the passion of expense, beyond all former precedent. The love of sensual pleasure is sweeping away the barriers which once separated the church from the world, and drowning men in destruction and perdition. The principles of men professing godliness are exerting less and less effect on their practice. To arrest this progress of worldliness must be especially difficult in churches which, theoretically or practically, directly or indirectly, admit the doctrine of hereditary membership. We profess to have escaped this error. It becomes us, therefore, when the enemy is coming in like a flood, to lift up a standard against him. Let us, then, review our principles. Let us assure ourselves of their truth. Let us, at all hazards, carry them out into practice. By so doing, rather than by following the example of others, shall we please the Master, and confer the greatest benefit upon our brethren of other denominations. Devout men of all persuasions are alarmed at the condition of religion throughout our country, and they would hail with joy the opening of a brighter day, from what quarter soever it might arise.

Wherever the standard of the cross is erected, the sons of God, by whatever name they may be called, will gather around it. Let us arise and lift up that standard, for this matter belongeth unto us.

I would ask my brethren who have been allured from the simplicity that is in Christ, and have yielded themselves to the maxims, the fashions, the luxury, and sensuality of a world that perisheth, What fruit have ye in the things of which ye were once ashamed ? Is not the end of these things death? What scriptural evidence do you possess that you are heirs of eternal life? Are your affections on things below, or on things above? Can you turn your eyes to the Saviour, and say to him, Lord, thou knowest all things, thou knowest that I love thee? Jesus Christ has said, Except a man deny himself, and take up his cross daily and follow me, he cannot be my disciple. Are you conscious of either one of these evidences of discipleship? Christ has said, How hardly shall they that have riches enter into the kingdom of heaven; and yet, is it not your all-absorbing desire to be rich? Are you not robbing God by using what he has lent to you, in the gratification of worldly desires? An apostle has told us that the lust of the flesh, the lust of the eye, and the pride of life, are not of the Father, but of the world; and for these lusts are you not sacrificing your souls? Are not your children eagerly drinking in the poison with which you so liberally supply them? Suppose that you, at their age, had been where your children are now, where would you have been at the present moment? Where, then, will they be, when they shall be of your age? What hope can you have of their salvation? You must meet them at the judgment day, and can you abide that meeting?

But I forbear. The subject is too painful to be continued. It is not too late to return. Let us do again our first works. God is yet waiting to be gracious unto us. Let us humble ourselves in the dust before him. Let us once more take up the forgotten cross, and walk in the footsteps of the lowly, self-denying Saviour. Let us bring our tithes into the storehouse, and see if God will not pour out upon us a blessing that there shall not be room enough to receive it. Then shall we know if we follow on to know the Lord.

XXXIII.

IMPORTANCE OF PUBLIC WORSHIP.—THE DUTY OF THE DISCIPLES OF CHRIST TO MAINTAIN IT.—WITH US, THIS DUTY REQUIRES A UNIVERSAL EFFORT.—DIFFICULTIES PECULIAR TO OUR CONDITION.

SOME months since, a correspondent of *The Examiner* requested me to discuss, more at large than I had already done, the subject of the Christian ministry in the Baptist denomination. I promised, perhaps incautiously, that if no one else would perform this service I would undertake it myself. It is in fulfillment of this promise that the following papers are written.

It is too obvious, to need illustration, that one of the great objects for which churches of Christ are established, is to maintain the public worship of God. Hence, also, one of the first duties devolving on those who profess Christianity, is to provide the means by which this object shall be accomplished. Under the former dispensation, those that feared the Lord spake often one to another, and the Lord hearkened and heard, and a book of remembrance was kept. Our blessed Lord, as his custom was, was seen every Sabbath day in the synagogue, to read and explain to the people the Law and the Prophets. An apostle has cautioned us not to forsake the assembling of ourselves together. Indeed, were there neither precept nor example to enforce this duty, the experience of every

Christian soul must bear witness to its vital importance. It is thus that we, once in the week at least, publicly testify to the world that we are looking for the Sabbath which remains for the people of God. It is thus that we strive the better to understand the word of God. It is in the sanctuary that we offer up, with one heart and voice, our prayers to him who is the giver of every good and perfect gift. Here we render public thanks for public as well as for individual mercies. It is to the sanctuary that we invite the thoughtless and impenitent, to hear the words by which they may, by the blessing of God, be saved. And we do all this, encouraged by the blessed assurance of the Saviour, "Wherever two or three are gathered together in my name, there am I in the midst of them."

The importance of this subject can hardly be exaggerated. Every one knows that the Christian who has begun to think lightly of the ordinances of the sanctuary, is already treading in the path of the backslider. Who that, by sickness, or other providential hinderance, has been kept for a time from the meeting of the saints, has not uttered the plaint of the Psalmist, "My flesh longeth, yea, even fainteth for the courts of the Lord." In a village or settlement in our own country, where the Sabbath is not honored by the public worship of God, how soon do parents and children relapse into almost heathenism! Suppose that any denomination should adopt the view, that as religion was a personal matter, the assembling for public worship was needless, and should sell off its churches and close its meetings for prayer, who does dot see that it would become extinct within a single generation? And, on the contrary, those denominations are most rapidly extending, which furnish the most abundantly, to all classes of the community, the means of hearing the preaching of the pure word of God.

Hence it is not remarkable that the making provision for public worship has been a leading object with all sects of Christians. Where religion is established by law, the State assumes this responsibility. The people are taxed to support religious worship, and they have an equitable claim on the State for the maintenance of teachers of religion. In the Episcopal form of church government, the oversight of a particular district, called a diocese, is devolved on a single individual. He has the power of admitting to the ministry—he has the whole field under his eye, and to him the people look for direction in their efforts to extend the kingdom of Christ. A Presbytery frequently exercises a similar influence within its limits. With us, however, there is no such organization. Every church with us is independent, and is not of necessity associated with any other. Every pastor is a Bishop, and holds the highest ecclesiastical rank which we acknowledge. Hence it is manifest that the responsibility for sustaining the worship of God, in our case, rests upon every church, and every individual member of a church. We have neither State, nor Bishop, nor Presbytery, nor Synod to fall back upon. We have assumed this responsibility as churches and individuals, and we must abide by the choice which—agreeably to the New Testament, as I conceive—we have made. Our progress—nay, our very existence—depends upon the vitality which pervades *the whole mass.* If every individual disciple would devote himself to the work of extending the kingdom of Christ, relying on the promised aid of the Holy Spirit, we should need no more organization than existed in apostolic times, when they that were scattered abroad went everywhere preaching the Word, and when, within a single lifetime, the civilized world was filled with the knowledge of Christ. If we rely on any thing else, it is evident that we must be covered with confusion. If, instead of putting forth our own power, in simple reliance on Christ, we are looking for aid in any other direction, we shall find that we have mistaken our principles, we have leaned on a broken reed which can yield us no adequate support, but will pierce the hand which presses upon it. So long as, universally vital, each disciple relies on himself, trusting only in God, we shall be irresistible. So soon as individual effort relaxes, and we trust to means of our own devising, we shall inevitably fail.

It is, besides, worthy of remark, that with us there are peculiar difficulties in maintaining throughout our whole country the public worship of God. Our people belong, in general, not to the class of capitalists. The capital of our members commonly consists in skill and enterprise, and not in houses, lands, ships, and bank securities. Hence, in the mighty exodus now going on from the East to the West, a large portion of the emigrants belong to our communion. The wealthy citizen, whose gains have been invested in real estate, yielding a rich rent, and doubling in value every five or ten years, or who holds his hundreds of thousands in securities paying eight or ten per cent. per annum, has no desire to leave his home in the metropolis. The rich agriculturist, whose well-tilled land is producing a fair income, and who sees yearly a new farm added to his noble domain, has no inducement to leave the place of his fathers' sepulchres, and the region where his single influence frequently decides the election for his town or county. It is the man of cultivated capacities, who knows how to do something well, but is destitute of the capital which can render his skill available, who is tempted to remove to the West. Such are the men wanted in the new States, and there, with the blessing of God, they are sure not only of competence, but abundance, both for themselves and for their children. Accordingly, if I have been correctly informed, you will rarely find a settlement of twenty families anywhere on our western frontier, which is not composed, in a marked proportion, of Baptists. These are the men who, with faculties developed by the exigencies of their new residence, will give character to the West, and in a few years find themselves equal to any thing they have left behind. They are everywhere manifesting power, of which they never supposed themselves possessed, and are laying broad and deep the foundations of society far beyond the mountains.

Hence it is, that the field which we are called upon to supply with the public worship of God, is vast in extent, and of a very diversified character. For instance, we have our great cities, in which are to be found numerous and wealthy churches. These are fully able to maintain public worship at large expense. The same may be said of our small cities, and large towns, in each of which may be found one or two Baptist churches of ample means. Besides these may be counted numerous large villages, where the Baptist community is fully accommodated by a single house of worship. In all these localities the worship of God is maintained in the regular manner, and our churches in general follow the examples of those around them. But even here, are these churches doing their duty? They secure the services of an able and acceptable preacher. Their houses of worship are as tasteful, and the religious services as expensive as those of other denominations. They maintain themselves at a point of what is called high respectability. But let us look a little further. Ascertain the population of that city or town, and ask how large a portion of it attend any religious worship at all? Inquire for the statistics of preceding years, and you will probably find that the proportion of church-goers is relatively diminishing. A large missionary field is spreading abroad on every side, in the immediate vicinity of our very churches. What are we doing to supply these perishing souls with the word of life? The houses of worship have no room for them, and the cost of attendance is beyond their means. No man cares for their souls any more than for souls in the center of Africa. Have believers any right to settle down at their ease, enjoying the privileges of the sanctuary, while their fellow-men are perishing around them in heathenish darkness? Suppose that converts on missionary ground pursued a similar course; how would then the kingdom of Christ be extended? The Karens take a different view of this subject, and are subduing Burmah to Christ. But what difference does the Saviour make between a church in Toungoo and a church in New York, Philadelphia, or Boston?

But leaving these classes, which after all, form but a moderate portion of our population, we come to churches of thirty or forty members, in the older settlements and in the vast regions of the mighty West. These churches are numbered by hundreds, I might say by thousands. They are wholly unable to support a pastor who shall devote his whole time to preaching, and were they able, they could not employ his whole time in labors among themselves. How shall the worship of God be maintained in such localities? These villages are rapidly increasing, and parents and children are growing up destitute of the means of grace so far as we are concerned.

But besides these, there is a still larger region of destitution. Our brethren and sisters are emigrating by thousands. In every town and village the members of Baptist churches are found in fives, and tens, and twenties, who have formed themselves into no organization, who are as sheep without a shepherd, and who, from neglect of the ordinances of worship, are losing the evidences of piety, and falling back into the world. What is to be done for these sheep scattered in the wilderness? Must they be left to perish? Could these scattered brethren be united in some organization, and engaged in maintaining the public worship of God, each little band would become a nucleus, attracting to itself similar elements, and thus the foundation of churches would be laid, and these silent brethren would each one become a noble witness for God. Is it not time that something was done? Can no remedy be found for a condition so much to be deplored?

XXXIV.

FACILITIES IN OUR CONDITION FOR EXTENSION.—OUR LATEST STATISTICS SHOW A GREAT NEED OF MINISTERS OF THE GOSPEL.

In my last paper, I briefly sketched the duty devolved upon us to maintain the worship of God in the United States. That the same obligation rests upon other denominations, does not diminish the weight of obligation pressing upon us. There are our cities fast sinking into heathenism, to whose hundreds of thousands of perishing men we are bound to carry the word of life. There are our smaller churches, unable to support a pastor, which, for want of the stated worship of God on the Sabbath, are annually diminishing, and will soon be numbered with the things that were. There are our small villages, containing from five to twenty Baptist families, too weak, as they consider themselves, to be formed into a church, who, almost unknown to each other, assume no distinctive badge of Christianity, merely attending worship, it may be, with other denominations, without being able, with a good conscience, to unite with them in church fellowship. How are we to maintain the worship of God in all these thousands of places?

The work, I know, is attended with difficulty; but if it can be accomplished, the results will be glorious. Every part of the denomination will become vital. Instead of being paralyzed at the extremities, the extremities will give evidence of the intensest life. Even our scattered condition has incomparable advantages, if we would only avail ourselves of them. They that were

THE INFLUENCE OF THE GOSPEL. 207

scattered abroad, went everywhere preaching the Word. In every settlement of the West, there may be found the nucleus of a Baptist church, if the members could be induced to unite, and hold forth together the word of life. The name of the Saviour would be honored in thousands of villages and settlements where now the Sabbath is almost unheeded. Sinners by multitudes would be converted to Christ, and the principles of the gospel would from the first be interwoven with the whole fabric of society. The Methodists only excepted, no sect of Christians enjoys half so great advantages as we for bringing this whole country into obedience to Christ.

Nor is it to be forgotten that our views on these subjects are peculiarly favorable to every form of aggressive Christianity. Meetings for conference and prayer, where every believer is invited to express his religious sentiments, to exhort his brethren, and to warn the impenitent, have always been considered a part of our religious services on the Sabbath or week day evening. While we respect every department of human learning, and believe it to be the duty of the minister of Christ to give attention to reading, and to every form of mental cultivation, that his profiting may appear unto all, we have never avowedly dared to require in the candidate for the ministry any other qualifications than those which the Holy Ghost has required. We generally believe that God designs for laborers in his vineyard, men of every variety of human culture. It was so in apostolic times, and we believe it to be so now. The Baptist, therefore, welcomes to the ministry of the Word every brother, whatever be his attainments, who to fervent and consistent piety adds the gift of speaking in public, to the edification of saints and the awakening of sinners. We have established no barriers of human invention to restrict the number of ministers. On the contrary, we receive joyfully every brother on whom the Holy Spirit has conferred the gift of teaching.

Enjoying these advantages for extending the kingdom of Christ, it is important to inquire whether we are improving them. Are we using the means which God has given us to subdue our country to the Saviour, or are we failing in this duty, and coming short of the blessing which has been so richly proffered to us by the head of the church?

The instrumentality which God has appointed for cultivating the worship of the sanctuary, is the ministry of the gospel. We are assured, in the most solemn manner, that the Holy Spirit confers upon his churches the gifts which qualify men for this office. When the Messiah ascended on high and led captivity captive, he gave gifts unto men; and what were these gifts, the most important which the ascended Messiah could bestow? He gave some apostles, and some prophets, and some evangelists, and some pastors, and teachers, for the perfecting of the saints, for the work of the ministry, for the edifying of the body of Christ. This was the object of his gifts. When they are not, therefore, enjoyed, the churches must suffer loss, and the progress of religion be arrested. It therefore becomes a matter of deep interest in any denomination, to ascertain whether it be supplied with the ministry of the Word, and other means for conducting public worship.

It is with this view that I ask attention to the following statistics. They are compiled from the *American Baptist Register*, for 1852, the latest authority on this subject with which I am acquainted. The figures may not perfectly agree with our present condition, but they are sufficiently accurate for the purpose which I have in view.

From this authority, which I believe has been prepared with great care, it appears that we had, in 1852, 9,584 churches, averaging 81 members in each.

We had ordained ministers 6,291, which deducted from the number of churches, leaves 3,293 churches destitute of pastors.

But of these ordained ministers, we find that about 730 are without charge. Of these, some are engaged in supplying destitute churches, but the greater part either do not preach, or else merely act as supplies when the stated minister is absent or sick. Besides these, there is a large number of our ordained ministers who are engaged as teachers, professors, editors, or agents. These are not enumerated in those without charge. If we therefore deduct 730 as without charge from the number of ordained ministers, we have 4,023 as the number which designates the deficiency of pastors among us. That is, out of 9,584 churches, there are 4,023 without regular pastors. Nearly one half of our churches then, it would seem, are destitute of the stated means of grace.

A deduction from this statement must, however, be made on account of licentiates. This is the natural source of supply for the ministry. In former times, these, among us, were far more numerous than the regular pastors. The number of licentiates, however, given in the *Register*, is 1,146, or about one to eight churches. Is it not strange that eight of our churches, on an average, should furnish but one licentiate in the ministry. The churches in Germany furnish a much greater number of licentiates than pastors, and these are the means of their wonderful increase. If we suppose every licentiate to be the regular supply of a church, which is, however, very far from the fact, we still have 2,877 churches without the regular means of grace. That is, about a third of our churches are, at this moment, without the preaching of the gospel.

Nor is this evil by any means diminishing. From the *Register* we learn that we had—

In 1792—1,000 churches, and 1,264 ministers, that is, 264 more ministers than churches.

In 1812—2,433 churches, and 1,792 ministers, leaving a deficiency of ministers of 611.

In 1832—5,322 churches, and 3,647 ministers, leaving a deficiency of ministers of 1,675.

In 1852—9,584 churches, and 7,393 ministers,* leaving a deficiency of ministers of 2,191, and if from the number of ministers we deduct those without charge, the deficiency will be 2,889, or very nearly what we have stated above.

It would seem, then, that in 1852, there were about 2,800 churches in the United States, with congregations expecting from us the word of life, for which we make no provision. It would also seem that this deficiency is increasing at a very rapid ratio. In 1792 we had 264 more ministers than churches, and in 1852 we had over 2,800 more churches than ministers, including all our licentiates. It may be said that some of these minis-

* This includes licentiates.

ters supply three or four churches. Be it so. It alters not the case, for if we take any one Sabbath in the year, in which all the pastors and all the licentiates are engaged in preaching, there would still remain the same number of churches without any supply. Or, if we took into the account those without charge, and all the editors, teachers, and agents, of every class, and supposed every one of them to supply a destitute church, there would still be more than 2,000 churches without a preacher of the gospel.

But let us look at the subject from another point of view. Suppose these 9,584 churches all supplied with pastors. The average duration of a pastor's life is not probably more than twenty-five years. I do not mean that no man lives more than twenty-five years after he enters the ministry, but that taking into account sickness, the leaving the ministry for other occupations, and removals by death, I presume that twenty-five years of service for each individual, is a large average. To supply these churches then, at their present condition, without any hope of increase, would require 383 ministers annually. But if we hope to increase by the multiplication of churches, and by cherishing those small collections of members to be found in every settlement in the West, and by calling in the thousands of heathen swarming in all our large cities, we should need, certainly, as many more. The number of our churches in 1832 was 5,322, in 1852 it was 9,552, that is, our increase in churches was 4,230. To supply this demand, we should then require 211 ministers annually. This number added to 383, equals 594, or the number demanded at our present rate of increase. About 600 ministers, as an annual supply, is no more than would be required to place us in a condition to occupy the field which God, in his providence has placed before us? After every deduction has been made, with 2,800 destitute churches, and an annual demand for 600 ministers, and this deficiency rapidly increasing, what are the prospects before us? It is for us who are now living, looking back upon the past, and forward into the future, to answer this question.

XXXV.

IN OUR PRESENT CONDITION WHAT IS TO BE DONE? CAN THEOLOGICAL SEMINARIES AND COLLEGES SUPPLY OUR NEED?—THE ANSWER GIVEN BY STATISTICS.—WE NEED A GREAT NUMBER OF MINISTERS, AND WE NEED THAT EVERY MINISTER BE MADE AS EFFICIENT AS POSSIBLE.

I THINK that no Baptist can have reflected on the facts stated in my last number, without grave concern. If the course which we are pursuing must soon arrest our progress, and end in fatal decline, it becomes us to look at the whole matter soberly, resolutely, and courageously; and, in the fear of God, to adopt such measures as may lead to a change for the better.

It may possibly be objected that the statistics which I have used are incorrect. Of the value of this objection, I have not the means of forming an opinion. I know not why their truth should be suspected. They were collected with great care, and on the most responsible authority; and they have been for several years before the public. It therefore becomes him who objects to their results, to show their inaccuracy. But let any one make all the deductions which he would consider reasonable, and I do not believe that it would be possible for him to modify, in any important respect, the conclusions at which I have arrived; namely, that we are in danger of coming short of our destiny, and of failing utterly to accomplish the work which God has mercifully set before us, in consequence of a fearful deficiency of ministers of the gospel.

Again, it may be said that we are in this respect no more culpable than other denominations. I very much doubt it. There is no other denomination that has within itself the same elements of increase as the Baptists, except the Methodists; and they are better supplied with ministers than we. But suppose it to be the fact that we are in the same case as others, does this render our case at all the better? If we, by adopting their practices, at variance with our own principles, are suffering as badly as they, does this render our case the more hopeful?

But a thoughtful man will naturally ask, If such be the case, what is to be done? When this question is asked, nine out of ten persons who hear it will spontaneously reply, We must look to our colleges and theological seminaries. These are the fountains from which our ministry are to issue, and it is by their aid that this deficiency is to be supplied. Our agents have repeated this in our ears so often, that we believe it almost as we do an axiom, without examination and without question. Let us then turn again to the *American Baptist Register*, and see what aid we have received, or are likely to receive, from this quarter.

On page 450 of the *American Baptist Register*, is a table exhibiting the statistics of all our theological seminaries and colleges. Since the year 1820, we have established ten theological seminaries. These, in the year 1852, contained 105 students, and 24 professors. Supposing the course of study in each to be three years, the annual supply from this source would be exactly thirty-five. If we deduct from this number those who are needed for foreign missions, those who become professors, teachers, editors, and agents—what is left for the supply of the ministry at home? Our annual demand for the supply of the ministry we have estimated at about 600. From our seminaries we may expect, at most, twenty-five or thirty, or about one to each professor. The seminary at Newton, Massachusetts, is better endowed than any other which we have established. It possesses spacious grounds and extensive buildings, a fund of $100,000 was lately raised for its support, and it besides receives large aid from the Education Society. Its number of graduates up to 1852, is set down at 201. It had been in existence then twenty-seven years. Its average number of graduates per annum has been about seven and a half, or not quite two to a professor. The whole number of those who had studied there, whether pursuing the complete course or not, is 300. The annual average of these is a fraction over eleven. These facts are sufficient to exhibit the amount of supply which the ministry may expect from this source.

On the same page are the statistics of colleges. Of these we have established twenty-two. In them, in the year 1852, there were preparing for the Baptist ministry three hundred and twelve. Supposing a college course to be four years, the annual supply from this source would be seventy-eight. It is well known, however, that a considerable proportion of those preparing for the ministry in college never enter it. On the other hand, a considerable number of Baptist students are found in other than Baptist colleges. It is, however, to be observed that almost all who at present attend our theological seminaries, are graduates of colleges. We can not, therefore, in estimating our supply, add the students at college to those at the seminaries. It is difficult to determine the number of candidates for the ministry, who annually come from our colleges and theological seminaries. Probably they do not exceed ninety or one hundred, and from this number must be deducted those who become professors, teachers, editors, agents, foreign missionaries, and those who relinquish their intention of entering the ministry. Making the most liberal calculation, it is manifestly absurd to rely upon any such means as these to supply our annual demand. Our present condition may be in a great measure owing to a too great reliance upon these sources for the supply of our necessities.

Since, then, the means which we have adopted have manifestly failed, shall we despair? Can no other means be employed? Are there no encouragements left us, or have we sought for them in a wrong direction? Let us look again. We are men and Christians, does the gospel of Jesus Christ teach us nothing upon this subject? Let us then look upon our condition in the light which comes from the Holy Oracle, and see whether we can discover a more excellent way.

What then is the object which is set before us as disciples of Christ? Is it any thing less than to subdue the whole world to God? "Go ye into all the world and preach the gospel to every creature." Is there a creature of God on earth to whom we are not bound to send this salvation? But if we confine ourselves to our own country, what is the object set before us as Christian citizens of the United States? Is it simply to build for ourselves, in wealthy places, expensive houses of worship, and surround our services with the means of gratifying the senses, and then sit down and enjoy an intellectual effort, sanctified by a tincture of religion? Oh, no! Christ has set before the whole of us an infinitely higher object for which to live. It is to subdue this whole nation to himself. This is the work which he has set before his church, and before every part of it. We, as a part of his church, are bound to consecrate our whole energies to this work, and to leave no effort unexpended until it is done thoroughly. This is the duty of every portion of the Lord's host.

But is this a work to which we are competent? Can we with a united effort, suppose we were to put it forth to the full, convert a single soul? We all know that this is impossible. Are we capable of devising, by our own wisdom, the best means for effecting this work? Every Christian soul will instantly, and with emphasis, answer, No. Hath not God made foolish the wisdom of this world? God makes use of what the world calls folly to confound the wise. The work itself, and all the means for accomplishing it, belong to God. We must work upon his plan if we ever anticipate success. The more humbly we look to him for direction, eschewing our own wisdom and relying on his omniscience, the greater must be the certainty of our triumph.

Indeed, under any other conditions, we must be condemned to palpable and disgraceful failure.

Now, so far as this subject is concerned, there are two necessities which press with great severity upon us. In order to carry forward the work which the Master has set before us, we need in the first place a great number of ministers of Jesus Christ; and, in the second place, we need to increase to the utmost the efficiency of every minister; for the work is vast, and requires the best use of all the talent which the Master has called to the service. I ask my brethren to consider these two points separately. It seems to me that they have been unfortunately confounded in most of our discussions of this subject, and that hence has arisen great confusion in our counsels.

In the first place, then, we need a vastly greater number of ministers of the gospel.

But how, let me ask, are ministers of the gospel created such? I ask this question, not in the light of worldly wisdom, but as a disciple of Christ and a believer in the New Testament. Under the old dispensation, God did not leave the selection of those who waited upon the altar to man. "No man taketh this honor upon himself, but he that was called of God, as was Aaron." Under the new dispensation the same principle was adopted. God chooses to select his own agents for carrying on his work. Every Christian knows that there are peculiar moral and intellectual gifts which alone can qualify a man to be a successful minister of Christ. But can we bestow these gifts? Will human knowledge or human training confer them? Will Latin, or Greek, or mathematics create a love for souls, or touch the lips even of a pious man with that burning eloquence which rivets the attention, arouses the conscience, and carries the naked truth directly to the heart, mighty through God to cast down every strong hold, and bring the man to obedience to Christ? I need not suggest the answer to these questions; it is made already by every disciple of Christ.

But for this necessity a provision is made in the plan of man's salvation. As I have said before, we are assured that when our blessed Lord ascended on high, he received gifts for men, and that among these gifts were evangelists, pastors, and teachers. It is Jesus Christ who, by the effusion of his Spirit in special bestowment and measure, appoints those whom he calls to his service. He does the work which we can not do. From him these gifts are derived, and by him are they maintained in the churches.

But have we nothing to do in this matter? I answer, we have much to do. Our Lord himself has told us what it is. These gifts are bestowed in answer to prayer. The harvest is great, the laborers are few; *pray ye therefore* to the Lord of the harvest, that he will send forth laborers into his harvest. If, in earnest prayer, we look up to him for those gifts which he has received for us, he will assuredly bestow them abundantly. Such seems to me to be the plan of the Master for the supply of the ministry. Can we devise a better?

XXXVI.

THE GIFTS WHICH CHRIST, ON HIS ASCENSION, RECEIVED FOR HIS CHURCH.—THESE GIFTS BESTOWED IN ANSWER TO PRAYER.—WHAT IS EFFECTUAL PRAYER.

I CAN readily anticipate the objections that will be made to the doctrine of the last number. Some will say that it is all theoretical, and that we want something practical. Others will style it fanaticism, or mysticism, and accuse me of vague and dreamy prosing.

There are, however, others who will understand me, the men who believe that there is a Holy Ghost, who have felt his power, who know what is meant by the prayer of faith, and who receive with childlike simplicity whatever the Master has said. The eye of faith can discover things invisible to the wisdom of this world. In this, however, there is nothing extraordinary. Each party looks upon the subject from its own point of view, and these points of view are exceedingly dissimilar. Revelation has made known to us the reason of this divergence in the simple announcement, "The natural man receiveth not the things of the Spirit of God, for they are foolishness unto him, neither can he know them, because they are spiritually discerned; but he that is spiritual judgeth all things, yet he himself is judged (discerned, comprehended,) of no man."

Taking then the simple teaching of Christ and his apostles, we learn that Christ received at his ascension gifts for the ministry, which he is ready to bestow upon his body, the church, and that he will bestow them in answer to prayer to the Lord of the harvest. Such is the divine method for proclaiming through the world the message of salvation, and thus is the church to be furnished with a ministry.

Let us pause for a while and attempt to develop the idea.

It is said by the apostle Paul that the ascended Messiah received the gifts of evangelists, pastors, and teachers, for the *perfecting* of the saints, for the *work of the ministry*, for the edifying of the *body of Christ*. Now it is manifest that the work of the ministry is a universal work. It is to be carried on wherever there is a creature to whom the gospel can be preached. Wherever there is a sinner to be saved, there is a demand for the ministration of the Word. Again, these gifts were for the edification of the body of Christ. I ask, Were they for the edification of the whole, or of a part of this body? Would food be for the nourishment of the body which supported only a hand or foot, or the head or the heart? Instead of symmetrically nourishing the whole body, would such food create any thing but monstrosity? So when Christ received these gifts for his *body*, was it not for the whole body, to its remotest extremities, for every muscle and sinew, for every artery and nerve, so that the most insignificant portion of his body might receive, equally with all the rest, the benefit of his completed mediatorial work?

The application of this truth to our present purpose is self-evident. Did Christ receive the gifts of evangelists, pastors, and teachers only for great cities, for metropolitan temples, where the rich, and the mighty, and the learned most do congregate? Has he who is now seated on the mediatorial throne, forgotten the poor to whom, in the days of his humiliation, he preached the gospel, and with whom in his houseless wanderings he most associated? Is Jesus Christ the same yesterday, and to-day, and forever, or has he, once the friend of the friendless, now chosen new associates? No, brethren, the Messiah is not changed. He has as rich gifts in store for the hamlet in the wilderness, for the few disciples, the twos and threes who meet in his name unnoticed and unknown, in the log-cabin, the school-house, or the barn, as for those who sit before him under Gothic arches, and are lulled to moral forgetfulness by the music of Rossini or Beethoven.

Again, these gifts are bestowed upon the body of Christ in answer to prayer. "*Pray* ye the Lord of the harvest."

But what do we mean by prayer? Is it merely the form of words in which the heart has no share? Is it any thing else than the earnest outpouring of a deeply affected spirit? Do we ever pray in truth, unless the object for which we supplicate exerts an absolutely controlling power over every opposing desire? Suppose a man pray long and much, and even tearfully for holiness, while his love of holiness is not sufficient to control his avarice, or vindictiveness, or any other evil passion, can this be prayer in the sight of God? "If I regard iniquity in my heart, the Lord will not hear me." Suppose that some object, innocent in itself, has become an idol, and has assumed the chief place in our affections, and we pray for holiness, but can not give up our idol, though we know that idolatry and holiness are incompatible with each other, can our prayer be "offered up with much incense?" And thus, if we pray for any blessing, we must surrender every thing incompatible with it, and do every thing that the earnest desire for such a blessing would indicate. This is the only condition on which the answer to our prayers is promised. "If ye *abide in me* and *my words abide in you*, ye shall ask what ye will, and it shall be done unto you." And yet more, if we pray in the spirit, we shall not restrict the Most High in the manner of his answer, believing that he knows, far better than we, what will best gratify our holiest desires and glorify his own name.

Now let us apply these remarks, to which I am sure every Christian heart responds, to our present case. I suppose that we all believe that God has placed us here to subdue this country to himself, that this is our calling above and beyond all others, and that we must give account unto God for the manner in which we discharge this trust, and occupy the talent committed unto us. Suppose this to be, as it ought to be, the sentiment that controlled all the departments of practical life, and which more than any other occupied our most earnest thoughts. Were this the fact, could we live as we do? Could we enter with those who know not God upon the eager pursuit of wealth? Could we be found among the votaries of almost every form of sensual pleasure? Would not this controlling object modify and chasten every desire, and render the things which earthly men strive after distasteful to our souls? Would it not entirely reform the maxims which govern us in the expenditure of wealth? Could we vie with earthly men in luxurious display, while the progress of the gospel is everywhere impeded for want of the wealth which we squander in that frivolous extravagance which is leading men by multitudes to destruction? Can we pray that the kingdom of God may come, while we stand directly in the way of its progress? Can we supplicate for the increase of holiness on earth, while we love our idols better than holiness? Can we ask men to come out from the world, while we ourselves are immersed in worldliness? Can we invite men to deny themselves and take up the cross, while we live in luxury, and touch not the cross with one of our fingers?

Brethren, it is a more solemn thing to pray than we are commonly aware of. If we really pray for the extension of Christ's kingdom, we must live like men who make the extension of that kingdom the great business of our lives. This will require the sacrifice of many an idol. It will cost many a self-denial, and will expose us to many a scoff and reproach. But will not the object be worth the sacrifice? Is there not a crown of righteousness in reserve for those who fight this good fight? If the Saviour gave himself for every one of us, is it much for every one of us to give up himself to Christ? If we pray, Thy kingdom come, can we do less than live so that the kingdom of God may come?

Were this accomplished, were any denomination of Christians, nay, were a single church thus to arise from the dust and put on its beautiful garments, how vast would be its moral power. Every disciple would be a witness for Christ. The gifts whereby the body of Christ is perfected and the work of the ministry accomplished, would be poured out abundantly. Saints— now buried under houses, and lands, and stocks, and merchandise, and aspirations for political office, and leadership in fashion—would arise as if from the dead, and Christ would give them life. They would look back with shame at the hole of the pit from which they had been digged, and henceforth resolve to know nothing but Jesus Christ and him crucified. Among these, how many would be found endowed with gifts which neither they nor their brethren supposed them to possess. The talent unrolled from the napkin would shine with the splendor of burnished gold. Evangelists, pastors, and teachers, would spring up among our lawyers, physicians, merchants, manufacturers, and mechanics. Each church would number its chosen disciples, who, on the Sabbath, would be carrying the message of salvation to the perishing; while, on the other days of the week, they would exemplify to the world the life of him whose affections are set on things above, where Christ dwelleth. Were all our churches such churches as these, the world would know something of the moral power which belongs to the gospel of Jesus Christ. Were the churches of our denomination such as these, in a single generation this nation would be the people of the Most High. Holiness to the Lord would be written upon our legislative halls, our executive chambers, our courts of justice, our marts of trade, and our country would be the first on earth to welcome the coming of the Son of God.

I need hardly add that if we thus live, and thus pray for the bestowment of ministerial gifts, we shall thankfully receive them in any form in which they may be presented to us. Whether they come to us adorned with classical culture, or rich in the blessed gift of natural common sense ; whether in the young disciple, or in the mature Christian ; whether associated with secular avocations, or under circumstances which enable men to devote themselves wholly to the work of the Lord, we shall welcome them all with hearty good will as laborers in the vineyard of the Lord. We should not hedge about the vineyard, and admit no one to labor within it unless he entered by the narrow wicket-gate which we had set up. Much less should we, either directly or indirectly, create the impression that no man was competent to teach men the way of salvation, unless he had spent several of the best years of his life in the study of heathen poets imbued with the licentiousness which Paul depicts in his Epistle to the Romans. While, under these circumstances, we should put all due honor on every form of valuable human learning, and give to every minister all the human means in our power to make his profiting appear unto all, we should not dare to limit the Holy One of Israel, or place any culture which we could furnish in comparison for a moment with the gifts of the Spirit of God.

I ask my Christian brethren whether, in such a religious state of the churches as this, there would be any want of ministers ? Would not every church be able to furnish the public worship of God to all the moral waste which surrounded it ? Is not this the plan which the Saviour himself has marked out for us ? Are any of the means which we now employ likely to accomplish the object ? Is it probable that we can improve upon the plan of the Master, or can we expect His blessing in doing His work, unless we do it after the example which he has left us ?

XXXVII.

DUTY OF BAPTISTS IN NEW SETTLEMENTS WHERE THEIR NUMBER IS SMALL TO KNOW EACH OTHER, MEET TOGETHER FOR WORSHIP, ORGANIZE SABBATH-SCHOOLS, AND SEEK OUT FOR GIFTS FOR THE MINISTRY AMONG THEMSELVES.

In my last number I endeavored to present the mode for increasing the ministry which the Lord has appointed. I ask, Have I not presented it truly? Has not Christ assured us that he has received these gifts, and when they are needed, has he not directed us to pray for them? If this is his appointment, can our wants be supplied in any other way? Men may call this fanaticism and mysticism, but so they frequently call the doctrines of regeneration and the influences of the Holy Spirit. We know these, nevertheless, to be realities. Is not one part of Christ's teaching a reality as much as the other?

But it may be desirable for us to consider this subject more in detail, and show how these truths should guide us in particular instances.

I will commence with those cases in which a few Baptist families only are found in a village or settlement at the West, or in any part of our country. Instances of this kind are innumerable. There may be churches of other denominations in the vicinity, or the whole locality may be destitute of any public religious service. We ask, What is the duty of these few scattered Baptist professors of the name of Jesus?

In answering this question, I suppose it is hardly necessary to state, that neither time nor situation changes the relations which exist between the believer and his Saviour. The commands of Christ are as obligatory in the West as in the East, in the country as in the city, in the new territory as in the old settlement. His command to us all is to preach the gospel to every creature, to let our light shine before men, to hold forth the word of life, and to forsake not the assembling of ourselves together. The more dense the surrounding darkness, the brighter should our light shine. The greater the dearth of the word of life, the more imperative the obligation resting upon us to make known to men the message of salvation. We must do this individually, but in order to do it more effectually, we must do it together. We must worship God by entering into our closets; but in order to reap all the benefits which Christ has promised, the various twos and threes scattered abroad must meet together in his name, and he has assured us that there he is present in the midst of them.

1. In the first place, to such brethren, who, in the providence of God, are thus scattered abroad, I would say, inquire for and know each other. A little inquiry will generally suffice for this purpose. When every one knows his neighbor, where he comes from, and who are his connections, and what his occupation, the religious associations of each may, without difficulty, be discovered. When Mr. Thomas, who preceded Dr. Carey in India, had been for some time in Calcutta, inquiring in vain for a Christian brother, he inserted an advertisement in the newspaper, requesting that if there were such a one there, of any denomination, he would make himself known. We should have no such difficulty here in ascertaining the existence of our brethren.

It frequently happens that a missionary, in a day or two, will find out eight or ten Baptist professors in a settlement who had been before unknown as such to each other. But what can be done by a missionary stranger, may be done by any one who will take the trouble to do it. Let any brother, who may chance to read these lines, at once undertake this labor of love. Or, if no brother will undertake it, let some Phebe, who "has been a succorer of many," become a "servant of the church" in this important matter. This is the incipient step. Until this be done, nothing can be accomplished, and in a multitude of cases, it will reveal the important fact, that each brother and sister is surrounded by brethren and sisters, fellow-helpers in the Lord, of whose religious profession he had thus far been profoundly ignorant.

2. In the second place, I would most earnestly urge these brethren and sisters to establish a meeting for the worship of God. Begin on a week day evening. Meet and read the Scriptures, and unite with each other in prayer and conference. Call in your neighbors. Tell them of the love of Christ. Confess your fault in not having done your duty to each other before. Confess Christ before all men, and pray for the effusion of the Holy Spirit upon your neighbors, your friends, and your families. Do not ask, Where shall we meet ? Where is the Christian who would not willingly open his house for such a service ? The first meeting of Christians after the resurrection was in a private house ; and it is in private houses that many of our most flourishing churches have been planted. Make sacrifices to attend this meeting. Business may press, cares may multiply,

inconveniences may thicken; but if Jesus has promised to be there, should any worldly business keep you away from meeting him? This life consisteth not in the abundance of the things which we possess. Is any earthly possession to be compared with Christ in us the hope of glory?

Having done this, the next step will be easy. Collect the children around you into the Sabbath-school. There instruct them in the knowledge of God, and in reverence for his holy day. Bring them up in the nurture and admonition of the Lord. This will, by the blessing of God, shield them from innumerable temptations, and lead them to the Lamb of God. But this is not all. Can you feed the souls of others without yourselves being refreshed with the bread which came down from heaven? He that watereth shall be watered himself. Thus you will assuredly find it to be. The change within and around you will gladden your own hearts, and the Lord will give you souls for your hire.

3. Assume, in the third place, a spiritual care for each other. This is a duty devolving upon every disciple of Christ, wherever his lot may be cast. If you see a brother liable to err, caution him. If he has done wrong, set the wrong before him in the spirit of meekness, and it shall be an excellent oil which shall not break his head, and his prayer shall be for you in the day of your calamity. Brethren, if any of you do err from the truth, and one convert him, let him know that he which converteth a sinner from the error of his way, shall save a soul from death, and shall hide a multitude of sins. If a few brethren in an irreligious neighborhood were thus to bear testimony for Christ, how

blessed would be the light which they would diffuse around them! Impenitent men would confess the reality of religion, and acknowledge that God is with them of a truth.

4. But you need for your progress and establishment ministerial gifts. You need some one who shall, in a greater or less degree, take the oversight of you. Where shall you look for such gifts? I would say without reserve, look at home, instead of abroad. Who has received for you ministerial gifts? Who is more ready to bestow all that he possesses upon you, than Christ? He is not afar off. He is in the midst of you. Why then should you not go to him directly, and tell him your wants? You may, in the full assurance of faith, go and ask for all that you require. You are laboring, not for yourselves, but for him. You are doing his work, and not your own. He does not require you to go into this warfare at your own charges. You may confidently ask of him all that is requisite for the work which he has placed in your hands. And while you thus pray, look out among yourselves, and inquire if there be not some brother who indicates talent which may be employed in his cause. Encourage him, and pray specially for him, and you may thus find yourselves supplied in a manner which you had least expected.

Whenever it is in your power, send for the nearest ministering brother to come and spend a few days with you, and if possible, administer to you the ordinances of the gospel. Do not ask him to labor at his own charges. Frequently a brother who would willingly aid you, has not the means for making the journey. Let one of you go and fetch him, or pay the expenses of

ORGANIZING A CHURCH. 231

his traveling. Receive him with all kindness, and let him feel that he is with his brethren. His heart will move him to come again, and thus he will be a joyful co-worker with you in building up the kingdom of our common Master.

In the next place, as soon as possible organize a church. It is not necessary that a church be large in order to be efficient. The smallest church, relying upon God and doing his will, is mighty to the pulling down of strongholds. The largest church, relying upon human means, or going down to Egypt for help, is frequently only a stumbling-block in the way of the progress of piety. But before this, if you have not been able to organize worship on the Sabbath, attend statedly on the worship of any evangelical denomination. Let your sentiments, however, be fully known. Let it be understood that you are Baptists, and that, as soon as the providence of God shall open the way, you intend to be organized as a Baptist church. Do not, in the mean time, neglect the assembling of *yourselves* together. Meet for prayer and conference, as I have before advised. Do all in your own power, and your power will rapidly increase. Cease to coöperate with each other, and you will soon be powerless.

Nor, in all this, is there any thing bigoted or sectarian. You have your own belief, and you hold it to be important; why then should you not sustain it? You have principles; why should not your practice conform to them? You have a work to do, as well as Christians of other denominations; why should you not do it? And while doing it, cultivate in your hearts, and exemplify in your lives, an earnest and fervent love for all that love the Lord Jesus Christ. Aid your Christian brethren of other denominations by all the means in your power. Sorrow in their trials, and rejoice in their success. Coöperate with them in every good design, as far as you can do it without a sacrifice of principle. Far be it from us to diminish the influence, or curtail the usefulness of any disciple of Christ. We war not against them, but against the powers of darkness, against spiritual wickedness in high places. While we firmly adhere to what we believe to be the truth, we steadfastly allow to others the liberty which we claim for ourselves. Such has ever been the practice of Baptists, as it was, of old, the practice of Roger Williams.

XXXVIII.

DUTY OF FEEBLE CHURCHES TO RELY, UNDER GOD, ON THEMSELVES; TO CULTIVATE TALENT FOR THE MINISTRY AMONG THEIR OWN MEMBERS.—ALWAYS HOLD WORSHIP ON THE SABBATH.—PAY A MINISTERING BROTHER FOR HIS TIME AND EXPENSES; BE NOT ASHAMED OF HIM IF HE BE A LABORING MAN.

I COME now to consider another class of cases, in which, however, the same principles are involved, though their application is slightly different. Asking my readers to bear in mind what has been already suggested, I will proceed to make a few remarks on the duty of what are called small and feeble churches. I here allude to churches composed of from twenty to forty members. Some of these are situated in villages, others in rural districts, sparsely settled, the members living at considerable distances from each other. They are generally composed of men in moderate circumstances, with here and there one, or perhaps two individuals of wealth among them. They have not the ability to support a minister who shall spend his whole time in laboring for them, nor even, if they should support him, would there be sufficient ministerial work to employ him in their service. Hence they are frequently destitute of a pastor, or else three or four such churches unite and employ a pastor between them. On the Sabbaths in which the pastor is absent, worship is not maintained. The young members of the congregation are growing up thoughtless and indifferent to the subject of religion, now and then a member is added, and thus the existence of the church is protracted, but it makes no progress, and is probably, at the present day, very nearly where it was some ten or twenty years since.

Now this is manifestly an unnatural condition for a church of Christ. The kingdom of the Messiah is always represented as *going forth* "conquering and to conquer." A church in such a state *goes not forth*, and it achieves no victories. It remains year after year in the same position, merely existing, a branch that bears few leaves, and no fruit. Are there not many such churches among us?

To such churches permit me to offer a few words of advice. In the first place, brethren, let me urge you to rely upon yourselves, under God, and cease to look abroad for help. It is this looking abroad for what you probably have at home that has been a fatal stumbling-block in the way of your progress. There are gifts for edification among you, if you will only look after them and employ them. Christ does not plant barren vines in his vineyard. When you were constituted a church, he meant that you should increase, having seed within yourselves. Or, if you have neglected to cultivate the gifts which he bestowed, until they have been lost, he has still gifts in abundance in reserve. Pray ye the Lord of the harvest, and he will send forth laborers into his harvest. Instead of imploring the aid of missionary societies and conventions, and sending an annual letter to the Association complaining of your weakness, go directly to the Master and ask him for all that you need. The cause is his. He came from heaven to earth to establish it, and now reigns supreme, having all power in heaven and earth to carry it forward. If you really want a minister, he will provide one for you, and more likely from among yourselves than from anywhere else. If you really desire to advance his cause, you have only to ask him, and he will bestow upon you all that you need. But you must ask in faith, and your actions must correspond with your prayers. You must show by your conduct that the cause of Christ is nearer to your hearts than any thing else, and that you are determined to know nothing among men in comparison with Jesus Christ and him crucified.

Let me entreat you, then, to meet weekly for prayer and conference. Among many of you this duty has probably been neglected for several years. Hence you hardly know each other as Christian brethren. Your Christian affections have grown cold. If you have a covenant meeting once a month, but few attend it, and you are almost strangers to each other. Meet together, then, more frequently, and let your hearts flow together oftener in prayer to God. Encourage every brother to speak for the Saviour, and to call upon sinners to repent and believe. You will soon find that, by exercise, your gifts for public address will improve, and others as well as yourselves will take a deeper interest in attending your meetings. Soon, it may be, you will find not one but several brethren who may become useful as licentiates or pastors.

When you see any talent which promises to be useful, encourage it. Assist your brethren who may give any indications of power in public address, by your prayers and counsel. Strive to build them up for Christ. Aid them in procuring books, and enable them to give themselves more and more to the work. At the very time when you are inquiring whether God has not called a brother to labor in public in his cause, probably the same inquiry is pressing upon his mind also, and he is looking forward in deep depression at the possible obligation that may be laid upon him. He needs your sympathy, and counsel, and encouragement. Let him see and feel that he has them. This trembling and self-diffident brother may be a chosen vessel whom the Master has appointed to some important service in his church.

I know very well that in sparsely settled neighborhoods, where roads are bad, and traveling inconvenient, it is difficult, and in fact almost impossible, for brethren to meet all in one place as often as might be desirable. In such cases, it may be better to have frequent neighborhood meetings, in the various districts occupied by the members of the church. A school-house or a room in a private house will furnish all the accommodation desired, and then women and children may be able to attend, who otherwise would have little opportunity of enjoying this means of spiritual edification.

I have thus far referred to meetings for spiritual improvement on week days. I now turn to the Sabbath. Suffer me to urge you never to omit meeting for worship on God's holy day. Do not be satisfied with merely meeting for worship when you have a minister present. This is idolizing the ministry, not honoring it. You gather together, not to meet the minister, but the Saviour. He has not said, When you come with a minister I am with you, but, Wherever two or three are met in my name, there am I in the midst of you. You can be profited as truly, if Christ be there, without a minister as with one. It is very desirable to have an under-shepherd, but if God has not gratified you in this respect, he may answer your prayers by being in a special manner present with you himself. Meet then with your families, whether you have a minister with you or not. Let some brother who, in your more private meetings has shown an adaptedness for this service, take the lead of the meeting. You can spend the time profitably in prayer, singing, reading the Scriptures, and exhortation. If every brother would, before the meeting, direct his attention prayerfully to some passage of Scripture, and when you come together would give his brethren the result of his reflections, the service would not lack interest. If you prefer a sermon, any brother may be called upon to read one. President Davies' are the best that I remember for this purpose. Plain, earnest, pungent, practical sermons are the best for such occasions, as they, in fact, are for any other. In this manner,

DEVELOPING SPIRITUAL GIFTS. 237

meeting statedly, and having a little concert with each other beforehand, you may readily conduct a service to mutual edification, and greatly to the advancement of the interests of godliness in your neighborhood.

I have said that your private meetings present an opportunity for observing the gifts of the several members of the church. The meeting on the Sabbath, when no minister is with you, is still better adapted to this purpose. Talent, of any kind, always shows itself when there is a demand for it. Give men an opportunity to speak for God, let occasions arise in which men feel that they are called upon to bear witness for him, and lips will be opened which have long been sealed in silence. You may thus find that what you have been asking for from man, in vain, God has sent you from among your own brethren. Some brother whom you have wholly overlooked, may be the very man whom God has chosen to minister to you in spiritual things.

But you are not able to employ all the time of a brother, if you desire him to serve you in the ministry. You are, however, able to pay him for all the time which he devotes to your service. Pay him, then, honestly, for this portion of his time. You have no right to ask that he should impoverish himself to serve you for nothing. If his labors are blessed, you will soon require more of his time, and you should pay him for all you require. When Dr. Baldwin first commenced his ministry, he was employed in carrying on a saw-mill. He was also pastor of the church to which he belonged. He was frequently called from home to perform ministerial service in different parts of the town and vicinity, and his business suffered. All he asked of his brethren was, that they would pay the wages of the workman whom he was obliged to employ in his absence. This they often promised, but never performed. When he had left his family in straitened circumstances, and could with difficulty meet his traveling expenses in aiding some destitute church, a wealthy brother would sometimes most affectionately squeeze his hand, and say, with great cordiality, "Thank you, thank you, Elder Baldwin, such men as you will never want," and having said this, turn away, leaving him to find a resting place where he could. Dr. Baldwin was tenderly attached to his people, and to the region where he ministered. A family was growing up around him, and the pressure grew year by year more severe. He was called to the situation in Boston, which he filled with such admirable success, and removed to that city. It is no disparagement to the Baptist ministers of New Hampshire to say, that thus far, Thomas Baldwin has there had no successor. A little more thoughtfulness might probably have retained him there. What changes would our churches in that State have seen, had Dr. Baldwin spent the last twenty-five years of his life among them!

Remember both of these things. What your minister does for you deserves remuneration, and he should receive it. It must be paid for by some one; must he pay for it, or will you do it? And thus, if you invite a minister from abroad, you will, of course, treat him kindly and hospitably, but this is not all. His time is his money; it is spent for you, and traveling is expensive. See that in neither of these respects he is a sufferer in consequence of doing you good.

Do not be ashamed of having a minister who is employed a part of his time on his farm, or in his workshop. The Master was the son of a carpenter, and it is reasonable to suppose that he worked at his father's occupation. The apostles were many of them fishermen. Paul wrought at tent-making in the shop of Aquila. Honest labor is everywhere honorable, and that it is honorable to combine it with the ministry, these instances abundantly prove. In later days, Bunyan was a tinker, and Carey a shoemaker, and both worked at their trades until the duties of the ministry absorbed all their energies. At this many will smile. When Carey was going out to India, Sidney Smith held him up to scorn and ridicule, because a cobbler was leaving England to convert the Hindoos. Yet, which is now and ever will be the object of universal admiration, the reverend jester, or the cobbler missionary? Yet, let me not be misunderstood. A man is no better fitted for the ministry because he labors with his hands. The work is open to all, and every variety of occupation may be called to engage in it. I only say that it is as truly open to men of one avocation, as another. The Lord requires every variety of talent and culture in his vineyard, and some of his choicest gifts to his church have been bestowed upon men whom the world would have rejected with contempt.

Once more I would say, while you are destitute of a pastor, take every means in your power to secure the assistance of ministering brethren in your vicinity. Have the ordinances of the gospel statedly observed, and never, if possible, omit them. This will be frequently more easily accomplished than is supposed. Use a minister kindly. Make your place a Christian home. Neglect not his comfort, but do not act as if he came merely to eat and drink. Treat him as a brother beloved, and show that you are earnestly engaged with him in building up the kingdom of the Redeemer. Make your church an attractive place for the best and holiest men, and the best and holiest men will love to visit you, and by every means in their power to build up the cause of Christ among you. Do thus, and the small nation will soon become a strong people.

XXXIX.

OBJECTION, WE ARE FEW AND WEAK, ETC.—WOULD THIS JUSTIFY YOUR COURSE IN CONVERTS FROM HEATHENISM, OR IN THE TIMES OF THE APOSTLES?—THIS EXCUSE SAVORS OF PRIDE, NOT HUMILITY.—EXAMPLE OF THE CHURCH IN HAMBURG.

IN my last paper I endeavored to set forth what seemed to me the duty of Baptist disciples of Christ, when they were few in number, in villages or small settlements throughout our country. To the views which I have presented, I know that many objections may be urged, but they may all be summed up in one. We are few and weak, and nothing can be done by a little handful, in the midst of a multitude who profess no religion at all, or if they profess any, it is in many respects at variance with our belief.

To this I reply, in the first place, suppose that as many persons as you now number had been converted from heathenism and were living in Rangoon, Bassein, or Toungoo, and that they adopted your principles.

They would say, There are but few of us among hundreds of thousands of idolaters. What can we do to reform a nation? We will therefore never meet to worship God; we will not care to have it known that we are the disciples of Christ. What should we think of such converts? What would they be worth to the cause of Christ? Their light, hidden under a bushel, would soon expire. Yielding no seed, they would soon perish, and the heathen world would be none the better for their existence. Now, I ask, in what respect do the disciples of Christ on one side of the globe differ from those on the other? What would be treachery to the cause of Christ in Burmah, is treachery in the United States. We can not answer it to the Master if we hide our light under a bushel. We can not answer it to the souls of our perishing fellow-men, if we do not, by our precept and practice, hold forth to them the word of life, and point them to the Lamb of God who taketh away the sins of the world.

Again, how was it in the times of the apostles? When the ministers of Christ went at first among the heathen, had they hearkened to such objections as yours, where would now have been the church of Christ? Had the one hundred and twenty in the upper chamber looked abroad upon the world, and considered the power, and wealth, and learning, and prejudice, and avarice, and vice which were arrayed against them, much more reasonably than any of us, they might have concluded that any attempt to convert the world was useless. They might have resolved to enjoy their religion by themselves, not meeting together nor exposing themselves to remark for the singularity of their behavior. But did they do this? No, they held to the prayer and conference-meeting. "They continued with one accord in prayer and supplication." And when the day of Pentecost was fully come, instead of scattering abroad and going up with the multitude to the temple to unite in the Jewish festival, they were found *all, with one accord, in one place.* It was then that the Holy Ghost descended, and before the sun of that day had set, " there were added unto them about three thousand souls." This was worth coming together for. And were there more such gatherings, there would be more similar outpourings of the Holy Spirit.

And when those who were scattered abroad went everywhere preaching the Word, into whatsoever city or town they entered, they were at first the only disciples of Christ within it. They, however, at once proclaimed their message. God gave it success. A few were converted. No sooner were men converted than the wrath of Jew and Gentile was aroused, and the ministers were obliged to flee for their lives to another city. They left, in every place where they ministered, a little band of disciples, perhaps eight or ten in number, as sheep among wolves. But what course was pursued by these few converts among hundreds of thousands of idolaters? They held forth the word of life. Amid persecution even unto death, they proclaimed Christ and the resurrection, and the Lord added to them daily of such as should be saved.

From these small beginnings arose the churches by whom the gospel was carried to every part of the then known world. In the great marts of trade, the centers of influence, on the shores of the Mediterranean, the apostle Paul continued longer. He abode for a year and a half at Corinth, and two years at Ephesus, because from these great cities the word of God could be carried to every town in the interior. So far, however, was this from his usual custom, that a vision from the Lord was necessary to induce him to tarry at Corinth. Such was the manner in which the gospel gained its wonderful triumphs at first. It was by the labors, and preaching, and example of little bands of two or three, or ten or twelve, planted in the midst of the heathen, from whom the word of God sounded out into all the surrounding country. How could it be otherwise? This was the way which Christ has chosen, and it was, as it ever must be, mighty.

But it is still said, What can we, a poor feeble band, do amid the multitude who fear not God? This question seems to savor of humility, but it is, in fact, the offspring of most unchristian pride. He who makes it must suppose that the work is his own, that man can accomplish it, and therefore the greater the number of men engaged, the more easily will the work be effected. Were this true, there would be force in the objection. I ask, then, How many men does it take to convert a single soul? If ten can not do it, can twenty, or a hundred, or a hundred thousand? You reply, No; it is the work of the Spirit of God exclusively. Christ alone by his Spirit can convert, renew, and sanctify the soul, and make it meet to be an inheritor with the saints in light. The work of converting souls, and of casting down the strongholds, does not therefore depend on the number of disciples meeting together, but upon the presence of Christ. And how many must meet together in order to expect the presence of Christ? He himself has specified the precise number. Wherever *two* or *three* are gathered together in my name, there am I in the midst of them. Two believers, then, met in the name of Christ, may plead the promise as effectually as two thousand. If only two meet together and Christ is there, all power in heaven and on earth is present, and in such a company where is there place for unbelief, despondency, or despair?

All this has been practically exemplified in every age of the history of the church. One of the latest, as well as one of the most remarkable, is the case of our brethren in Germany. They numbered at first precisely seven souls. They were in a great city given over to the love of wealth, as most great cities are, and in a nation of formalists sternly opposed to evangelical religion, especially that form of evangelical religion which we profess. They, nevertheless, were constituted into a church, and as true disciples, undertook the work of converting Germany to vital and spiritual religion. They gave themselves to the work. They met together for prayer on week days, and for the worship of God on the Sabbath. They called in their neighbors and friends to hear the word of God. The Lord began to add to their number. When men were converted, for fear of the authorities they were obliged to perform the ordinance of baptism in retired places, in the darkness of the night. The work needed more laborers; they prayed to the Lord of the harvest, and ministerial gifts were poured out upon them. The church at Hamburg was soon able to send laborers into the neighboring towns. In these, also, churches were established, partaking in rich measure of the spirit of the church from which they sprang. No sooner was a little band of believers gathered together, than they, at once, commenced the work of evangelizing not only their own town, but the towns in their vicinity. Gathering strength in their progress, they have already advanced to the borders of Russia; and it may be almost said that they are filling Germany with their doctrine.

But, in the mean time, the enemy was not idle. Persecution at an early date arose in Hamburg. The pastor was thrown into prison, their place of worship was closed, and their enemies believed that thus the movement was permanently quashed. But it was not so; for God was in the midst of it. The pastor preached from the grated windows of the prison, and the brethren, driven from their sanctuary, met in private houses, so that instead of one, sixteen places of worship were established. The pastor was at length released. Soon after occurred the great fire at Hamburg, and then the self-denying charity of these poor disciples so completely disarmed their oppressors, that persecution died of very shame, and they have not since been molested.

Not so, however, in other places. Wherever these brethren went preaching the Word, they were met by the envenomed opposition of the priesthood, and, I regret to say, of a Protestant priesthood. They were imprisoned, fined, maltreated, and driven from place to place, but they went everywhere preaching the Word. Every church, in addition to its pastor, had its little band of licentiates, whom it sent out, Sabbath after Sabbath, to carry the Word to neighboring towns. The little one has become a thousand. From these seven disciples in Hamburg, there have sprung up a multitude of churches, and thousands of disciples of Jesus. Thousands have emigrated to this country, and have established flourishing churches in the West. And, in all this work, the church has always supplied its own wants. The gifts which were needed were found to exist in the midst of her, and these gifts were, for the most part, bestowed upon men in common life, mechanics, journeymen, brethren whose power consisted in the spirit that resided in them, and not in any culture which could be bestowed by the schools.

Nor is this all. The question that was continually presented in these cases of persecution, was this : What are the inalienable rights of conscience, and what right has civil government to interfere with religious belief? This question has been pressed upon the attention of thoughtful men in every part of Germany. The personal views of the King of Prussia are understood to have become favorable to freedom. At length the Chevalier **Bunsen**, one of the ablest and most enlightened statesmen in Europe, has pleaded with irresistible power the cause of religious liberty, and has spread before the world the injustice suffered by our defenseless brethren. Behold, how great a matter a little fire kindleth! But it must be fire from the altar, fanned by the breath of the Spirit. The seed planted by the Master can never die.

Here, then, is the result of the Christian labors of seven poor disciples of Jesus—the result only up to the present time. To what it will spread in the future, God only knows. Had they lived as hundreds of sevens of our brethren are living; where had been the evangelical churches and the religious liberty of Germany? The same men, acting on the same principles, settled in any city of the West, would have made every village beyond the mountains vocal with the name of the Redeemer. Brethren, who of us will follow their example?

We can do what others are doing. The Methodist class-meeting is an institution specially designed to gather together the scattered members of that communion into an organization that shall be the nucleus of a church. It is an admirable system, and has been of infinite service in developing ministerial talent, and in extending the cause of Methodism in our country. It has done much more than this. In ten thousand instances it has kept alive the flame of piety, where it would otherwise have been extinguished, and trained up thousands and tens of thousands for the heavenly Jerusalem. We do not need the name, or the form, but may we not have the essential thing with all its attendant benefits?

XL.

CHURCHES IN CITIES.—THEIR SPECIAL NEED OF OPPORTUNITY TO LABOR FOR CHRIST.—ITS EFFECT UPON INDIVIDUAL PIETY.

I COME now to the case of churches in cities, and would respectfully present the application of the law of Christ to them. They are, in comparison with the churches in the country, few in number, and they contain but a small portion of our entire membership.

They are, however, of an importance which is but imperfectly indicated by their number of communicants. They are composed, in a considerable degree, of the wealthy and the more highly educated. They have in their power vast means of doing good, means which, if improperly used, must work extensive evil. The manners, the maxims, the opinions, the practice of cities, are always rapidly carried into the surrounding country. They are the centers of influence, by which the character of the circumference is determined.

The condition of such churches is peculiar, and worthy of special consideration. Wealth is accumulated in cities with great rapidity. Temptation here assumes every variety of form, and clothes itself in its most alluring dress. Secresy in wrong-doing may be secured much more successfully than in the country. Where human beings are collected in so large masses, the power of public opinion becomes vastly more intense and omnipresent. The fact that other men do so, becomes a justification for almost any moral obliquity. The natural love of wealth is inflamed by emulation, and the apparent necessity of following the example of others. Expensive habits can be indulged only by excessive gains, and when large gains are indispensable, the means by which they must be secured are not apt to be scrutinized, if they can only find shelter under the customs of the trade. The lust for political power is here most rampant, as here there are dispensed its most coveted prizes. In every department of life, in every grade of society, the whisper of the Arch Tempter is unceasingly heard, "All these things will I give thee, if thou wilt fall down and worship me."

In such a moral condition as this, the most active antagonistic moral and religious forces are absolutely necessary, in order to guard the soul from that sensuality and worldliness which tends directly to final apostacy. The most direct and pungent appeals to the conscience, the clearest scriptural exhibition of the evidences of piety, the most discriminating delineations of unconscious hypocrisy, the plainest setting forth of easy besetting sins, the most fearless exposure of the various forms of prevailing vice, the loftiest views of Christian attainment, the glorious hopes which animate the pure in heart, the crown of righteousness which the Lord, the righteous judge, shall give to all who love his appearing—these truths, and truths like them, need to be held up before the eye of the believer, if we would guard him from the moral perils by which he is here environed. That the circumstances which surround a city pulpit are peculiarly favorable for the earnest exhibition of these momentous realities, I will neither affirm nor deny.

But, in order to insure our spiritual progress, it is necessary not only that these truths be believed, but that they be acted upon; and that, in fact, they form the basis of our practical, every-day character. It is not enough that we believe that there is a world of ineffable glory, to be secured only by strenuous moral effort—we must, individually, make that effort. It is not enough to believe that we must take up the cross and follow Christ—we must feel the pressure of that cross upon our own shoulders, and plant our own feet in the footprints made by the Son of God. If we act not thus, our belief is liable to work our undoing. Nothing conduces more to insensibility of conscience, than the distinct knowledge of duty, while we neglect to perform it. Hence, evidently, a Christian in a city requires, above all men, the means of carrying out to their practical results the truths which he believes. Without this his principles will become absolutely inoperative, and believing all the solemn revelations of the New Testament, he will be living without God in the world, and worse than all, he will become contented to live thus. He needs to retire to his closet for prayer; but he needs also to meet his brethren for prayer; he needs the opportunity in public to avow himself a follower of Christ, and to call on other men to follow his example. It is absolutely necessary to his growth in grace, nay, to the preservation of his piety, that he be seen, on all possible occasions, testifying for Christ, and doing those very things, despised and scorned though they be, which Christ has made the duty of all his disciples. His character must be formed, and his life must be governed by the principle of direct, positive, and unyielding antagonism to a world which lieth in wickedness. The ice must be broken, the barrier must be passed. He must be crucified to the world, and the world unto him. The line of separation between the man that feareth God and the man that feareth him not must be broad and visible, or the disciple of Christ, borne down by the incessant pressure of worldliness, will be swept away by the current, and find himself, in fact, in the company of those who deny his Master, and it is well if he be not in sympathy with them also.

All this every one sees. But as our churches are now constituted, what opportunities are presented for this practical manifestation of Christianity? Every religious service is devolved upon the minister, and he is hourly sinking under it. The merchant rises early on Monday morning, and hurries to his counting-room, the mechanic to his place of business, the lawyer to his office. He hears through the day not a word on any subject except gain and politics. He returns home in the evening wearied and harassed, but must participate in the round of amusement which the customs of society impose upon his family. He arises in the morning from unquiet sleep, to spend another day in the same manner. On Sunday he attends the worship of the sanctuary, his mind recovers a little from the intense pressure of worldliness, and it may be that in the evening a beam of light breaks through the cloud, and discovers to him for a moment the nature of the life that he is leading. On Monday morning the impression is, however, to a considerable degree, obliterated, and he plunges headlong into the current of trade, with the same heedlessness as before. The arrangements of the household hardly allow of family devotion. The demands of business sadly interfere with private prayer. The disciple of Christ gives occasionally a little money to the cause of religion, regretting that the expensiveness of his family renders it impossible for him to do more. Such is his life from year to year, unless sickness or other calamity arouses him from this stupor. He awakes, calls upon God, disentangles himself for awhile from the world, but soon again he yields to the pressure, and things go on as they were wont. I ask, Does piety such as this possess the vitality necessary to resist the moral contagion of a great city?

What, then, is the remedy? Is it not evident that it must be found in furnishing, for private members, the opportunity for laboring more actively for God, and in rendering our churches earnest and zealous associations for the promotion of Christianity? Our meetings for prayer must be multiplied, and these should be conducted mainly by private members of the church. Our dwellings should be frequently opened for such meetings, rather than for routs and fashionable entertainments. Every brother should be encouraged to speak at such meetings in exhortation, in encouragement, in warning, or in exposition and application of the word of God. The church itself should earnestly inquire for places in the city where the destitution is the sorest, and where those are to be found in the greatest numbers, who, in their homely garb, would be ashamed to appear in the temples commonly erected for the worship of Jesus of Nazareth. These places the church should supply with Sabbath-schools and religious services, not by employing here and there a city missionary, but from its own members. It should be the primary object of every church to cultivate all the talent for this service which it possesses, and employ it systematically in the work of evangelization. There is scarcely a city church among us, which could not furnish a large number of intelligent Christian men, abundantly competent to this work. Many of them would labor without a license. Others should receive a license, and they might, with great profit both to themselves and others, frequently occupy any of our pulpits on the Sabbath, while, on the other days of the week, they devoted themselves to secular avocations. From these would arise a large body of efficient pastors, men whose talents were manifestly designed for extensive usefulness, and to whom the ministry became so attractive as to disengage them from every other pursuit. Such a man was the late Dr. Sharp, whose praise is in all the churches. While engaged in mercantile business, he believed that he might be useful in preaching Christ, without charge, to the destitute in the suburbs of New York. He was licensed by the church to which he belonged, and for some time labored successfully in this manner. It soon became evident that the pulpit, and not the counting-room, was the place in which he could most effectually serve the Master, and after spending some time under the instruction of the late Dr. Staughton, he commenced that career of usefulness which has endeared his name to the whole church of God.

The effect of such a course upon the religious character of individual members, need not be here spoken of. The man who had spent his Sabbaths in calling men to repentance, could hardly fail to testify for Christ on the other days of the week. By a large and more thoughtful reading of the Scriptures, his mind would be more deeply imbued with divine truth. Communion with God would render the pursuits of worldly men distasteful. He would walk through the midst of temptation unharmed, protected by an invisible arm, for he that dwelleth in the secret place of the Most High shall abide under the shadow of the Almighty.

Could these ideas prevail, it is manifest that a new era would open upon our churches. Every church would become a living fountain, diffusing on every side the waters of salvation. Instead of looking to organizations polluted by political ambition—instead of relying on policemen and material force, the disciples of Christ, trusting to his aid, would go forth to regenerate the world around them. And they would do it. The wilderness and the solitary place would be glad for them, and the desert would rejoice and blossom like the rose.

But it will be said that there is and must be a division of labor in this work; some must accumulate wealth to support those who give up themselves to the ministration of the gospel. I ask, Is this so? Is one man to give up *himself*, and another his *wealth*, and another his love of *pleasure* to Christ, while each withholds the remainder? Is this the piety of the gospel? Christ gave himself *wholly* for us, and should not we give up our *whole selves* to him? So Saul was very jealous for the Lord of Hosts, but the bleating of the sheep and oxen revealed his hypocrisy. We may be sure that the man who gives up but a part to Christ, always reserves for himself all that he loves best, and yields to the Saviour only the remainder. But you say, We are acquiring property for Christ. Can you, my brother, say that to him? Does he not know better? If you are accumulating for him, you are spending for yourselves, and leave him only the fragments. My dear brother, the word of God is quick and powerful, a discerner of the thoughts and intents of the heart.

But it may be said, men will not do as you recommend. It may be so, but what then? What becomes of the cause of Christ? Who is prepared to suffer the punishments of disobedience? Indications are not few, that judgments for our sins are rapidly approaching. Who of us shall stand when God riseth up, and who shall answer when he appeareth? If this is the way to obey Christ, the only way in which Christianity can exert its legitimate effect on the minds of men, and we say we can not and will not pursue it, we surrender Christ to his enemies, we give up the contest, and yield the victory to the powers of darkness. Sinner, redeemed by the blood of Christ, are you prepared to do this?

XLI.

MEANS TO BE USED TO IMPROVE THE WHOLE MINISTRY.—THEOLOGICAL SEMINARIES.—COLLEGES.—ACADEMIES.

In my preceding papers I have endeavored to show the manner in which the ministry may be increased in number. It seems to me to have been the way devised by the Master. It has always proved eminently successful. The evil which we complain of is universal. It must arise from some universal error, either in our theory or practice, or both. It can not be removed but by a change in that theory or practice. I have endeavored to point out the change which seems to be required. We must return to the theory and practice which prevailed when we had more ministers than churches. In no other manner can we hope to make progress, or to perform that part in the conversion of the world which the Master has assigned to us.

I hope it will be admitted, that by the use of the means which I have suggested, the number of ministers would be greatly increased, may I not say, so much increased as to be adequate to the supply of our wants. It will be a ministry composed of men of different ages, coming from various occupations in life, and of great diversity of intellectual culture. They will all agree, however, in many particulars. They will have entered the ministry because they believe that the Holy Spirit has called them to this office, and their brethren will have come to the same conclusion respecting them. Most of them will have given themselves to the work at the cost of personal sacrifice, and a large portion of them will, by early labor, have attained to vigor of constitution, firmness of nerve, and a power of overcoming difficulties, which hot-house cultivation never confers. I ask, What better material for a ministry could be found than a body of just such men?

I come now to the second part of my work. I proposed to show, first, how the number of our ministers could be increased; and secondly, how their efficiency could be promoted. I proceed to the second consideration. Suppose that annually six or eight hundred of such ministers are given to us; how shall we, so far as we can, make them able ministers of the New Testament?

Before answering this question, let us determine what is the object to be aimed at. Let us look at this question calmly, as reasonable men, capable of forming an opinion for ourselves, and without turning to the precedents set before us by other denominations. Is it our object merely to carry to a higher point of education, one in twenty of these brethren, leaving all the remainder without sympathy or aid? Shall we say to brethren who pant for knowledge, but who are unable to devote more than one, two, or three years to preparation, " Go and study for five or six years, and then we will aid you;" and by this decision shut them out from all aid whatsoever? Or shall we say to brethren whose time is thus limited by the providence of God, " If you will promise to go to an academy, and study two years with boys, and then go through college, and add to this a three years' course at a seminary, we will assist you; but if you will not or can not do this, we have nothing to say to you?" Is this right, is it wise, is it kind, can it be acceptable to the Master? Is this really zeal for educating the Baptist ministry?

We take a different view of this subject. We urge the necessity of giving to *every* brother whom God has called to the ministry, as large an amount of culture as the circumstances in which he is placed render expedient or practicable. We should look upon the farmer or mechanic, who gives evidence that he has been called of God to the ministry, with just the same respect, and extend to him the hand of fellowship as cordially as if he had spent his whole life in study, and bore in his hand a dozen diplomas. We should *more* cheerfully aid him than the other, for the simple reason that his need is more pressing. I will not, however, pursue this question any further. I do not conceive that there can exist, among brethren at large, more than one opinion concerning it.

The question before us, then, is, In what manner shall we proceed, so as best to increase the usefulness of the whole mass of ministerial talent?

I need say but little of Theological Seminaries. They have their utility; but they educate so few that they can affect, but in a small degree, the multitude whom we wish to benefit. Besides, they are under the special guardianship of learned and able brethren, who are thoroughly acquainted with the subject of education—who have made theological education their peculiar study, and have arranged their courses of instruction with special reference to their view of the wants of our own denomination. Of such institutions, so conducted, it becomes us to speak with becoming reverence. If, however, a suggestion in respect to them might be made without presumption, I would ask, Could they not be rendered more efficient? By the tables already referred to, they graduate annually about one student and a half to each officer of instruction. Could not this proportion be somewhat exceeded? The labor of teaching such classes can not be oppressive; might not other courses, adapted to other classes of students, be introduced? So long as our seminaries admit none but those who have pursued a collegiate course, or its equivalent, their number of students must be small, and the labor of instructors not burdensome. Might they not add something to their courses of instruction?

If it might be done without offense, I would ask, Might not more direct effort be exerted to make *preachers*—I say preachers, in distinction from philologists, translators, professors, teachers, and writers on theology? Other professional schools aim to render men able in the *practice* of their several professions. The law school is satisfied if it makes good lawyers. The medical school is satisfied if it makes good physicians. Why should not the theological school aim more simply at making good and effective preachers? Men need instruction and practice in the everyday duties of the ministry. They should acquire the power—and it is a great power—of unwritten, earnest, effective speech.

I rejoice to perceive that all the changes in our seminaries are in the right direction. In the catalogue of Newton Seminary it is said that the course is designed for those who have passed through a collegiate course, or what is equivalent to it; they nevertheless add that other students are welcomed to their instructions, and arrangements are made for their especial improvement. I have not the catalogue at hand, but this is, I think, the substance of the announcement. In the Institution at Fairmount, Cincinnati, as it has been stated in the public papers, the course of instruction, in the main, coincides with the suggestions which I have offered. Students are made to acquire practice in preaching, and candidates of a much greater diversity of acquisition than usual, are admitted to the Institution. All these are hopeful indications. Let the principles on which these changes proceed be carried out to their results, and the usefulness of these institutions will be indefinitely increased.

But besides theological schools, we have a large number of colleges and academies endowed by our brethren, which ought to render efficient aid in the improvement of the ministry. By following the example of others in founding schools of learning, while our intention has been to benefit the ministry, we have contrived to render them, in the least possible degree, capable of accomplishing our object. We have, with one exception, adopted in all its strictness, the old academic course, which prescribes a fixed succession of certain studies for four years, and unless a man pursues the preparatory routine, and enters for the whole course, he can derive from them but little advantage. Thus, a person who wishes to study such branches as would be of service to him in preaching, and has neither time nor means for doing more, is effectually excluded from their benefits. Now it is manifest that a college intended to benefit the ministry, should conform its arrangements to the actual condition of the ministry. Our colleges should be so constituted that licentiates, to say nothing of any others, should be enabled to pursue such studies as they need, and under the same advantages as any other students. To many who are unable to pursue the languages and mathematics, a course embracing physical science, rhetoric, history, intellectual and moral philosophy, would be invaluable; or, if the student could not pursue all these courses, he might take only such of them as he most needed. The same remark applies, in substance, to our high schools. Arrangements in these seminaries should be made, which shall facilitate the education of young men somewhat advanced in life. It is not necessary that such men be obliged to sit in the school-room and recite with boys and children. A young man, who, in obedience to the call of God, leaves his occupation for the ministry, has trials enough to meet, without being called on to bear any that are superfluous.

But we might, with great reason, go further than this. It would be very desirable even to have a course of instruction for licentiates especially. Many of our institutions have courses arranged especially for teachers; and lectures are delivered for their exclusive benefit. Why should not the same plan be adopted in behalf of licentiates? Why should not courses of lectures be delivered in our colleges on the evidences of religion, on the principles of interpretation common to all languages, on the essential doctrines of revelation, on the rhetoric of the pulpit, and on pastoral duty? I rejoice to see that at Waterville College, arrangements are in progress for accomplishing this object. I do not know how a college could more effectually serve the cause of ministerial education, than by devising some such plan. Professors who would undertake such a service, would be abundantly rewarded in their own souls. They need some effort of this kind for their own spiritual edification. Were this course pursued by all our colleges, it would add greatly to our ministerial power.

XLII.

OUR GREAT RELIANCE FOR THE IMPROVEMENT OF THE MINISTRY IS ON THE MINISTRY ITSELF.—WHAT A MINISTER MAY DO IN THIS WORK.—THE BLESSING THAT WILL FOLLOW SUCH LABOR.

IN my last paper, I attempted to show what could be done by the colleges and schools endowed and supported by Baptists, for the improvement of the Baptist ministry. It will, of course, be said, in the first place, this would render our colleges peculiar. Be it so. Are we not able to determine what is best for ourselves? Are we so bound to other examples that we must follow them to our own destruction? A great deal is written and spoken on the subject of ministerial education among us. Platforms thunder with the eloquence aroused by the exciting theme, and the agent repeats for the hundredth time his narrative of the wants of the denomination. It has all resulted in leaving us more imperfectly supplied with ministers than before. Let us now take up the subject in earnest. Let us make a serious, universal effort to accomplish something, and then something will be accomplished.

But it may be said, that if we made these provisions, no one would avail himself of them. I do not know on what authority this should be said, until the experiment has been fairly made. I say *fairly* made. Let the instruction be valuable, and adapted to the wants of licentiates; let them be treated, not as outsiders who should be thankful even for the crumbs that fall from the table of science, but as men respectable and respected; and let the churches encourage every promising young man to improve himself, as far as the providence of God renders it practicable, and the experiment will not fail. If neither of these things can be done, it must fail, and it will deserve to fail.

But it is manifest that if the door of the ministry is opened as widely as I have suggested, a part, indeed the greater part, of those who enter it, will be composed of men so bound by prior engagements that they can not leave home at all; much less can they leave it for a prolonged and expensive residence in some distant part of the country. What shall be done to aid this large portion of our brethren, the very men who most of all need our aid?

Here, as every one must anticipate, I turn at once to the ministry. We look to you, brethren, for we have nowhere else to look. You, above all other men, can aid in giving efficiency to the ministry of the gospel. The work to be done is great. The laborers must be many, and they must labor in earnest. The wall must be built, and it can never be built, unless every man builds over against his own house.

I say, then, let every minister of Christ, in the first place, seek out and bring forward all the talent for the ministry which exists in his church, and let him pray, and encourage his brethren to pray, that such talent may be bestowed in abundant measure. We have the promise of Christ that such prayer shall be answered. Let us go to him freely, asking in faith, nothing doubting.

Suppose, now, your prayers to be answered, and a number of your brethren come forward desiring to labor in the work of the ministry. You and your church need great wisdom in this matter. See that you act wisely, in the fear of God. If you think a brother has misjudged his calling, and you obtain no evidence from his communications that he is designed by the Master for public usefulness, tell him so, kindly and plainly. If he is not satisfied, give him longer time for trial, but do not place him in a work to which you do not believe he has been called. You are acting for Christ in this matter, and you have no right to please either yourselves or any other men.

But having acted according to your best judgment, you find, to your joy and rejoicing, that there are several of your brethren whom you believe Christ has called to labor in the ministry. You find them exceedingly dissimilar in character and circumstances. Can the same rule reasonably be applied to them all? Can we wisely advise them all to pursue the same course? They range from the age of fifteen to that of twenty-five or thirty years. They are of great variety of education and culture. Some are under no previous engagements, others have entered into contracts, and are engaged in business which can not now be honestly brought to a close. It will be a question whether some had not better become preachers without giving up the business in which they are engaged. Others may appear promising, but it is evident that they had better preach for a time as licentiates, and wait for the openings of Providence to determine the future. Others are young, and can devote some years to education. But here a question arises: Have they the kind of talent which will be benefited by the ordinary course of education? Many good men go through college without acquiring any additional mental power. They are essentially the same men after ten years' study as they were before, with greater accuracy, more fearful of making a mistake, but with no greater vigor and no higher promise of usefulness than when they commenced. And yet such men may be useful in no common degree—they are made for action and effort, rather than for investigation and solitary study. There may be some, again, who exhibit talents which point them out as young men whom the Master has chosen for labor in which extensive education is manifestly required. It is in the highest degree desirable that such brethren should be encouraged to pursue a liberal course of education. They may not be any more useful than others of their brethren, but the Master seems to have designated them for a peculiar field of labor, and they should be prepared to enter it. Still, if such be the case, it does not follow that the church should assume the whole responsibility of their education. If they possess unusual talent, they are the better able to educate themselves. This they should be encouraged to do. They should proceed upon the principle that it is a work to be done by themselves, and that they will do it as far as they are able. When they are in straits, let them always be assisted. Let every kind thing be done to aid them in their meritorious undertaking. But let not the responsibility be taken from the men themselves. If a young man of promise, in this country, desires an education, he will be educated. He may not complete his course in the same time as another, but he will do it, and do it mainly by his own exertions. And this very exertion will, in the end, prove the most valuable part of his whole education. Yet, let me not be misunderstood. Never let a promising young brother be left to sink into despondency. Let him know that if he does all he can for himself, he will not be left to fall to the ground. And beyond question, the members of his own church, those who know him and have an opportunity to observe his walk and conversation, are the proper persons to aid him. Why should they contribute their money to strangers, who shall give it to him, instead of giving it to him themselves?

But we pass these cases to consider those that remain. There will probably be a portion of those who manifest talent adapted to usefulness, who may grow into the successful pastor, or the earnest evangelist, or the faithful licentiate, but who are chained at home for the present, by the providence of God. They may have relinquished their studies at boyhood, and have since enjoyed small means of improvement. They do not know where to begin, or what course to pursue. They feel their need of intellectual cultivation, while the space between their present position and that which they would attain, seems veiled in thick darkness. Now, to such persons, a judicious pastor would be of the greatest advantage. By free conversation, he could learn the bias of each individual, and ascertain his precise intellectual position. He might then mark out for him the course which he could most profitably pursue. In most cases, he could easily refer a brother to such teachers in the vicinity as would give him the needful assistance. Where this was impossible, he might undertake the work himself. This, however, would rarely be necessary. There are few districts in our country, except the newest settlements, where the ordinary branches of a solid English education may not be pursued under a competent instructor. A teacher by profession, or any other person of generous sentiments, would cheerfully give assistance to a pious man, struggling to obtain that knowledge which would render him more useful in the work of the ministry.

But suppose this done, the licentiate requires important aid in the special work to which he has given himself. Here the older ministering brother may be of essential service. He may direct the reading of the licentiate, set before him in a connected view the doctrines of the gospel, point out to him the proof-texts, show him the objections to them which he has himself met, and the best way of answering them, exhibit to him the various subterfuges of the heart, explain to him the mode of interpreting the word of God, remove the false views which he may have derived from an incautious reading of the Scriptures, and thus add much to his efficiency as a preacher of the gospel. He may also teach him to form the plan of a sermon, show him the errors of the plans which he presents, hear him preach, point out his awkwardness in language and delivery, encourage him in all that is good and acceptable, and prune away all that is the reverse. In this way a pastor may be of invaluable advantage to his younger brother in the ministry. Nor need this be done in the form of stiff and formal lectures. It may nearly all be accomplished in the way of pleasant fraternal conversation, while riding to visit the sick, or while walking together to attend a meeting, or working together in the garden or the field. Older brethren in the ministry have little idea how greatly they might improve their juniors by conversation of this kind. One of our most distinguished and most eloquent ministers, on whose lips the first men in the nation have hung with solemn attention, once told me that all the instruction which he had ever received in preaching, was contained in a single remark addressed to him by an aged father in the gospel. " Tell the people," said he, " precisely what they tell you." He had the good sense to understand the precept, and reduce it to practice. In visiting his people, he remarked the various forms of religious experience, in affliction, in joy, in conversion, remorse, repentance, faith, doubt, trust, in sickness and health, and in the hour of death. He told the people what they told him, and hence his preaching was distinguished for vivacity, knowledge of the human heart, and richness of religious experience, which has been rarely excelled. Probably in no six months of his life did that old minister ever do so much to advance the cause of Christ, as by uttering these few words of advice to a younger brother.

Do not say, brethren, you have not time for this labor. I know you are pressed with care; but how could you spend your time more profitably to the cause of Christ, than in just this manner? Could you not devote to it one afternoon in the week? This, probably, would suffice for all that would be demanded. While teaching others, you would greatly improve yourself. And besides, your younger brother would soon abundantly repay you, by the aid he would render in the discharge of your duties. What could be more delightful than for a minister to have three or four brethren uniting with him in carrying forward the work of God, all animated by the same spirit, all aiming at the same object, and filling the whole district in which they live with the preaching of the word. Under such a state of things, how rapidly would converts be multiplied, and how many new ties would bind ministering brethren together. I may add, how greatly would the power of the elder ministry be increased. He that watereth would here in a special manner be watered himself.

XLIII

MINISTERS COMPETENT TO THIS WORK.—WITHOUT THEM IT CAN NOT BE DONE.—SUGGESTIONS TO THOSE THAT HAVE THE MINISTRY IN VIEW.

To the remarks in the preceding paper I know it will be said, "We are not competent to this work." It must be left to the professors of theological seminaries. To this I reply, that one of the most popular objections made against theological professors is, that they *have not* precisely what you *have*, practical acquaintance with the working of the ministry. Not to mention ministers abroad, Dr. Stillman, Dr. Baldwin, Dr. Chapin, and more than either, Dr. Staughton, while engaged in the work of a laborious ministry, were thus instrumental in introducing to the pulpit a host of our most eminent preachers. But consider for a moment. Can you not always teach another what he does not know so well as you? You can surely impart to another all the knowledge you have yourself. This is all that is required. If every minister would do this, he would confer an invaluable benefit on those who are coming forward into the ministry. But I know, from my own observation, that brethren who make this objection underrate themselves. I could enumerate scores and hundreds, who, by devoting a portion of their time to this object, might not only greatly increase the number, but add vastly to the efficacy of brethren who have no other means of improvement.

But this is not all. It by no means follows that the licentiate will go no further than you can find the time to carry him. Set a man of sound mind and earnest purpose upon the right track, and he will go on by himself. Some of those whom you have thus cultivated, may, after feeling their own biases, pursue wider and more extended courses of study. Others, bent on self-improvement, will go on in a rapid course of self-development. The seed which you sow, though as a grain of mustard-seed, yet falling into good soil, may become a great tree. You may have the pleasure of seeing your pupils advancing in knowledge, piety, and influence, until they are much abler ministers than yourself. What higher reward than this can an instructor either expect or desire?

You see then, brethren, the object which is uppermost in my mind. It has seemed to many who have thought on this subject, that the Baptists in this country fail to accomplish one half of what is obviously and imperatively demanded of them by the Saviour. One of the reasons of our failure is, that we have not felt the importance of universal, individual effort. We have relied on voluntary associations to do what each one should do himself. The individual church members stand still, and yet expect the church to go forward. The church sees a great work before it, and instead of doing it, looks to the Home Missionary Society, or the Convention to do it. The minister sees the necessity of greater numbers and greater efficiency in the ministry, but instead of doing the work himself, he turns it over to the Education Society. The Societies turn over the work to their Boards. The Boards turn it over to their Executive Committees. The Executive Committees turn it over to the Secretaries. Thus, in fact, the work of extending the cause of Christ among us, which belongs essentially to every disciple, is devolved on some fifteen or twenty men, who, overburdened with business, do all they possibly can; but what does this amount to, in comparison with the universal effort of six or eight hundred thousand communicants, each laboring in his own sphere, each building over against his own house, all animated with the same spirit, each determined to do with his whole heart the whole service which the Master has appointed to him individually, and casting loose from all entanglements, resolved, whether minister or private brother, to know nothing but Jesus Christ and him crucified.

In the work specially of enlarging and strengthening the ministry, the ministry must, of course, take a prominent part. To them it especially appertains. Without their whole-hearted aid, we may, by Associations and Societies, do here and there a little good, but nothing far-reaching, universal, and effective can be accomplished. You, my brethren, see our condition. Does it not call for a universal effort? Will you make it? Will you put forth your hands, and uniting as one man, labor under God to place us in the position to which we should aspire, that of the foremost denomination on earth, in extending the kingdom of the Lord Jesus? We have among us no delegated authority; we have no central power; we are all independent churches. Does not every one see that our efficiency must depend, not on organization, but on individuality? If every one labors, and if all labor for the same object, and all labor in the same spirit, we shall possess a unity and efficiency of action which no form of organization can possibly confer. Love to the Redeemer binds every individual to Christ and to each other, and all live, not to themselves but to Him who died for them. Shall we not make one universal effort to be such a church—to be such representatives of our Lord?

But it may very likely be said, Physician, heal thyself. You are urging us to undertake the instruction of our younger brethren, Why do you not undertake it yourself? Set us an example, and we will follow it. I acknowledge the obligation, and am willing to perform the duty. If my observation or experience is of the least value to a brother in the ministry, he is welcome to it. I will, therefore, in the remainder of this series, offer a few suggestions for the benefit of just such licentiates as I have alluded to. I propose to present no systematic treatise, but shall throw together, in a familiar manner, precisely such thoughts as would have been useful to me, when I was at the age and in the condition of my younger brethren. These remarks, then, are not designed for those who have spent several years in passing through the "regular course." My remarks are intended for persons, who, from secular avocations, have entered, or are thinking of entering, the ministry; and who are of maturer age than is common for students. The path before them seems dark and almost impassable. My object is to throw a little light upon it, and relieve them, if possible, of some of that burden under which they now so painfully labor.

There are, however, a few preliminary considerations to which I would refer, before I enter upon the subject of preaching.

One of the most common sources of deep and anxious disquietude in the minds of men who, under the circumstances supposed, have thought of devoting themselves either wholly or in part to the work of the ministry, is a feeling of mental and moral incapacity for the work. Of the moral incapacity I need not here write; for though it exists, it is common to all stations and all conditions. The feeling of mental incapacity is not merely absolute, it is also relative; the man not only feels his want of intellectual power to grasp the mighty truths of revelation, but also his inferiority in these respects to those who have spent many years in the study of books, in acquiring familiarity with several languages, and who have been subjected from youth to all the discipline of the schools. Now, in so far as this feeling is absolute, that is, so far as it relates to the inability of man to comprehend the ways of God, it is true and salutary, and in harmony with the teachings of the Spirit. It is this feeling, when it is founded on a comparison of ourselves with others, that I would here consider. The notion to which I refer may be expressed somewhat in words like these : " How can I, who have received nothing more than an English education, and that perhaps imperfect and nearly forgotten, open my mouth in the presence of men, some of whom have spent half their lives in study, and who have been trained in all the discipline of colleges and seminaries ?"

Now, to such a brother, I would say in the first place, Who was it that marked out the bounds of your habitation, who placed you in the very course of life which you have thus far pursued? Was it not a Being of omniscient wisdom and infinite love? Did he not, from the beginning, know the precise work which he wished you to perform, and did he not direct your past life with special reference to it? Has he called you, or will he call you to any service for which he will not qualify you? He will not send you into this warfare without furnishing you with the armor which he wishes you to wear. The history of the world has not shown, moreover, that God has always employed human learning in carrying out his most important purposes. Cromwell was a man of no more than a plain English education. Milton was learned in all the knowledge of his age. The life of the former was certainly as important to mankind as the life of the latter. Burke was a man of acquisitions which astonished his contemporaries. Washington spent his early life as a surveyor, and had enjoyed no other advantages than those common to every respectable Virginia farmer. Which of them was chosen to confer the greatest blessing on humanity? The age of Cromwell and Charles II. was fruitful in theologians of great learning, but where among them all can we find a name that shines so brightly as that of John Bunyan, who, according to Macaulay, could not spell correctly, and did not understand the grammar of his own language? I mention not these instances to depreciate learning. This would be absurd. All I wish to affirm is, that the field of usefulness is open to all who wish to enter it, and that God assigns to us places in his vineyard according to his will, and that he qualifies his servants for the place which he intends them to occupy.

But again, it may be observed, that this feeling of unpreparedness for any new duties is almost universal. You will scarcely ever converse with a man respecting his early education, who does not wish that it had been different, and who will not tell you that under different training he would have been much more successful. The son of a man of wealth repines over the fact that he had not, by early poverty, been compelled to rely upon himself. The son of a poor man regrets that he was obliged in youth to contend with difficulties and to suffer hardships while the other was enjoying all the advantages of the most expensive culture. If you take men who have been through the same course of education, the complaint is the same. One wishes that he had entered college earlier, another that he had not entered it so early; one that he had pursued the languages more extensively, another that he had neglected them entirely for mathematics, and another that he had thrown them both aside, and devoted himself to philosophy and physical science. The feeling of our own insufficiency for any new and important undertaking is thus very common, and every man naturally refers his deficiency to the circumstances of his youth. This feeling, then, the licentiate shares with humanity. Were he to converse with men whom he considers the most favored, he would find that they look upon their previous training, if they are thoughtful men, with a feeling similar to his own. The conclusion from all this seems to me evident. Let us all set ourselves earnestly to the work which God has placed before us, trusting that he will give us all the aid necessary to do his will, if we humbly and faithfully rely upon his assistance. If we work, he will work in us.

XLIV.

OBJECT OF EDUCATION.—EDUCATION NOT CONFINED TO THE STUDY OF BOOKS.—DIFFICULTY OF ACQUIRING THE HABIT OF CONTINUOUS THOUGHT.—AIDS IN ACQUIRING IT.

On the subject of the last paper, allow me to add another remark. The object of education is, I apprehend, very generally misunderstood. It is commonly believed that there is some magical power emanating from the knowledge of Latin, and Greek, and mathematics, just as, in the dark ages, it was believed that evil spirits might be summoned or exorcised by drawing triangles on the floor, or by addressing them in scraps of the ancient languages. There is no magic whatever in this matter. The Latin word for a horse, expresses precisely the same idea as the English word. The fact is, that this knowledge, unless in exceptional cases, is, to all practical purposes, very soon forgotten, and all that remains is the mental power gained by acquiring it. If young persons are accustomed to daily intellectual tasks, which they are obliged to perform, it is natural to suppose that they will acquire the power of continuous thought, and the ability to direct their attention at will to any particular subject. If, together with this, the knowledge which they acquire is living and vital, if it be remembered through life, and serves to form the basis of sound opinions, and thus guide a man wisely through untried vicissitudes, the great object of education is accomplished.

But it is not to be supposed, because a man has had no opportunity of studying books, that his life has been of necessity a blank. God, in mercy, has not left the means of mental cultivation so much to the sport of accident. He has endowed every man with senses, the inlets of knowledge, and has given him the power of elaborating this knowledge into general facts and principles. Every man who is capable of thinking, and who has the gift to believe that there is something in his own thoughts, is thus educating himself every day, or rather, I might say, is receiving his education from his Creator. But besides, and above this, if he have his own fortune to make, and is obliged to decide upon actions by his own unaided intellect and conscience, he is acquiring a discipline of the very best character. Being obliged to think for himself in matters which deeply concern himself, he learns to govern his conduct by principles, to examine every condition of an action with caution, to observe and remember the results of different decisions, and thus he forms for himself a character, in which strength of common sense essentially preponderates.

The conclusion at which we arrive from these facts is this. There is not, by any necessity, such a difference as is commonly supposed between one thoughtful man, who has had the opportunity for acquiring the learning of books, and another thoughtful man, who has been deprived of this opportunity. Between a thoughtful man, under any circumstances, and a frivolous man, no comparison need be instituted. A man who has arrived at the age of intellectual development, if he has cultivated the habit of thinking for himself, need, by no means, suppose that he has passed his life without any education. He has no need of deferring, on all subjects, to men of supposed learned culture. With modesty, and yet with confidence, he may advance his well-considered opinions, and he will find that men of sense will hear him with attention. Such a man, while he feels his deficiencies, will labor strenuously to remove them. He will seek for knowledge from every quarter, and he will seek the more earnestly, because he is both aware of his want of it, and he knows how to use it.

So far as preaching is concerned, however, there is one deficiency which such a man frequently feels: it is the difficulty of continuous thought, the power of arranging a series of ideas, so that each one individually, and all collectively, may bear upon the point which he wishes to enforce. He can give an opinion on a particular subject of discussion—he can exhort on the instant to a particular duty, but to construct a connected discourse of half an hour long, in order to exhibit or prove a particular truth, he finds almost impossible.

That there is here a real difficulty, it would be useless to deny; but there is in it nothing whatever peculiar. It is precisely the same difficulty which meets us every hour of the day, when we attempt to do any thing to which we are not accustomed. It meets us when we first begin to handle a saw, to wield an axe, to guide a plow, or to sing a tune. The body has not become accustomed to this kind of action, and it moves awkwardly, sometimes so awkwardly that we fear lest we should never learn to do what we see other men doing with ease. The second and third trial, however, show some signs of improvement, and if we make the effort frequently, and at short intervals, we look back with wonder that any difficulty ever seemed to exist. It is the same with any mental effort. When we are required to do what we have never been in the habit of doing, our minds act awkwardly, or seem to refuse to act at all. The remedy is the same; make the effort, make it again and again, and we shall soon perceive that we have made some progress. Let a man continue in the same course, determined to secure for himself this habit of mind, and he will, before long, find that in any important matter, it is just as natural for him to think consecutively, as it is to think at all.

There are several modes of improvement which a man, desiring thus to educate himself, may pursue with advantage. One of these is to study carefully any science that is presented in a well-arranged form, carrying in his mind the leading and the subordinate divisions, until he can go through all the principal topics without looking at the book. Suppose him to study English Grammar, using Green's Analysis, the best book on this subject with which I am acquainted. Let him take the first section, and make himself so familiar with it, that he can think it out for himself. He then proceeds to the next section in the same manner, and, at one view, connects them both together. As he advances, let him always connect his present with his past acquisition, and hold in his recollection the thread which binds the whole together, until he has completed the subject. Let him study every thing in this manner. If he reads a sermon, let him take it to pieces, write down for himself the divisions and subdivisions, and then criticize it, observing its excellences and its defects. If he read, or hear, a plea at the bar, let him take the same course. He who will take this trouble, in order to render himself a more useful laborer in the vineyard of the Master, will find himself abundantly rewarded.

A most excellent means for cultivating this habit of mind is, to take up a book of Scripture, and proceed with it in the manner I have described. At the beginning, he may take an historical book, say, for instance, Genesis, and note down, as he proceeds, the several important points of the narrative. Let him fix them in his mind, in a consecutive series, so that he can recall them at will. After taking a few books of the Old Testament, he may proceed to the Acts of the Apostles, and treat it in the same manner. He may then take up the Harmony of the Gospels. If he does not read Greek, the English Harmony of Dr. Robinson for this purpose, is just as good. Let him study this in the order of the events, until he is able by himself to go over the whole narrative of the life of the blessed Saviour. When he comes to an extended discourse of our Lord, he should treasure up, not merely the sentiments, but the thread of thought which binds them together. Last of all, he may take up the Epistle of Paul to the Romans, and study out its entire analysis. It is by far the most thoughtfully and systematically composed of any of the apostle's writings. By the time he has done this, he will have no difficulty in making out a train of thought for himself on any subject connected with revealed truth.

Of the advantages of such a mode of study, I surely need not speak. It must be seen that it will cultivate, in a remarkable degree, that power of consecutive thought which is so indispensable to a public speaker.

This, however, is but its smallest benefit. We readily perceive that any one who will study the Scriptures in this manner, will very soon be a scribe well instructed, able to bring from the treasury, things both new and old. The various relations of revealed truth to each other will spontaneously manifest themselves to him. Illustrations will crowd upon him from every part of the Scriptures, whatever subject may be under discussion. Objections, as they rise from any quarter, will find their ready reply from the word of God itself. His mind will thus be enriched with the very thoughts and words of God, and he will be accustomed to consider them in the very relations, and with the very connections, established by Omniscience itself. All this a thoughtful and earnest man may do for himself, by the study of the English Bible, in the received version.

But this is not all. This habit can never be acquired, without putting it further into practice. A man who intends to become a preacher, must devote his attention to the construction of plans of sermons. He should at once make a book, which must be ever at hand, in which he may write down any verse, which seems like a good text, as it occurs to him in his reading of the Scriptures; writing out any thought, or plan, or division, that presents itself to him concerning it. These notes will be of great advantage to him when he is looking for a subject, and will frequently save him many hours of valuable time. And besides, in this, as in other cases, our first thoughts are frequently our best thoughts, and a division or a plan suggested, as it seems, by accident, may be much better than he could have elaborated by long-continued effort.

But, besides this, he must acquire the habit of forming plans of sermons on all occasions, when walking, when riding, when at labor or exercise. These let him write down in another book prepared for this purpose, giving the divisions and subdivisions as much in detail as possible. Having made a plan, let it lie a few days, and then he may subject it to a second examination. If there be a minister in his neighborhood, it would be very desirable to secure his aid. Let him criticize your plan, and point out its defects. Take it and try again, and do not leave it until you have made it as perfect as possible.

When this is done, however, the work is in a great measure completed. When you have such a plan in your mind, you will have no difficulty in speaking from your text. Words will flow readily when you know what you have to say, or if, at first, you have difficulty in this respect, it will easily be overcome by a little perseverance and practice. Whether you use written or oral delivery, the case is the same. Knowing what you have to say, and having the natural order in which to say it, all the rest is easy. You have broken the back of the difficulty, and it can not hereafter trouble you. Relying on the grace of God, you may go forward confidently in your work.

XLV.

PULPIT ASSISTANTS.—DIFFERENT CLASSES OF SERMONS.—DOCTRINAL SERMONS.—PRACTICAL SERMONS.

I closed my last paper with some remarks on the necessity of forming the habit of making plans, or skeletons of sermons. It will be understood, that by this I do not mean the mere putting together such thoughts as may occur to us, until we have enough to occupy the appointed time of a discourse; but thoughts arranged in a natural order, so that one introduces another, each one strengthening all that have gone before it, and all bearing upon the point to which we desire to bring the mind of the audience. This process is exceedingly improving to the mind and heart, and is one of the most delightful of all intellectual efforts.

Here, however, let me offer a caution. A strong temptation frequently assails a man, when preparing a sermon, to look around for helps. He can easily find a book of skeletons made to his hand, and it seems to him very convenient to make use of it. Let me urge every brother, as he values his self-respect, his honesty, his ministerial usefulness, as he values his own soul and the souls of others, to resist this temptation at the outset. If he have any of these crutches, let him commit them at once to the flames, or he will never learn to walk. The habit is absolutely fatal. If commenced, it will increase until the power of original thought is lost. The man who begins to borrow from others will borrow more and more, and he will at last be a preacher of other men's sermons, acting a lie every time he goes into the pulpit. I never knew a man addicted to this habit whom it did not ruin. Fear of discovery drives him from place to place, and at last drives him into some secular office, or some agency, in which one sermon will last him for a year. Whatever you have, then, be it little or much, let it be your own. If you draw from your own fountain the waters will continually arise clearer, sweeter, and more abundant. If you neglect it for other men's cisterns, it will rapidly dry up, or its sluggish water will breed slime and filth, so that you yourself will turn away from it with disgust. I say this to the licentiate who is just commencing his work, and whose advantages for improvement have been limited. I fear, however, that these are not the only persons who are in danger from this habit. Men of thorough training, as it is called, sometimes fall into it. Is it not sad, that a man who has spent nine or ten years in preparation for the pulpit, must thus confess his inability to make a sermon, but is obliged to buy sermons ready made for him? Such a man must certainly have mistaken his calling. I hope that in these remarks I do not seem censorious. I should not have made them if booksellers had not informed me that no books were more saleable than these various forms of "pulpit assistants."

Sermons have been divided into several classes. What the divisions commonly made are, I do not remember; it will, however, readily occur to every one that they may be Doctrinal, Practical, Experimental, Expository, or Hortative.

The object of the doctrinal sermon is to explain and prove some truth of revelation.

In this kind of discourse, two things are specially to be observed. First, the exposition of the truth, and secondly, the proof of it.

The exposition of the doctrine is, of course, a matter of the utmost importance. If we attempt to prove any thing, the first matter demanding attention is, to know for ourselves, and to exhibit clearly to others what it is that we desire to prove. From the neglect of this caution, men frequently announce the doctrine to be proved, and then prove something else, or really prove nothing at all. It is, therefore, not sufficient that we recite some expression of the doctrine derived from books, we must think it out for ourselves, and be sure that we understand it clearly. This will enable us to separate the truth from all extraneous matter, and present the simple statement distinctly to the minds of others. We shall thus guard the doctrine from abuse, and answer beforehand many objections which lie, not against the truth itself, but against the conceptions which men have erroneously associated with it.

The *proof* of any truth of revelation must be essentially revelation itself. God has not made a revelation of that which has been already made known by natural religion. The highest authority for our belief of any truth, is that God has said it. Why, then, should we go to the weaker evidence to support the stronger? We may present the texts in the Bible which affirm the truth directly, showing by a brief exposition that this is their exact and legitimate meaning. We may adduce other truths from Scripture which harmonize with what we affirm, or which take it for granted. We may appeal to the experience of inspired men, who have relied on this truth as the foundation of their trust and hope, and thus, from every inspired source, derive confirmation and proof of what we affirm to be true. If we wish to answer objections, we may show that this truth is in analogy with the truths of natural religion, but we should not, I think, appeal to this latter and feebler light, to *prove* any thing which we believe God to have spoken.

I beg leave to call attention to these last remarks. There has seemed to me a growing disposition to omit the proof of a revealed truth from revelation, and attempt the proof from every other source than the Bible. Why should this be? If the Bible be true, why should we ignore its evidence? To do thus may seem more philosophical, and may be more pleasing to unregenerate men, but is it really according to the mind of the Spirit? Do we not thus practically lead men to the conclusion that there is a higher authority than the word of God, by which *it* is to be judged, and to which its teachings are to be subjected? When we have done this, what is left to us but natural religion? We take such portions of the Scriptures as natural religion can prove, and the remainder is laid aside as unproved, and therefore valueless.

In doctrinal discourses, it is important to remember that it is useless to prove what is self-evident; and what, of course, all men acknowledge. When we attempt to prove a self-evident truth, we must, of course, fail; for there is nothing more evident which can be brought forward as proof. I have frequently heard men deliver discourses of this character, and the result has been that those who fully believed the doctrine at the commencement of the sermon, doubted the truth of it at the close. They said to themselves, If this is all the evidence on which it rests, we may, after all, have been in error. Such must always be the consequence of attempting to prove what is self-evident.

But though the establishment of a doctrine be, formally, the object of a doctrinal discourse, it is not the preacher's whole, or even his principal object. He wishes this truth to have its moral effect on the minds of men. Hence he should never fail to apply it to men's consciences, and show the manner in which such a truth must affect our eternal interests. It is possible to prove a doctrine very clearly, and leave an audience as much unmoved, as if we were discussing a mathematical proposition. Paul did not thus exhibit the doctrines of revelation. The Epistle to the Romans is the most logical of all his treatises. It is a systematical view of the plan of salvation. All the latter part of it, however, is made up of earnest practical exhortation. Nor is this enough. The apostle frequently suspends his argument, to introduce some practical or experimental truth flowing from the doctrine which he had established. The same remark applies with equal force to the Epistle to the Hebrews.

I find, however, that I am in danger of going more into detail than I intended, and of making a treatise, instead of offering a few desultory suggestions. I therefore hasten to offer a few thoughts respecting practical sermons.

A practical sermon is a sermon intended directly to influence our conduct, and conform it to the word of God. Here, I presume, we should endeavor to understand clearly what the word of God commands or forbids, and then fearlessly apply the rule to the conduct of men who hear us. Unless we do the first, we shall not be sure that we are uttering the commands of the Most High. Unless we do the second, our hearers will go away wholly unaffected, or applying the truth liberally to other men, but never seeing its bearing upon themselves.

Take, for instance, the commandment, Thou shalt not steal. To steal is to take the property of another without his knowledge or consent. But, according to our Saviour's interpretation of the commandments, it forbids not only this form of transgression, but any mode of appropriating the property of another inconsistent with the precept, Thou shalt love thy neighbor as thyself. Having clearly shown this meaning, and the broadness of the law of God, we should apply it to the audience directly before us. If we are preaching in a city, we should apply the command to the frauds of commerce, and show the manner in which they violate the precept of God. We should analyze these transactions, and exhibit precisely the point of the transgression. Under this would be included frauds on the revenue, and other similar sins. We should show that customs of trade do not alter the law of God, or our obligation to obey it. Were we preaching on the same text in a manufacturing or an agricultural district, our application would be different, as it would refer to the forms of violation of the command to which our hearers were most likely to be tempted. A sermon was preached on this text, some years since, in one of the most moral and exemplary towns in New England. The manner in which the subject was treated, may be learned from the results. On the next morning, the streets were alive with men and women, carrying books, household utensils, and a multitude of articles which they had long since borrowed, but had neglected to return. How would the light of the church shine, if practical sermons were preached in every pulpit of our country, with precisely the same results?

Here, however, we must guard against censoriousness. We must apply the command to the evil practice, avoiding all personality, and above all, taking care that we do not fall into the sin of rebuking sin for the gratification of our own evil passions. There is no occasion in which we need to be so deeply imbued with love, as when we are exposing sin. In no other manner can we render our reproofs effectual. Here, emphatically, we need wisdom from on high. We must be plain, simple, scriptural, fearless, and yet affectionate. There is abundant need of this sort of preaching. Many men have sat for years under the sound of the gospel, continuing in the practice of some common form of dishonesty, or prevarication, because they have never been taught the simple principles of honesty and truthfulness.

XLVI.

EXPERIMENTAL, EXPOSITORY, AND HORTATORY SERMONS.

In my last paper, I offered a few suggestions respecting doctrinal and practical sermons. I proceed to consider those denominated experimental.

This class of subjects occupies far less attention, as it

seems to me, than its importance deserves. A soul is dead in sin, its affections are fixed on the things that perish, and it is surrendered up to the dominion of its lusts and passions. By the Spirit of God it is made sensible of its condition, it repents, believes, and a new principle of spiritual life is created within it. Its affections are changed. It is henceforth in antagonism with the world which it once loved. It is now living for heaven, but it is sanctified only in part. The remains of sin within it create a continual warfare with that which is spiritual. Faint, yet pursuing, it still maintains the conflict, surrounded with doubts and fears, yet upheld by an invisible arm. It is under the discipline of a kind and indulgent parent, who chastises it for its good, that it may be made partaker of his holiness. It struggles on, looking for the recompense of reward, until it arrives at that blessed consummation where the pure in heart see God.

Now every one must see that there is here revealed an internal history of most absorbing interest, which the world knows not of. It is, in short, the narrative of the working of the new nature, in opposition to sin within us and without us, the life-struggle of an imperfectly sanctified soul after perfect holiness. The exhibition of divine truth on these subjects is always intensely interesting to the true believer. He thus learns, that in all his internal trials, he is following in the path of those who have fought the good fight, and have entered into rest. When he has mistaken the true moral character of his exercises, he is thankful to be corrected. He learns to examine his own heart more closely, and gains confidence as he discovers that his spot is the spot of

God's children. I can not but believe that the piety of the church would be much more vigorous and consistent, and that mistakes for eternity would be much less common, if experimental religion were much more frequently the subject of our discourses.

The common error of discourses from experimental texts is, that they are prone to become doctrinal. Thus, if a minister should take as a text, "My soul thirsteth for God, the living God; when shall I arise and appear before God?" he would be very likely to go into an *argument* to *prove* that the devout soul longed after God, and show the reason for it, closing with a string of miscellaneous inferences. How much better, after explaining distinctly what was meant, to illustrate the fact from the experience of David, as given in the Psalms and elsewhere, from the experience of Paul and other eminent saints, whose lives have been recorded by the pen of inspiration, and from the experience of pious men of a later age, closing with the blessed assurance of our Saviour, that those who hunger and thirst after righteousness shall certainly be filled. It may be said this is not logical, it is merely declamatory. Good, but it is just such declamation as the Holy Spirit has used abundantly. It is such declamation as strengthens and confirms the soul of the saint, and marks the line of separation between the saint and the sinner. Can logical preaching do more than this?

The source from which we are to derive experimental as well as all other religious truth, is, of course, the Holy Scriptures. If we would read the lives of holy men as the Spirit has given them, meditating on them devoutly, placing ourselves in their condition, and comparing and contrasting our sentiments with theirs, we should both improve ourselves in piety, and find much matter for preaching. The lives of Christians under trial, in sickness, bereavement, discouragement, and joy, especially in times of persecution and martyrdom, afford a rich field for the illustration of experimental religion. Another source from which the experimental preacher will draw an abundant supply of truth and illustration, is found in the examination and observation of his own heart, and the observation of the working of religion in the hearts of others. Why should a man hesitate to exhibit the dealings of God with his own soul, the struggles against indwelling sin, and the best modes of resisting it, his doubts and fears, and the means of their removal? He need not, of course, mention his own name, nor obtrude *himself* on his people, but by thus unfolding what he has himself felt, he will find that he is binding himself to them by a tie that nothing but death can sever. And then he will learn much by visiting his people, and conversing from house to house on their religious condition and progress. If they become familiar with him, they will love to unbosom their whole souls to him. In sickness and affliction, he will be their dearest friend, their chosen spiritual counselor. It is thus that the pastor acquires a rich fund of experimental knowledge which he returns to his people with interest, from the pulpit, or in the conference room. It is from want of this intercourse between pastor and people, from the neglect of pastoral visiting, that sermons are so frequently dry, abstract, and general; all true, and all well expressed, but they lack the vitality that carries them to the heart. They may be "successful efforts," but they awaken no moral emotion, and they make no one any better.

The expository sermon is employed in illustrating and enforcing, not a particular sentence, but a chapter, or what is better, a paragraph of the word of God. This is a most instructive and profitable exercise for both preacher and hearer. It teaches us to read the Scriptures with greater attention, and to observe not only the meaning of single sentences, but the connection which binds the several sentences together, limiting or expanding the sense, and giving point and meaning to them collectively, which they lose when considered individually.

The preacher, in an expository discourse, should take great pains to ascertain the circumstances under which the passage selected was spoken, its relations to what has preceded and what follows it, so that he may place himself as much as possible in the condition of the writer. He must meditate on each sentence, and recall similar sentiments in other parts of Holy Writ, and thus form a distinct conception, which he can convey in his own language, of the meaning of the writer. But these sentences were never delivered as isolated and disconnected truths. No man in his senses, unless he writes or speaks proverbs, ever writes or speaks in this manner. While each sentence is the announcement of a particular truth, every sentence is closely connected with what precedes and what follows, and all have a distinct bearing upon the leading idea which it is the design of the writer to enforce or illustrate. Now it is this idea which the expositor should seize upon, and thus exhibit in the clearest manner the thread which binds all these gems together. It is frequently surprising to observe what unexpected richness of meaning flows from a passage when it is thus skillfully analyzed, and how firmly it fixes itself in the memory, recurring to us ever afterward, whenever we read that portion of God's word.

But it will occur to every one that a minister's duty is not performed when he has done all this. He may have done it, and yet have gone through with an interpretation as a simply intellectual exercise, with all the indifference of a German neologist. He must go further than this. As he proceeds, he must enforce every successive portion on the conscience of his hearers, and bring the truth home to their business and bosoms. He must interweave these divine sentiments with their whole course of thought, and the whole practice of their lives. One verse is doctrinal, another is practical, another devotional ; one arouses to energy, another agitates us with fear, and another enkindles Christian hope and encourages doubtful faith. All these uses should be made in the progress of the discourse. Nothing is more profitable than an exposition thus carried out. Some Protestant churches require that one of the services of the Sabbath shall always be of this character. Nor is this without reason. When the Scriptures, in their connection, are thus explained from Sabbath to Sabbath, the people will become familiar with the word of God, and false doctrine can rarely find an entrance among them. The late Dr. Mason, of New York, was peculiarly happy in this mode of preaching. He enjoyed it himself more than any other, and he believed that it had, more than any other, been blessed to his people.

Hortatory preaching consists in an exhortation to the performance of some particular duty, as, for instance, faith, repentance, etc., or to avoid some special evil, as lying, Sabbath-breaking, hypocrisy, impurity, etc.

Hortatory preaching is liable to a fault which greatly detracts from its usefulness : it is sameness. Hence, it is sometimes said, disparagingly, of a sermon, it was nothing but an exhortation which we have heard a hundred times before. Now, I think the proper remedy for this evil is to present the exhortation precisely as we find it in the Scriptures, confining ourselves strictly to the text. Thus the exhortation to repentance, if urged on general principles, will be all exhausted by one discourse. If we take the Scripture reasons as they are presented, each one makes a discourse, as, for instance, Repent, for the *kingdom of heaven* is at hand, or the new dispensation has now appeared ; repent, *for God has appointed a day in which he will judge the world ;* repent, on account of the *mercy of God ;* the goodness of God *leadeth thee to repentance,* etc. Each idea furnishes a different reason, and the ground-work of a different discourse.

While I thus refer to these several forms of discourse, I do not suppose that a sermon need to be, or ought to be, either the one or the other exclusively. Nevertheless, either one or the other form will commonly predominate. A doctrinal sermon would be imperfect without exhortation, a hortative sermon frequently requires both doctrine and exposition. While this, however, is true, the main object of the discourse will be different, and by this its character may be designated.

Of what kind soever a sermon may be, it should never terminate in abstract discussion. Its object is to move men to faith, repentance, and reconciliation to God. We must not suppose that it is enough to convince the understanding; and that men will make the application themselves. This is, in fact, the last thing they are disposed to do. We must do it for them. We must make them feel that they, individually, are the persons addressed, and that their own personal salvation is involved in the truth which we set before them. That is the best sermon which leads the hearer to think the least about the preacher, and the most about himself and his relations to God and eternity.

XLVII.

TEXTS.—WHY SHOULD A TEXT BE TAKEN AT ALL?—HOW MAY IT BE USED?

I proceed to add a few thoughts on the subject of texts.

I will in the first place inquire, What is the use of taking a text at all?

Is it to indicate that the man who addresses us is a minister? This is, I believe, quite a common notion. It is by many persons believed that no one has a right to address his fellow-men from *a passage of Scripture*, unless he be of the clerical order. Hence, when a minister wanted a lay brother or a student for the ministry to speak from the pulpit in a revival, or on some missionary subject, I have often heard him combine with his request the remark, "You know, you need not take a text." I think that few of my readers will, upon reflection, consider this a sufficient reason for placing a sentence from the word of God at the commencement of our discourses, when we speak to men as the ambassadors of Christ.

Again, do we use a text as a kind of motto to indicate that we are to discourse on some religious topic? If this be so, it is not without its uses; it would distinguish a sermon from a lyceum lecture, or a speech at a public meeting. To take a text for this purpose, would certainly have its advantages, but they might easily prove illusory. A text might still be used to usher in, and give additional weight to a political harangue; or, to save a minister the labor of pulpit preparation, it might be prefixed to a lyceum lecture, so that the same discourse would answer either purpose, according to circumstances.

The taking of a text by a Christian minister is justified by far higher reasons than these. It proceeds upon the supposition that the Bible is the word of the living God; the only manifestation that has been made to us of the will of our Creator and our Judge, the only record of what he has done for our salvation; the only volume on whose pages are inscribed the conditions on which we may escape eternal wrath, and enter into the rest which remaineth for the people of God. This is the truth which the minister of the gospel is sent forth to utter. This is the beginning, and middle, and end of his teaching. He comes to us with a message from on high. He claims to be an ambassador. It is meet, therefore, that he should take for his *subject*, not merely as his *motto*, some part of the revelation from God, so that when he speaks to us, we may know that he keeps within the limits of his commission. It is this truth alone which God has promised to accompany with that energy of the Holy Spirit, without which we know that no soul is ever made wise unto salvation.

But suppose a text taken from the volume of inspiration, What use shall we make of it? There are several ways in which it may be treated. We may draw an inference from it, and make the inference, instead of the text, the subject of our discourse. Thus, suppose we take the text, "I have heard of thee with the hearing of the ear, but now mine eyes seeth thee; wherefore I abhor myself, and repent in dust and ashes." From this we may infer, that we are more affected by the sense of sight than of hearing, and hence the superiority of the former sense to the latter. We may make this fact the subject of discourse, and amuse our hearers with a description of the nature of both these senses, then a comparison of them with each other, and then with a dissertation on the various points of the superiority of sight.

Or we may generalize a truth into some general law, and discuss the general law, instead of the particular case of it presented in the Scriptures. Thus we might take the text, "Godly sorrow worketh repentance unto salvation," and generalize it into the law, that a permanent change of action is always preceded by a permanent change of character. This is no doubt true, and is a general law, under which the case in the text is comprehended. We might take this as our subject, and enter into a metaphysical examination of motives, and their effect on the will, and illustrate our truth from history, sacred and profane, from our own consciousness, and a hundred other sources.

Sometimes a text is taken, and the object of the preacher is not to exhibit *the* meaning of the writer, but to show how much meaning *he can get out of it.* Thus a narrative, or a parable, is sometimes taken, and it is allegorized, or spiritualized, as it is called, and the whole plan of redemption, or any particular view of it which pleases the preacher, is evolved from it. Thus the beautiful parable of the good Samaritan has been allegorized, and people have wondered at the skill of the preacher who found in the wounded man the sinner under condemnation, in the priest and Levite the ceremonial and the moral law, in the good Samaritan the Saviour, and in the inn the church of Christ.

Now, who does not see that thus treating the Scriptures we can make them teach any thing, natural philosophy, metaphysics, political economy, social philosophy, or whatever you please. The Bible ceases to be to us a revelation from God, for we can make it, at the pleasure of the speaker, teach wisdom or nonsense, solemn truth or flippant frivolity. If we may take such liberties with the Scriptures, we might take any other book as a repository of texts, as well as the word of God ; and we might derive from it just as good a meaning. Such can not, surely, be the way in which we should use the truth revealed to us by God himself for our eternal salvation.

In what manner, then, having taken a text, are we, as disciples of Christ, permitted to use it ? I answer, we profess to believe that the revelation of God is pure truth from heaven ; that the teaching found in that revelation is dictated by the Spirit of God, and contains within it the *mind of the Spirit*. We are bound, then, first of all, to ascertain, as far as we are able, what is the mind of the Spirit in that particular text, and having found this, to explain and enforce it upon our hearers. What else can we do if we are, as we claim to be, ambassadors of Christ? What should we think of an ambassador, who, instead of governing himself by his instructions, and diligently seeking for the meaning attached to them by his government, should deduce from them his own inferences, and propose terms derived from these inferences, or from the principles which he might generalize from them, or the views which he might obtain by considering them merely as allegories? We should certainly consider such a man wonderfully unfit for an ambassador. If we are ambassadors for Christ, why should we not be governed by the same principles? How else can we be ambassadors at all? What right have we to take the words of inspiration, and drawing our own inferences, cover them ostensibly with the authority of God himself? This is surely to handle the word of God deceitfully.

If, on the other hand, we ascertain the mind of the Spirit, and enforce this upon our hearers, we know that we are delivering to them the message which God has committed to us. We preach the preaching which he has bidden us, and He has promised to accompany this, and this only, with the saving influences of the Holy Spirit. Observe, also, the effect of this habit on both minister and people. The minister will soon acquire an extensive and accurate knowledge of the word of God, and while he is doing this for himself, his people will be nourished with the pure word of life. They will be indoctrinated neither into this or that *ism*, but will be sober, sound, whole-hearted, Bible Christians, well instructed in what God has spoken, knowing little and caring less for the opinions and doctrines of men. A large portion of the dissension and disagreement of Christians, proceeds from our teaching the doctrines of men as a part of that which God has revealed as his own truth. Should we not all come nearer to each other, if we all endeavored to learn precisely what the Spirit has taught, and nothing but what he has taught. The nearer we all come to the truth, the nearer, assuredly, shall we be to each other.

Nor is this all. If we ascertain the precise meaning of the Spirit, and make this the theme of our discourse, we shall attain to endless variety. We can scarcely find two texts of Scripture which, if attentively considered, give us exactly the same idea. Sometimes a truth is presented under one aspect, and sometimes under another. In different places, the same duty is enforced by different considerations. By observing these different phases of the same truth, we shall be able to present it continually in different aspects, and thus avoid the necessity of ever repeating ourselves. If, on the other hand, we pay no attention to the variety of circumstances with which the Spirit of God has associated it, we shall fall into abstract views of truth, and say all we have to say on a particular doctrine in one sermon. Hence, we shall, if we preach on the same subject again, repeat essentially what we have said before, or, as we frequently are tempted to do, preach again the old sermon.

I know it will be objected to what I have here suggested, that to preach in this manner, will require an accurate knowledge of the word of God. I grant it, but is it not desirable that a minister should have an accurate knowledge of the word of God? Is not this a far better and higher acquisition than a knowledge of the words of men? Why should we attempt to teach men out of the Scriptures, if we do not seek to know more of the Scriptures than they? I know that the tendency is in the other direction. We have all manner of contrivances for obviating the necessity to ministers, of a familiar acquaintance with the word of God. We have sermons made for them, and Scripture selections for different occasions and services, so that a man may perform ministerial duty, with no more knowledge of the Scriptures than might be expected from any intelligent layman. While, however, we do this, we cease not to speak of the solemn responsibility of ministers, and the great amount of preparation necessary in order to explain to others the word of God. If preaching and the work of the ministry can be thus made easy, a very small amount of preparation will surely be requisite for the satisfactory discharge of its duties. We believe that the best preparation for preaching is a familiar acquaintance with the true meaning of the word of God, and that any thing which renders such an acquaintance unnecessary, will weaken the power of the ambassador of Christ.

XLVIII.

MORAL REQUISITES FOR UNDERSTANDING THE SCRIPTURES.—INTELLECTUAL PREPARATION.—A KNOWLEDGE OF THE MEANING OF THE WORDS, OF THE CONTEXT, AND OF THE MANNERS AND USAGES OF THE TIME.

I HAVE referred, in my last paper, to the mind of the Spirit, and have said, that to ascertain this, was the first work to be done in preparing a sermon.

It may be well for us to ask, How can we ascertain the mind of the Spirit ? On this subject, it may be worth while to offer a few suggestions.

It is obvious, that in our present condition of moral and intellectual darkness, we are incapable of knowing the things of God, unless the Spirit of God enlighten us. The presence of that Spirit has been promised to us whenever we seek it. If any man lack wisdom, let him ask of God, who giveth to all men liberally and upbraideth not, and it shall be given him. If ye, being evil, know how to give good gifts to your children, how much more shall your Father in heaven give his Holy Spirit to them that ask him. Relying on these promises, we may then ask in faith, nothing doubting, and confidently expect that the Spirit will lead us into all necessary truth, if we ask for it in an humble and childlike temper. We may ask for the aid of the Spirit with special confidence in this particular case. We are obeying the command of Christ, and he has promised to be with us. We are laboring to convert and sanctify the souls for whom he died. We are doing his work, and not our own, and if we go to him for the aid we need, he assuredly will not disappoint us. If we desire to ascertain the mind of the Spirit, our first duty is to pray for light to that Spirit by whose inspiration the text was revealed.

Again, it is of great importance, if we would know the mind of the Spirit, that we maintain habitually a spirit of thoughtfulness and devotion ; and that our souls be, in a moral condition, in harmony with the truth on which we are meditating. A worldly, vainglorious, ambitious, pleasure-loving, frivolous soul, can not surely discern the things of the Spirit, for they are foolishness unto him, neither can he know them, for they are spiritually discerned. He may repeat the formula of doctrine to which the text is analogous, as he finds it in the standard of his sect ; or may present the view of the doctrine found in the volumes of systematic theology ; or instruct us with a synopsis of the views of commentators ; but he will not taste the water from the pure fountain, which is opened only in the heart in which the Spirit resides. With him the study of the text is mainly an intellectual exercise, with which the soul has very little to do. His hearers, if at all acquainted with the movements of the human heart, perceive that he is merely repeating a lesson, and that he is not, with his own hands, handling the word of life.

But, besides this, we shall be much more likely to arrive at the mind of the Spirit in any particular text, when our minds are specially in harmony with the truth which the text reveals. For instance, let a man read the 51st Psalm with a thoughtless, irreverent spirit, and he will see in it nothing peculiar, and it would be difficult for him to select a verse from which he could

INDWELLING OF THE SPIRIT. 305

make a sermon. Let now, the same man, bowed down with penitential sorrow, read the same Psalm, and every verse will overflow with meaning, every sentiment will find a response in his inmost spirit, and he would be able, from any verse, taken at random, to pour out the feelings of a contrite soul, and call others to the exercise of godly sorrow. Take another instance. Let a man, with but low ideas of the work of redemption, read the parting words of the Saviour from the 14th to the 17th chapters of the Gospel of John, and they will probably seem to him figurative, abstract, and almost enigmatical. But let him read them when the love of God is shed abroad in his heart, so that he is able, in some humble manner, to appreciate the love of Christ in offering up himself for his soul, and how deeply touching, how intensely affecting does every word appear! The heart of the Christian holds, as it were, direct intercourse with the heart of the Saviour, and the redeemed sinner seems with the beloved apostle at the Supper, to recline his head on the bosom of the Redeemer.

It would seem, then, that if we would in any case arrive at the mind of the Spirit, we must cultivate the indwelling of the Spirit in our own hearts. We see the effect of this habit of mind in the case of Payson. You could not, in conversation, mention a passage of Scripture to him but you found his soul in harmony with it—the most apt illustrations would flow from his lips, the fire of devotion would beam from his eye, and you saw at once that not only could he deliver a sermon from it, but that the ordinary time allotted to a sermon would be exhausted before he could pour out the fullness of meaning which a sentence from the word of God presented to his mind.

The above suggestions refer specially to the *moral* preparations required, in order to arrive at the mind of the Spirit. Those which follow have respect mainly to what may be called intellectual preparation.

It is obvious that, no matter in what language a sentiment is written, we can never understand it, unless we understand with sufficient accuracy the meaning of the words of which it is composed. If we attach to them no meaning whatever, or an inaccurate, vague, exaggerated, or insufficient meaning, the simplest sentence may seem to us involved in the deepest obscurity. This, then, is our first business, to ascertain, as accurately as possible, the meaning of the words which the Spirit has chosen as the medium by which the thoughts of God shall be revealed to man. A sufficient degree of attention to this simple direction will render many a passage luminous, which now seems hopelessly beyond the reach of our understanding.

Having done this, we must next examine the course of thought of the writer, as seen in the context. This is a matter of the very greatest importance. Without it, we can never know the meaning of any thing which we either read or hear. Every sentence in a connected discourse is closely associated with what goes before and what follows after it. Its abstract meaning is modified by that of its immediate adjuncts, and by the general scope of thought of which it is an integral part. It is on this account that proverbs are so frequently either incorrectly understood, or not understood at all. When they appear as isolated propositions, they stand out alone, with neither antecedent nor subsequent matter to furnish us with a clew to their meaning, and though we may acknowledge the general truth, we see not its particular application. We grow weary of this disconnected thought, and never read a large portion of it at the same time, with any particular advantage. To illustrate what I mean by an example. The Arabs use the following proverb, "When the Pasha's horses went to be shod, the beetle stretched out his leg." Now, taken abstracted from all associations, this proverb might have several meanings. It might intend to say of some mean Pasha, that the beetle mistook his horses for beetles; or that the beetle was, of all insects, the most given to imitation; or that shoeing was so universally useful, that even beetles felt the necessity of submitting to it. But suppose the speaker had been discoursing upon the character of a feeble-minded, pompous, vain-glorious man, who was always arrogating to himself the reputation due to others, and placing himself where no one else would ever place him, among the men most conspicuous for wisdom of counsel and energy of action, and should close his description with the proverb I have quoted, "When the Pasha's horses went to be shod, the beetle stretched out his leg," who then could doubt the meaning it was intended to convey? From illustrations of this kind, and every one can multiply them at will, we readily see the absolute necessity of studying the scope of thought in the whole passage from which the text is taken, if we would learn the mind of the Spirit in any particular passage. Unless we do this, we shall be led into inevitable error.

I may perhaps remark in passing, that the division

of the Scriptures into chapters and verses has greatly increased the liability to error in this respect. We read no other book where the sense is broken up in this manner. A chapter in some cases divides a sentence. There are no paragraphs, a form of division so important to the understanding of the course of an author's thought. We have no minor division but verses, and they chop up the meaning at random, so that the most continuous narrative is printed like a book of disconnected sentences. We soon form the habit of considering every verse as an isolated proposition, separate from every thing else in the book. When the Bible is read in schools, it is commonly read by apportioning a verse to each scholar. To the child, each verse is the announcement of a distinct proposition. The habit grows up with us. We cease to follow the train of thought, and look upon it as so many broken and independent fragments. The effect of all this is most unfortunate, and we must deliver ourselves from it if we would understand the Scriptures. Many of the most absurd and heretical views of the Scriptures are maintained by this mode of treating the word of God. A distinguished theological teacher used to caution his pupils, never to allow the use of any text as proof, unless the person quoting it gave chapter and verse, so that the passage might be examined in its place, and the meaning of it definitely ascertained. The young minister will save himself from many an embarrassment, by adhering strictly to this rule.

Besides this, the sense is frequently illustrated, modified, limited, extended, or adorned by the circumstances of the speaker, his age, country, and previous culture, by the habits and manners of the time, the course of thought, and the progress in civilization of the people. A knowledge of these not only throws light upon the sense, but gives great variety and vivacity to the discourse, provided it be not carried too far. We want Christianity, not Christian antiquities, and the latter only as they may subserve the illustration of the former. Thus the question of our Lord, " If David in spirit call him Lord, how is he his son ?" loses all its point unless we remember the boundless precedence which the Orientals, and especially the Jews, awarded to parents and remoter ancestors. The reason why the Jews heard Paul in silence until he spoke of being sent to the Gentiles, when they drowned his voice by a tumultuous outbreak of popular indignation, would not be apparent, did we not know that the Jews held themselves to be the special favorites of God, while all other nations were unclean outcasts, and that to offer the blessings of salvation to others besides themselves, was to insult the national character by sinking it to the level of the hated and despised Gentiles.

XLIX

CONSTRUCTION OF A SERMON.—WHAT IS A SERMON?—ACQUAINTANCE WITH THE HUMAN HEART, HOW ACQUIRED.—NECESSITY OF UNFLINCHING MENTAL EFFORT.

IN my last paper, I supposed the minister to have attained a clear view of the teaching of the Spirit in any particular text. The foundation is laid, the first important work is done. He knows what the truth is, which he intends to enforce, and if he have arrived at it in the way I have proposed, his soul is moved with the thought which he is about to set before others.

What is the next step? This truth he is to use for the purpose of producing a particular effect upon his fellow-men. He wishes, by means of it, to create in them conviction, repentance, faith, hatred of sin, striving after holiness, deadness to the world, trust in God, endurance of hardness for the cause of Christ, or any other Christian grace. He wants so to exhibit the truth before him, as to produce this particular result. I say this truth now before him, not any, or every, or all truth. He is not to take a text and aim at a particular result, and then bring all the truth in the Bible to accomplish it. He would then use himself up in a single sermon. He succeeds in making a sermon, as he renders this particular truth subservient to his particular purpose. His *sermon* is to be his text *expanded*, his *text* his sermon *contracted*. Keeping within these limits, as I have said, he will enrich and invigorate his own mind, and he will present an endless variety to his hearers.

We see then his position, what he intends to do, and the means by which he intends to do it. Here is an audience before him of immortal souls, on whom he hopes to make a given impression; here is a particular truth revealed by God himself, by means of which this impression is to be made. A train of thought, evolving this truth, is to be presented in such a manner as to lead to this result. This train of thought is the sermon, and it is successful or not, as it accomplishes this purpose. Here, then, we have the text on the one hand, and the audience on the other, and the sermon is to be so constructed as to bring this text to bear on the hearts and consciences of these immortal souls.

It would seem evident from this statement of the case, that the next business of the preacher was to be acquainted with the human heart. He should know its different moral biases, its endless subtlety, the various forms in which the love of honor, pleasure, indolence, human esteem, social position, wealth, sensual gratification, etc., oppose the entrance of truth. He should understand, on the other hand, the nature and office of conscience, its power, its authority, and the character of those teachings, which, as the voice of God, it utters even in the tumult of passion, as well as in the hour of solitude. When I say this, however, I do not refer to the study of books, though these may render him assistance. I do not propose that a man in preparing a sermon should go to his books for the purpose of learning how this motive would excite men, or how that other would depress them. What I urge is, that he acquire such an habitual acquaintance with his own heart, by constant reflection on these subjects, that the right motives and views will suggest themselves spontaneously and without effort, as the very views which most naturally suggest themselves to his mind.

But how shall a man acquire this knowledge of the human heart, which shall enable him most effectually to address men? It is, I suppose, greatly a gift of God. It is one of the talents which God gives to him whom he designs for a preacher of the gospel. Without it, a man may preach correctly, logically, and beautifully, but it is all abstract discussion, which leaves the heart untouched, and shows that God did not design the man for a preacher, and the gifts and callings of God are without repentance.

Yet, granting that this particular bias of mind is a gift of God, it is bestowed in different degrees, and like every other talent, is capable of cultivation. Much may be done by the study of the Scriptures, and bringing our hearts into daily communion with them. Much may be done by self-examination, turning our thoughts inward, and observing honestly the effect of truth upon ourselves. If a man wants to know the human heart, he has the means always at hand—let him look into his own. I know of no preacher who manifests a deeper insight into human nature than Massillon, who secluded himself from the world and lived almost entirely in his cell. When he was asked how he, who saw so little of men, should be so intimately acquainted with the most retired recesses of the human heart, he replied that he learned it all from the study of himself. We all are guilty of a twofold fault in this respect. In the first place we do not retire within ourselves to observe the workings of passion and conscience, and in the next place, we do not think the knowledge that we thus obtain of any value, or we are ashamed to use it, lest it should reveal our own imperfection. That man would be an unusual, as well as a most effective preacher, who, if endowed with any intensity of feeling, should, without of course the most remote allusion to himself, present his own experiences, the workings of indwelling sin, the conflict between sin and holiness, the ineffectual struggles to grow better, the humblings of the soul after backsliding from God, the doubts and fears which daily beset him, the victory over temptation and the means of deliverance, the glimpses of the better land, and the joy of the soul when she holds intimate communion with the Redeemer. He who will do this with entire simplicity and devout earnestness of purpose, may be sure that he will be designated as a man of intimate acquaintance with the human heart.

But the preacher has to do not only with men in general, but with particular men, the men of his own congregation, the men now before him. They have their own peculiar biases, temptations, and trials. He needs to become intimately acquainted with their peculiar state of mind, that he may bring forth from the treasury things suited to their wants, and adapted to their individual necessities. Hence the need of pastoral visitation, and religious conversation with all the members of his flock. It is from neglect of this special duty that our sermons are apt to be abstract discussions, addressed neither to men as men, nor to any man in particular. He who will cultivate the habit of intimate acquaintance with the religious condition of his own people, will never be in want of subjects nor of the most effective means of bringing them before an audience. He will find in the conversation of the sick, the afflicted, the sorrowing, and the bereaved, endless illustrations of the truth of the Scriptures, and will be enabled to bring the word of God home to the bosoms of men in a way of which the abstract, general preacher can form no conception. I have heard a minister of the gospel relate the following incident. He had occasion to visit a pious member of his church who had lost a daughter, the only child of her mother, and she was a widow. The bereaved parent gave him a narrative of the child's life, how, for so many years, she had been her only earthly solace, and specially with great simplicity described her feelings when the daughter, who had from infancy laid in her bosom, was for the first time separated from her for a single night. Soon after, the minister had occasion to use the parental relation in order to illustrate some scriptural truth, and he described the feelings of a mother as nearly as possible in the words he had so lately heard. The appeal went to the heart of every mother in the house, and touched sensibilities that were not often aroused. The wonder did not soon subside that a young man should know any thing about the inmost feelings of the heart of a mother.

So much then for a knowledge of the audience. Suppose now this to be acquired, the two things are distinctly before the mind of the preacher—the truth of revelation on the one hand, and this particular people in their present state on the other. He desires to bring this truth into contact with these hearts. How shall he do it? It is an original effort of mind, and can not be simplified or explained. Some suggestions, however, may lead us more readily to the exercise of it. In the first place, much depends on the resolute determination of the mind itself. Here is a work for the mind to do, and the mind must do it. It can not and shall not be let off from its work. It can not be allowed to play with it. It can not be permitted to think for a few minutes and then take up a novel, or a newspaper, or run over to the neighbors to make a call, or turn away to write a letter, or run into the other room to play with the children, or make a kite for the older boy. The mind must be kept down to this particular work. The door must be shut and bolted. Every distracting occupation must be laid aside. The man must put himself to the work, and determine that it must be done. He must then fix his mind upon the truth, and the object to be accomplished by it, and *think, think, think,* until he sees his way through the subject, and the train of thought is plain to his own mind.

This may seem a hard lesson. It is so at first. It will take time and self-denial, and severe mental labor. But having been done once, the second time it will be less difficult, and soon the formation of a train of thought will become almost a matter of amusement. There is no mental exercise which yields a richer reward than this, none which more surely cultivates vigor, acuteness, and alertness of mind. Any man who will resolutely determine to train himself in this manner, will not be disappointed.

One thing here deserves to be remembered. A man who has taken a text and commenced this sort of labor is strongly tempted, if he does not readily develop a train of thought, to leave it and take another, which seems to him much more manageable. He turns from the first to the second. When he attempts to construct a sermon from the second, he finds the same difficulty, and more readily turns to a third. Thus, after repeated trials, he consumes more than the time which would have been sufficient to complete the first, and has not yet accomplished any thing. His labor then, thus far, has been entirely thrown away. Nor is this all. His mind has lost confidence in itself. It has been overcome by difficulties, and is by so much, less able in future to overcome them. The habit of mental quiddling has been strengthened, and the man is much less fit than at the beginning to do any intellectual labor. Let me then advise the young preacher, having taken a text and fixed his mind upon it, never to leave it. Go through with it at all hazards. If you can not make what you wish of it, at least make something. You may, it is true, do badly. You may spoil a sermon, but you will have rendered yourself less liable to spoil a sermon in future. Never yield to the devices and tricks to which the mind naturally resorts for the sake of shirking labor. Keep your mind steadily at work, and it will soon love work.

L.

IMPORTANCE OF SELF-RELIANCE.—SAVING FRAGMENTS OF THOUGHT.—INTRODUCTION AND CLOSE OF SERMONS.—STYLE PROPER FOR SERMONS.—MISTAKES ON THIS SUBJECT.

In my last paper, I endeavored to set before my brethren what was necessary, when we have before us a text, and an object to be accomplished by it, and no train of thought is apparent. We must then set ourselves deliberately at work, and think it through. I will add, do not, in such a case, run to books to aid you. Go not down to Egypt for help. Your help is in yourself, under the direction of the Spirit of God. The more you rely on yourself the stronger will you become, and you will use your strength with greater skill. Let A and B be two preachers of equal talents and advantages. A relies on himself, and whether it be much or little which he produces, it is all his own. B dares not rely upon himself, but always goes to the best authors for ideas when he attempts to make a sermon. For the first year B may be esteemed by far the best, most accurate, and the most finished preacher. Look at them again in ten years. B has remained where he was; he struck twelve the first time, and he can not go beyond it. A has steadily advanced in power and skill, and has already passed his companion. People have found out that there is in him something original, and out of the beaten track. It has been ascertained that he thinks for himself, and hence, in other matters besides preaching, men think his opinion worth having. He is on an ascending path, the other is on a level plain, with a gradual descent at the further extremity. The case of A and B is a very common one.

But I hope that none of my readers will be led to the belief that a sermon can not be prepared without a process such as I have described. The fact is far otherwise. I have mentioned a strong case, to show what we are to do when we have a certain text in our minds, and feel it to be a duty to preach from it, and yet the train of thought does not present itself. If, however, our minds are earnestly fixed upon our business, if the condition of our people is ever in our recollection, and especially if a part of every day is employed in pastoral visitation, and that visitation is employed in personally religious conversation, subjects and modes of treating them will be rising before us daily. Texts, with the proper points of discourse derived from them, will suggest themselves in walking, in riding, at the bedside of the sick; or if we are employed in secular occupations, while we are holding the plow or gathering in the harvest, in the shop or in the factory, in the mart of business or the counting-room. If our hearts are fixed upon the subject, nothing will more readily spring up in our minds than sermons.

But, it is evident that while this is the general fact, it may frequently happen that the right sermon may not occur to us in the right place. Hence the importance of husbanding our resources, and having always on hand a supply for the time of need. We may accomplish this, as I have said before, by keeping near us a blank book, in which to record any text that occurs to us in reading the Scriptures, or in our pastoral visits. Sometimes we may write down only the text and the subject to which it refers, at other times the divisions of the subject as they at the moment occur to us, and sometimes a full plan of a sermon, if the subject seems to spread itself out before us. A book of this kind will be found a great help to us, and will frequently save us from fruitlessly employing half a day in looking up a text. Besides this, it is well for a minister to have always on his table a few sheets of paper sewed together for the purpose of noting down any thought which occurs to him that may be used in preaching. Three or four sheets of common foolscap folded lengthwise is the best for this purpose, and I am persuaded that a man who will once make the trial of using so simple an aid, will not readily be without it. It is told of the first President Edwards, that he was extremely careful to allow no thought to escape him which he supposed might be useful in the course of his studies. He found that valuable suggestions, inferences, and inquiries frequently occurred to him in his daily walks. To rescue them from forgetfulness he adopted the following expedient: he never went to walk without taking with him blank paper, a pencil, and some pins. If a thought occurred to him which he considered worth preserving, he would tear off a bit of paper, write down the thought, and pin the paper on his sleeve. It is said that he would sometimes return from a walk with both sleeves, from shoulder to wristband, covered with these bits of paper. He then retired to his study to examine and arrange them, and record them in a common-place book which he appropriated to this purpose.

In preparing a sermon, we should beware of too long an introduction. A minister sometimes fears that he shall not be able to find material for a sermon of the ordinary length, and hence he prolongs the first part by long discussions on the context, or any other miscellaneous matter which happens to occur to him. This is dry and uninteresting to his audience, and they become weary before he really begins his work. A preacher of this kind was once asked by Dr. Stillman to preach for him. The brother declined on account of his inability to meet the expectations of Dr. Stillman's congregation. "O," said the Doctor, "you will do well enough, if you are only willing to say your best things first." He took the advice and succeeded.

The close is a most important part of a discourse. Whatever may have been the subject, we should here endeavor to fix it with a nail in a sure place on the consciences of our hearers. If we have not preached what can be thus impressed, we have not probably delivered a gospel sermon. If we know our people as we ought to know them, we shall, instinctively, feel that there are persons there to whom the truth especially applies, and we shall impress it upon them with all the power the Lord has committed to us. It is of no use to persuade ourselves that the hearers will apply it for themselves, we must do it for them. We must aim at bringing them to a resolution, not six months or ten years hence, but now, and here. Why should not the sinner now repent and believe, why should not the saint now lay aside every weight and the sin that easily besets him? Now is the time to urge every motive, to press home every consideration, that can be derived from heaven and hell, from time and eternity. Never close a sermon until you are conscious of having done your duty; never bid adieu to your audience until you can say, I am pure of the blood of all men, especially of those who now hear me. Surely, a minister at the close of every sermon ought to be able to say this, for there is almost always some soul present whom he will meet no more, until both he and his hearer stand together at the judgment-seat of God.

As I have before remarked, when the train of thought is completed, the chief labor of making a sermon is performed. The rest is nothing more than clothing it with language. This is done either orally or by writing. Of the separate advantages of these methods I have already written, and I need scarcely refer to it again. It, however, seems strange that after having thought out a course of remark, a man should be obliged to write it all down, before he can communicate it to others ; I say a man, I mean a minister, for no other man ever feels the need of this sort of aid. No speaker at the bar, or in the senate, or on the platform, would ever hope to interest an audience for five minutes in this manner. I must, therefore, urge that every preacher should learn to preach, that is, address men from oral and not written preparation. If he insists upon writing let him write, but let him by all means acquire also the unwritten style of address.

The language of a sermon should be that of popular address, plain, simple, and easy to be understood. It should approach as nearly as possible to that which the hearers use in thinking, and ordinary conversation, purified, of course, from vulgarity and provincialisms, from cant, slang, and technicality. This is the style best adapted to any miscellaneous audience. It was greatly owing to his mastery of this style that the writings of William Cobbet exerted such an influence over the people of England. Now, whether a sermon be delivered from written or unwritten preparation, the style should be the same. To this I know the objection will be made, how shall a minister then learn to be a fine writer ? I answer, writing for the press, and writing for an audience, are very different things ; and in preaching we are to use the style best adapted to preaching. Beside, did Christ ordain the ministry of the word for the sake of making fine writers ? Have we a right to make the ministry of reconciliation a means for the acquisition of rhetorical reputation ? If a man wishes to be a fine writer, let him write reviews, dissertations, or any thing else, but let him choose for his medium of communication in the pulpit, that mode of address which will come most directly home to the hearts and consciences of his hearers.

The vice of preaching at present, in most of our pulpits, is that we do not aim correctly. We strive to please the few, and not the many, and the result is that the conscience of both parties is unmoved. The pulpit is dying of the proprieties. We dare not introduce an anecdote into a sermon. We shrink from an illustration, unless we can account it classical. We are averse even to the delineation of character, lest we should detract from the dignity of the pulpit. When a man is afraid of losing his dignity by attending to his own business, we generally think that he has very little to lose. We fear that the pulpit is liable to create a similar impression. Look at the highest example of preachers. How simple is the teaching of Christ, how perfectly adapted to the audience by which he was surrounded. How it abounds in illustrations, parables, and even every-day proverbs, so that the common people heard him gladly. Paul tells us himself how he preached at Corinth and Ephesus, and he is surely a good model for a cultivated man. Look at Bunyan, one of the most eloquent and effective preachers of his time, how plain, how simple, how earnest, and yet how full of incident and illustration were his discourses. Observe President Davies, how plain, forcible, earnest and direct were his sermons. We sacrifice vivacity and interest to a vague pedantic notion of what is *proper* for the pulpit, as though a preacher of the gospel were lecturing to a class on the proprieties of rhetoric. Is it not time that a change came over us, and that a preacher aimed more at interesting and converting men, and less at the reputation of refinement of style, and exquisiteness of propriety? A minister once said that a sermon without a fault would spoil a revival. Are not such sermons one reason why revivals are so rare among us?

LI.

DELIVERY OF A SERMON.—THE NATURAL TONES OF EMOTION.—LENGTH OF SERMONS.—ALL THE SERVICES OF WORSHIP TO BE IN HARMONY WITH THE SERMON.—FOPPERY.—TALKING IN THE PULPIT.

I HAVE in the previous papers stated the principles on which a sermon is to be constructed. It may, however, be proper to remark, by way of explanation, that it is by no means to be supposed that a minister should never preach unless he has had time to think out a train of thought such as I have suggested. Frequently he will be called upon in haste, and sometimes, with every effort he can make, he will be unable to satisfy himself. In such cases he must do as well as he can, and may preach as usefully as after long, and, in his own opinion, successful preparation. We are called upon to do precisely as well as the providence of God has permitted to us. Having done this, we may rest contented. The reason for offering the suggestions contained in the previous paper is, that we may know what is required in a good sermon, that we may attain as near to it as we are able, and thus guard ourselves against that unconnectedness of discourse which renders any sermon ineffective.

When a sermon is prepared, it is to be delivered. It may be worth while to offer a few suggestions on the subject of delivery. It is a common remark, that preachers acquire a worse delivery than any other men who address their fellow-citizens in public. How far this is just, it may be hard to determine. Suppose, however, a lawyer at the bar should read his plea, or the speaker at a political meeting should read his speech, just as ministers read their sermons, would they be at all endured? Or, suppose that, in an ordinary meeting of friends, any one should attempt to converse in the precise tones of voice which men use in the pulpit, would not the whole company stand amazed? When men preach without notes, it is not commonly as bad, but here there is frequently some evil habit which very much detracts from the effectiveness of the discourse. One speaks so rapidly that it is difficult to follow him, another drawls, another has a solemn ministerial tone, to which all his sentences are subjected; one is unmoved when uttering the most solemn truth, another is boisterous from beginning to end, and as much excited while uttering the most common remark, as in delivering the most solemn announcement. Now all this is unfortunate. Whoever attempts to improve a brother minister, should pay special attention to these defects, and labor assiduously and faithfully to correct them.

The great defect of all our speaking, is the want of naturalness. When we become confined to written discourse, this is almost inevitable. Men can not read as they speak. The excitement of thought in extemporary speaking awakens the natural tones of emotion, and it is these natural tones which send the sentiment home to the heart of the hearer. Any one must be impressed with this fact who attends a meeting of clergymen during an interesting debate. There is no lack of speakers on such occasions, and no one complains that he can not speak without notes. It is also remarkable that they all speak well, for they speak in earnest, and they speak naturally. We have sometimes thought, if these very brethren would speak in the same manner from the pulpit, how much more effective preachers they would become. In the pulpit we tend to a solemn monotony, which is very grave, very proper, very ministerial, but it is very wearisome to the vocal organs of the speaker, and to the ear of the hearer, and its tendency is decidedly soporific. We frequently hear a discourse delivered even with a good deal of earnestness, when not a single word has been uttered in a natural tone of the voice.

The tones which lie at the foundation of all good speaking, are the tones of earnest conversation. Here we never drawl, or fall into tone, or sing-song, but speak out what we mean, with the pauses and emphases which most readily convey the sense, modifying every sentence by our own feelings and the impression which we desire to produce upon the hearer. This is the basis of all good speaking. If a man could carry these tones into the pulpit, rendering them somewhat more grave, as becomes the solemnity of the subject, speaking more slowly, as he must do if he would be heard by a large assembly, abating somewhat of the suddenness of transition, and rising, when the occasion demands it, to an impassioned and sustained earnestness, he could not fail to be a most attractive preacher. This, then, should be the great object of a preacher, to address an assembly in the tones and the manner which he would use in earnest conversation. If we can only attain this excellence, every other will follow as a matter of course. If he once learns to stand up before an audience, and speak to them freely, without embarrassment on the one hand, or pompousness on the other, simply as any man might rise and address his fellow-men on a subject of importance, he may proceed from this to the highest efforts of eloquence, or at least to as high efforts as have been granted to his particular endowment. In order to impressiveness of delivery, however, it is essential that a man aim at *immediate* effect. No man can be eloquent if he be affirming truth which may be of use some ten years hence. He thus excludes all use of the emotions, for there is nothing for the emotion to do. His discourse becomes a mere abstract discussion, addressed to the intellect, and having no bearing on present action. When Demosthenes closed one of his orations, the whole audience burst into a unanimous shout, uttering simultaneously the words, "Let us march against Philip." If he had contented himself with discussing matters and things in general, telling them what might be necessary to be done sometime or other, they would have gone away quietly, remarking upon the beauty of his sentences, and the melody of his voice, and have complimented him upon "the success of his effort." Three days afterward, hardly any man in Athens would have been able to give an intelligent account of his discourse.

A word may be said respecting the length of sermons. Cecil remarks that a written sermon should not exceed thirty or thirty-five, and an unwritten sermon forty-five minutes. This is probably a judicious direction. As sermons are of frequent occurrence, and as they had better be confined to a single topic, or to a phase of a topic, the length of time which they occupy may profitably be confined within these limits. It is of small benefit to an audience to be wearied with the length of a sermon. A preacher should always bear this in mind, and by no means continue his discourse after his hearers have lost the power of attention. Sinners are rarely converted or saints edified, when they are half asleep.

The nature of the sermon governs all the other exercises of public worship. The object of the preacher is to produce a single impression. We all know how difficult it is to fix religious truth in the mind of man, especially when the reception of that truth imposes the necessity of corresponding action. We all know how easily the mind is diverted from the subject of discourse to every passing trifle, how soon a train of association arises and leads the mind far away from the words which are falling upon the ear. Now, of this the preacher should be aware. He should have every other part of the service so ordered as to coöperate with the sermon in producing one effect; and every source of distraction should be carefully avoided.

If we adhere to these principles, we shall of course select such Scriptures for reading as are conducive to the main design. The hymns should prepare the mind for the subject that is to follow. The tunes should express the emotion uttered in the hymns. For this purpose the old hymns, enriched by innumerable solemn associations, are greatly to be preferred. The more directly every thing bears upon the point to be attained, the greater will be the effect. And on the contrary, every thing is to be avoided which would lead the mind of the audience in a different, especially an opposite direction. Music which expresses no sentiment, but only exhibits the skill of the performer, especially music that awakens associations of the opera or theater, is sufficient to destroy the effect of the most solemn discourse, if, indeed, solemn discourses are ever found in such company. Notices, announcements of intention of marriage, etc., etc., if they must be made a part of the service of God, should be put as far out of the way as possible, that they may not interfere with the unity of design which should govern a religious service.

I hope I may mention without offense that the conduct of a minister in the house of God is of more importance than is commonly supposed. There is no holiness conferred by licensure or ordination. A minister is just as frail and erring a man as any of his brethren. If he attempts to separate himself from them by manner or address, by wearing any particular garb which shall create an artificial reverence for him or his office, he is welcome to all that he gains by it. But while this is so, it is yet to be remembered that the business of a minister is one of passing solemnity. No man should presume to address men on the subject of their interests for eternity without feeling deeply and earnestly the momentous nature of the truth which he discusses. This state of mind will give to his whole demeanor an aspect of simplicity and sobriety which becomes him as an ambassador of Christ. He will sedulously avoid all tricks and awkwardnesses which would detract from the effect of his message. His dress, like that of any other well-bred man, will be such that no one would be tempted to remark upon it. It has been well said that no one is well-dressed if his dress attracts notice, and the remark is specially true of a minister. Foppery of every kind, whether displayed in extreme care or in extreme negligence, is always to be avoided. Either of them shows that a man wishes to attract attention to his person. A suspicion of this kind detracts immeasurably from the usefulness of a minister.

There is another practice to which I regret to refer. It is the habit of talking in the pulpit when two or more ministers occupy it together. We frequently see two or three ministers engaged in earnest and apparently trivial conversation before the services commence, and in the intervals of singing. They appear to be looking together over the audience, and making remarks upon it, or upon some particular person or persons whom they discover in the midst of it. Or, it may be that after the sermon they are talking of the discourse. Now what a tempest of righteous indignation would it arouse in the bosom of a minister, if his *people* should act thus in the house of God. But I would ask, with all deference, what distinction is to be made here between the minister and his people? Is he not at least *as* strongly bound to show reverence in the house of God as those to whom he ministers? Is not the law for one precisely the law for the other? Nothing detracts more effectually from the impression of a sermon, than any thing which betokens levity in the man who has delivered it.

LII.

WEEK-DAY SERVICES.—LECTURE OR CONFERENCE MEETINGS.—PASTORAL VISITS.—CONVERSATION ON RELIGION.—CONCLUSION.

I HAVE thus far considered the services of the Sabbath. A few more remarks, on some other duties of a minister, will complete the suggestions which I propose to offer on the present subject.

The other duties of a minister, in the way of public service, appertain to week-day evening, and conference meetings.

In most churches there is an evening service once in the week, which is either occupied by the minister in a familiar discourse, or by the brethren for conference and prayer. Sometimes both are united, the minister occupying a part, and the brethren the remainder of the time.

These meetings are of great importance to the spiritual prosperity of the church. Christians are prone to lose the impression of one Sabbath before the next Sabbath arrives. An intermediate meeting of some sort is useful to break the hold of the world upon the heart, and turn the thoughts upon God and eternity. Such meetings should by all means be encouraged, and they will be found to have great effect upon the soul of the believer.

The preaching, on such occasions, may be more familiar than on the Sabbath. The audience is composed of men and women who have turned aside from the pressure of worldly business for the sake of spiritual refreshment. They need it, and they should have it. Dry discussion and learned interpretation are here out of place. Practical or experimental truth is far more apposite. Something is needed which shall enable the man, with a deeper sense of Christian obligation, and a firmer hold upon Christian hope, to enter anew upon the cares of every-day life. He who will devote himself to furnishing this refreshment to pilgrims on the way to Zion, will not lose his reward.

Meetings for prayer and conference have a similar effect. The gospel requires that a Christian should be not only a receiver, but a dispenser of spiritual benefits. By watering others he is also watered himself. By unfolding those views of truth which at the present most deeply affect his own mind, he himself becomes more strongly impressed by them; new trains of devotion are awakened in the minds of others, and a community of feeling is created in the members of a church. In this manner, also, the gifts of a church are called into active exercise, and those who have any talent for public address are readily discovered. Such meetings as these are the nurseries of the ministry.

Only a day or two since I received a letter on this subject from a pious and efficient layman, whose praise is in all the churches, and who has been honored as the means of the conversion of sinners beyond most clergymen. The letter is so apposite to the matter in hand that I can not resist the temptation to transcribe a part of it: "When, as is too generally the case, the prayer and conference and covenant meetings are neglected, I find that the ministers too often either pay no attention to these meetings, or, if they attend them, they occupy all the time, and prevent laymen, especially young ones, from participating in them. It is with me a most lamentable fact that a very large portion of the male membership sinfully refrain from ever opening their lips in any sort of religious service. We have in all our weekly papers glowing accounts of the number added by baptism to our churches, and I can rejoice in this, but a long experience has taught me that a great want exists in the general practice of our churches. In thousands of instances the whole of a Christian profession amounts simply to this: an individual is found *willing* to join the church, and is introduced by the pastor, perhaps with the consent of the deacons. A very few stereotyped leading questions are asked only by the pastor, with a whispered yes or no in reply to them, a listless non-negative vote, the baptism, the right hand of fellowship, a seat at the Lord's Table, the name recorded on the church book—and they are in the church, too often on the shelf. The work seems now completed, while in fact it is only the enlistment: the labor and the fighting have hardly begun yet. They have no positive specific duties assigned to them; no one to mark their progress or take note of their delinquencies if they fail; no regular plan of operations to employ the tongue, the hand, and the heart of every member. The Bible is plain enough—'They that feared the Lord *spake often one to another*,' 'exhorting one another,' 'speaking to yourselves'—but we fail in the practice of these duties. Ministers fail in fostering these duties, and then often complain that their preaching is powerless, without seeing and feeling that the iron must be *heated* before you can work it, that a religious atmosphere, by prayerful, active duty among all the membership, must be kept up, or nothing can be effectually done. Our Methodist brethren have their weekly class-meetings, for conference and contributions both, and these, I feel assured, are the sources and ground-work of the immense increase of that denomination, now largely ahead of us, though we had a century or more the start of them. Their class-meetings 'keep them all at it, and always at it.' Here every absentee is noted and inquired for, and not one present can be a mute-tongued Christian. All participate, and every warm-hearted real Christian enjoys it, and here all the talent for usefulness possessed by every member must be brought out and duly appreciated." These are the words of a lay brother, whose opportunities for observation have been as large, whose labors have been as abundant, and whose sacrifices for the cause of Christ have been as great, as those of any Christian of my acquaintance, at whose feet I would willingly sit for counsel. I hope they will be duly pondered by all my readers. If ever we mean to do our duty in the conversion of the world, we must be " all at it, and always at it." Every brother must do his part of the labor, and then the house of the Lord will be builded.

It may not be amiss to add a word on the subject of pastoral visiting, a duty which is in danger of being almost forgotten. When I say pastoral visiting, I do not mean merely ceremonial visiting, calling two or three times a year on all the members of the congregation to inquire after their health, and talk over the events of the day, and thus keep up a personal acquaintance with our hearers. This is not without its important uses, and hundreds of ministers, from the want of it, are almost strangers to their people; their people lose all personal interest in them; their preaching wants the directness which arises from the speaking of friend to friend, and some new attraction draws away now one and then another of their congregation.

I do not, however, refer to this form of visiting, but to something more. By pastoral visiting, I do not mean merely visiting in the manner I have suggested, but visiting as often as practicable every individual of the congregation, for the purpose of personal religious conversation. In such visiting, the pastor should make it his business to enter into the religious condition of every individual. With the Christian he should converse on the evidences of personal piety, the motives to a holy life, the value of souls, and the importance of a life of entire consecration of ourselves to Christ. He should warn the believer against the allurements of the world, and ascertain, as far as may be possible, his individual state in the sight of God. Frequently he will find the pious laboring under doubts and discouragements—these he should seek to remove. Sometimes they are in sorrow and bereavement, in need of the consolations of the gospel—these consolations he will delight to administer. In sickness he will be their comforter, and in the hour of death their dearest friend. He will pay particular attention to the children of every family, calling every one of them to early repentance, and pressing home upon each one the gracious offer of mercy through the blood of the cross. Such conversations they will never forget, and as they grow up they will look upon their pastor as their best counselor and the special well-wisher of their souls. No words will fall with such weight on their ear as his, and nothing can ever allure them away from his ministrations. To the worldly and unrenewed in heart, he will kindly and yet faithfully speak of the vanity of the world, the hollowness of its pleasures, and the treachery of its promises, and will urge them, without delay, to seek for an interest in Christ. When he has preached with peculiar solemnity, he will especially follow up the sermon with such conversation, addressed to those who seemed to be at all impressed on the Sabbath. He will thus attempt to fix in the mind the truth which he has publicly delivered, and foster every impulse which the Holy Spirit has given to the conscience of his hearers. Every one of his congregation will be assured, from his own personal knowledge, that the great object of the minister is the salvation of his soul; he will hear him with tenfold interest, and cleave to him with undying affection. The preaching of the Sabbath is a paid service, a professional performance; but here, of his own accord, as a friend who loves his soul, the minister seeks to save him from the misery of a lost eternity. One of the old ministers of Boston used to say, that on the Sabbath his people were like a row of empty bottles; he passed along, and with a sponge dashed water upon them, and here and there a few drops entered the bottle. When he visited them for personal conversation, he took up each bottle by the neck, and poured the water into it from his pitcher.

Nor is this all. Like priest like people. If a minister does not cultivate the habit of conversing individually with his people on personal religion, they will not converse with each other, or with men of the world, on this subject. Religious conversation will grow out of date, and a company of the disciples of Christ will meet and converse on every trifling event, without uttering a word on the great salvation. If, however, the minister makes the work of saving souls his great business, in season and out of season, his people will catch his spirit, they will speak often one to another, and words of religious warning, expostulation, and encouragement will be heard in the office, the sick chamber, the counting-room, and the workshop. The disciples of Christ will be the salt of their neighborhood, from them will be sounded out the word of God, and multitudes will be added to them of such as shall be saved.

I have thus fulfilled my promise. I have showed the need of ministers in our denomination, the manner in which the number of ministers is to be increased and their efficacy improved. I have, moreover, very imperfectly, as I am aware, endeavored to set a proper example, by doing what I could to aid the improvement of my younger brethren. I trust that this example will be followed, and that every minister of Christ will do what may be in his power to help those who are beginning to labor in the gospel. We must work all together, and work with a will, if we love the cause which Christ has committed to us. Ministers or private brethren, let us stand in our lot, and give up ourselves, without reserve, to the service to which God hath appointed us. So prays your brother in the Lord.

THE END.

A Biographical Sketch of Francis Wayland (1796-1874)

By
John Franklin Jones

A Biographical Sketch of Francis Wayland (1796-1874)

Francis Wayland was born New York, March 11, 1796, the son of Francis Wayland, also a Baptist minister (Armitage).

Wayland graduated from Union College at seventeen and began to study medicine but was called to the Gospel ministry prior to completing medical studies. He entered Andover Theological Seminary (1816) and became a tutor at Union College, continuing as such for four years (Ibid.) (1817-21) (*DEB*).

He was called to the First Church, Boston as its pastor and served there from 1821 to 1826 (Ibid.). He exhibited strong biblical convictions and moral turpitude in his sermons, "*The Moral Dignity of the Missionary Enterprise*" (1823) and "*Duties of an American Citizen*" (1925) (Armitage).

Wayland returned to Union College in 1826 as professor (Ibid.) of moral philosophy (*DEB*). He became the president of Brown University and continued therein from 1827 (Armitage) to 1855 (*DEB*). From that position Wayland, restored Brown's reputation, raised its educational standards, and pioneered elective studies in education (Armitage). In latter years, he served as pastor of the First Baptist Church, Providence (*DEB*).

JOHN FRANKLIN JONES

Francis Wayland is recognized as the leading Baptist mind of his day. He was an anti-slavery advocate. He promoted public schools, prison reform, and free trade. He aggressively advocated congregational polity. His mental and moral philosophy textbooks remained very important in pre-twentieth century higher education (Ibid.).

Wayland authored seventy-two works. The most outstanding of his works were *Moral Science, Political Economy, Intellectual Philosophy, University Sermons, Memoir of Dr. Judson, Limitations to Human Responsibility*, and *Principles and Practices of the Baptist Churches* (Armitage).

He died August 19, 1874 (Armitage) (*DEB* dated his death September 30, 1865 at Providence Rhode Island).

BIBLIOGRAPHY

Armitage, Thomas. *A History of the Baptists; Traced by their Vital Principles and Practices, from the Time of Our Lord and Saviour Jesus Christ to the Year 1886.* With an introduction by J. L. M. Curry. New York: Bryan, Taylor, & Co., 1887.

Dictionary of Evangelical Biography, 1730-1860. S.v. "Wayland, Francis," by William Ringenberg.

Wayland, F., Jr, and H. L. Wayland, *A Memoir of the Life and Labours of Francis Wayland*, 2 vols. New York: N.p., 1867.

BY JOHN FRANKLIN JONES
CORDOVA, TENNESSEE
JULY 2006

THE BAPTIST STANDARD BEARER, INC.

a non-profit, tax-exempt corporation
committed to the Publication & Preservation
of the Baptist Heritage.

CURRENT TITLES AVAILABLE IN
THE BAPTIST *DISTINCTIVES* SERIES

KIFFIN, WILLIAM   A Sober Discourse of Right to Church-Communion. Wherein is proved by Scripture, the Example of the Primitive Times, and the Practice of All that have Professed the Christian Religion: That no Unbaptized person may be Regularly admitted to the Lord's Supper. (London: George Larkin, 1681).

KINGHORN, JOSEPH   Baptism, A Term of Communion. (Norwich: Bacon, Kinnebrook, and Co., 1816)

KINGHORN, JOSEPH   A Defense of "Baptism, A Term of Communion". In Answer To Robert Hall's Reply. (Norwich: Wilkin and Youngman, 1820).

GILL, JOHN   Gospel Baptism. A Collection of Sermons, Tracts, etc., on Scriptural Authority, the Nature of the New Testament Church and the Ordinance of Baptism by John Gill. (Paris, AR: The Baptist Standard Bearer, Inc., 2006).

CARSON, ALEXANDER	Ecclesiastical Polity of the New Testament. (Dublin: William Carson, 1856).
BOOTH, ABRAHAM	A Defense of the Baptists. A Declaration and Vindication of Three Historically Distinctive Baptist Principles. Compiled and Set Forth in the Republication of Three Books. Revised edition. (Paris, AR: The Baptist Standard Bearer, Inc., 2006).
BOOTH, ABRAHAM	Paedobaptism Examined on the Principles, Concessions, and Reasonings of the Most Learned Paedobaptists. With Replies to the Arguments and Objections of Dr. Williams and Mr. Peter Edwards. 3 volumes. (London: Ebenezer Palmer, 1829).
CARROLL, B. H.	*Ecclesia* - The Church. With an Appendix. (Louisville: Baptist Book Concern, 1903).
CHRISTIAN, JOHN T.	Immersion, The Act of Christian Baptism. (Louisville: Baptist Book Concern, 1891).
FROST, J. M.	Pedobaptism: Is It From Heaven Or Of Men? (Philadelphia: American Baptist Publication Society, 1875).
FULLER, RICHARD	Baptism, and the Terms of Communion; An Argument. (Charleston, SC: Southern Baptist Publication Society, 1854).
GRAVES, J. R.	Tri-Lemma: or, Death By Three Horns. The Presbyterian General Assembly Not Able To Decide This Question: "Is Baptism In The Romish Church Valid?" 1st Edition.

	(Nashville: Southwestern Publishing House, 1861).
MELL, P.H.	Baptism In Its Mode and Subjects. (Charleston, SC: Southern Baptist Publications Society, 1853).
JETER, JEREMIAH B.	Baptist Principles Reset. Consisting of Articles on Distinctive Baptist Principles by Various Authors. With an Appendix. (Richmond: The Religious Herald Co., 1902).
PENDLETON, J.M.	Distinctive Principles of Baptists. (Philadelphia: American Baptist Publication Society, 1882).
THOMAS, JESSE B.	The Church and the Kingdom. A New Testament Study. (Louisville: Baptist Book Concern, 1914).
WALLER, JOHN L.	Open Communion Shown to be Unscriptural & Deleterious. With an introductory essay by Dr. D. R. Campbell and an Appendix. (Louisville: Baptist Book Concern, 1859).

For a complete list of current authors/titles, visit our internet site at:
www.standardbearer.org
or write us at:

The Baptist Standard Bearer, Inc.

NUMBER ONE IRON OAKS DRIVE • PARIS, ARKANSAS 72855

TEL # 479-963-3831   FAX # 479-963-8083
EMAIL: Baptist@centurytel.net   http://www.standardbearer.org

Thou hast given a standard to them that fear thee; that it may be displayed because of the truth. — Psalm 60:4

www.ingramcontent.com/pod-product-compliance
Lightning Source LLC
Chambersburg PA
CBHW021135230426
43667CB00005B/118